5 STEPS TO A 5

500
AP Physics 1 Questions
to Know by Test Day

5 STEPS TO A >5™

500
AP Physics 1 Questions
to Know by Test Day
Third Edition

Anaxos, Inc.

New York Chicago San Francisco Athens London Madrid
Mexico City Milan New Delhi Singapore Sydney Toronto

ISBN   978-1-260-44199-4
MHID   1-260-44199-7

e-ISBN   978-1-260-44200-7
e-MHID   1-260-44200-4

CONTENTS

ABOUT THE AUTHOR

For more than twenty years, Anaxos, Inc., has been creating educational and reference materials for some of the nation's most respected publishers. Based in Austin, Texas, the company uses writers from across the globe who offer expertise on an expansive array of subjects.

INTRODUCTION

Congratulations! You've taken a big step toward AP success by purchasing *500 AP Physics 1 Questions to Know by Test Day*. We are here to help you take the next step and score high on your AP exam so you can earn college credits and get into the college or university of your choice!

This book gives you 500 AP-style multiple-choice and free-response questions which cover all the most essential course material. Each question has a detailed answer explanation written to help instruct and fill in any missing gaps in your understanding. These questions provide valuable independent practice to supplement your regular textbook and the groundwork you are already doing in your AP classroom.

Among other enhancements, this new edition has added the following components to this book:

- A section at the beginning of each chapter with 15 review questions. This is designed for students who need to review essential knowledge with basic problems before moving on to the additional 35 higher-level, multi-concept questions characteristic of the AP exam.
- 160 brand new multiple-choice and free-response questions that are rich with concepts historically emphasized on the AP Physics 1 exam. These include over 60 new graphics and images!

This and the other books in this series were written by expert AP teachers who know your exam inside out and can identify the crucial concepts and questions that are most likely to appear on the AP exam.

You might be the kind of student who takes several AP courses and needs to study extra questions a few weeks before the exam for a final review. Or you might be the kind of student who puts off preparing until the last weeks before the exam. No matter what your preparation style, you will surely benefit from reviewing these 500 physics questions, which closely parallel the content, format, and degree of difficulty of the questions on the actual AP exam. These questions and their answer explanations are the ideal last-minute study tool for those final few weeks before the test.

Remember the old saying "practice makes perfect." If you practice with all the questions and answers in this book, we are certain you will build the skills and confidence needed to do great on the exam. Good luck!

—Editors of McGraw-Hill Education

5 STEPS TO A 5™

500
AP Physics 1 Questions
to Know by Test Day

Kinematics

Questions 1-15 are easier practice questions designed to allow the student to review specific AP learning objectives and essential knowledge of kinematics.

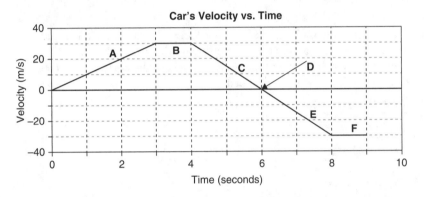

1. What is the acceleration rate of the car at the 6-second clock reading in the velocity vs. time graph above?

   (A) 0 m/s^2
   (B) -15 m/s^2
   (C) -30 m/s^2
   (D) $+30 \text{ m/s}^2$

2. The position–time graph shown here is typical of which type of motion?

   (A) Motion with a constant negative velocity
   (B) Motion with zero velocity
   (C) Motion with a constant positive acceleration
   (D) Motion with zero acceleration

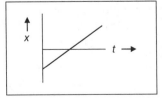

3. A 10-g penny is dropped from a building that is 125 m high. The penny is initially at rest. Approximately how long does it take the penny to hit the ground?
   (A) 3.2 s
   (B) 5.0 s
   (C) 10 s
   (D) 15 s

4. A car in a drag race started from rest and accelerated constantly to a velocity of 50 m/s when it reached the end of a 500-m road. What was the car's rate of acceleration?
   (A) −5.0 m/s²
   (B) −2.5 m/s²
   (C) 0.5 m/s²
   (D) 2.5 m/s²

5. An airplane is flying horizontally at a velocity of 50.0 m/s at an altitude of 125 m. It drops a package to observers on the ground below. Approximately how far will the package travel in the horizontal direction from the point that it was dropped?
   (A) 100 m
   (B) 159 m
   (C) 250 m
   (D) 1,020 m

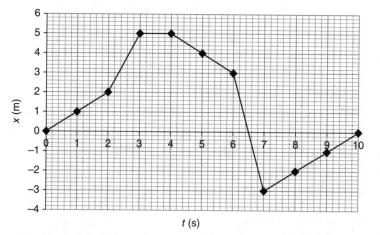

6. This graph depicts the motion of an object on a coordinate system for 10 seconds. During which time interval is the object at rest?
   (A) 0–2 s
   (B) 2–3 s
   (C) 3–4 s
   (D) 6–7 s

7. A car is initially traveling at an unknown velocity. It accelerates constantly for 5.0 seconds of elapsed time at a rate of 3.0 m/s² to reach a velocity of 30 m/s. What was the initial velocity of the car?

   (A) 1.0 m/s
   (B) 5.0 m/s
   (C) 10 m/s
   (D) 15 m/s

8. A plane takes off from rest and accelerates constantly at a rate of 1.0 m/s² for 5 minutes. How far does the plane travel in this time?

   (A) 15 km
   (B) 30 km
   (C) 45 km
   (D) 90 km

9. If a ball is thrown straight upward with an initial velocity of 30.0 m/s, how much time does it take to reach its maximum height?

   (A) 1.0 s
   (B) 1.4 s
   (C) 1.5 s
   (D) 3.0 s

10. On an airless planet, an astronaut drops a hammer from rest at a height of 15 m. The hammer hits the ground in 1 s. What is the acceleration due to the gravity on this planet?

   (A) 10 m/s²
   (B) 15 m/s²
   (C) 25 m/s²
   (D) 30 m/s²

11. A car uniformly accelerates from rest at 3.0 m/s² down a 150-m track. What is the car's final velocity?

   (A) 30 m/s
   (B) 90 m/s
   (C) 150 m/s
   (D) 450 m/s

12. A student launches projectiles with the same velocity but at different angles (0–90°) relative to the ground. She measures the range of each projectile. Which angle pairs have the same range?
    (A) 10° and 20°
    (B) 30° and 45°
    (C) 30° and 60°
    (D) 45° and 60°

13. A boy drops a stone from a cliff and counts 3.0 seconds until he sees the stone hits the base. How high is the cliff?
    (A) 3 m
    (B) 10 m
    (C) 45 m
    (D) 90 m

14. A girl is riding a bicycle at a velocity of 5.0 m/s. She applies the brakes and uniformly accelerates at a rate of -2.5 m/s². How much time does it take for the bicycle to stop?
    (A) 2.0 s
    (B) 2.5 s
    (C) 5.0 s
    (D) 12.5 s

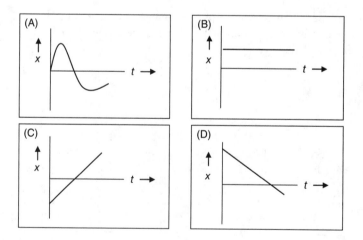

15. The position–time graphs of four different objects are shown in these graphs. If the positive direction is forward, then which object is moving backward at a constant velocity?
    (A) Object A
    (B) Object B
    (C) Object C
    (D) Object D

Questions 16-50 are higher-level, AP-style questions designed to test enduring understanding of AP content.

Questions 16 & 17 refer to the following diagrams which show possible scenarios of a dynamics cart going through two photogates:

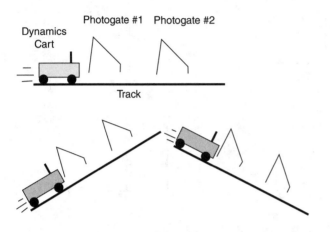

16. Photogate #1 measures a 0.02-second elapsed time for the cart's vertical rod (diameter = 1.2 cm) to block the infrared beam and then unblock the same beam. Photogate # 2 works in the same manner and measures a 0.06-second elapsed time for the rod to pass through the beam. Based on this data, describe the motion of the cart and calculate the magnitude of its acceleration.

    (A) Speeding up with |a| = 0.5 m/s/s
    (B) Slowing down with |a| = 0.5 m/s/s
    (C) Speeding up with |a| = 0.8 m/s/s
    (D) Slowing down with |a| = 0.8 m/s/s

17. Given the data in the previous question and assuming that the friction on the track is negligible, which of the following graphs best displays the future position of the cart on the incline versus time. Assume that the positive direction on the coordinate system is to the right.

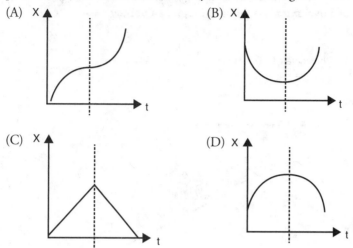

(A) X

(B) X

(C) X

(D) X

18. Starting at a speed of 34 m/s at the base of a hill, a car experiences a uniform acceleration as it rolls to a stop in 4 seconds of elapsed time. Is it possible to determine how far the car rolls on its way up the ramp? Why or why not?

(A) No, the angle of the ramp must be known to determine the rolling distance.

(B) No, the value for the uniform acceleration must be known to determine rolling distance.

(C) Yes, the distance may be found by multiplying the average speed by the elapsed time.

(D) Yes, the distance may be found by multiplying the starting speed by the elapsed time.

19. The position (X) vs. time (t) graph below shows the motion of an object on a given coordinate system. Select the corresponding velocity vs. time graph.

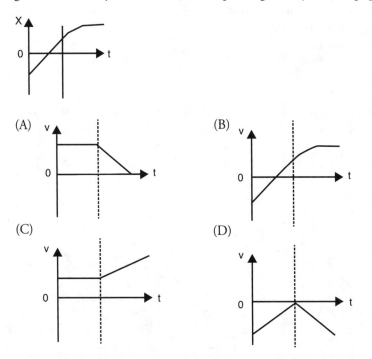

Questions #20 and #21 refer to four different projectiles that are fired from the surface of the Earth with negligible air drag. The following data table compares the four projectiles:

Projectile	Angle fired above the horizontal (degrees)	Initial velocity (m/s)
P1	30	40
P2	45	40
P3	60	20
P4	90	10

20. Rank the vertical acceleration of the four projectiles.
    (A) $a_1 = a_2 > a_3 > a_4$
    (B) $a_4 < a_2 < a_3 < a_4$
    (C) $a_1 = a_2 = a_3 = a_4$
    (D) The masses must be known in order to rank the accelerations.

21. Given the masses of P1, P2, P3, and P4 are respectively 1 kg, 2 kg, 3 kg, and 4 kg, determine the value of the greatest horizontal range of the four projectiles, assuming they land at the same height that they were fired at.

    (A) $80m$
    (B) $80\sqrt{3}m$
    (C) $160\sqrt{2}m$
    (D) $160m$

22. An object free-falls from rest a distance D in a given amount of time. How far will the same object fall from rest in twice the elapsed time?

    (A) D
    (B) $\sqrt{2}\,D$
    (C) $2\,D$
    (D) $4\,D$

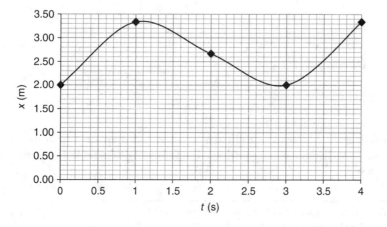

23. An object's position vs. time is depicted in the graph above. Based on the graph, at which time points will the object's velocity be closest to zero?

    (A) 0 s and 2 s
    (B) 0 s and 4 s
    (C) 1 s and 2 s
    (D) 1 s and 3 s

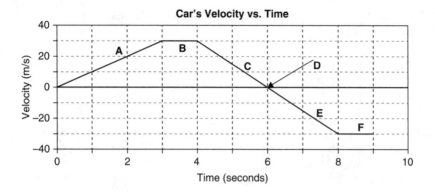

24. Which of the following best describes the motion of the car in regions C, D, and E of the velocity versus time graph in the problem above?

(A) It is slowing down until it reverses direction and speeds back up again.

(B) It moves at a constant velocity in the negative direction.

(C) It accelerates at a constant, nonzero acceleration except at point C when its acceleration is zero.

(D) Its position changes at a constant rate.

Questions 25 and 26 refer to the following graph:

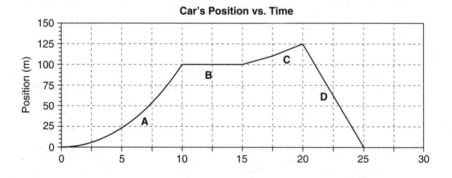

25. Which of the following best ranks the displacement of the car in each region of the graph above?

(A) A > B > C > D

(B) A > C > B > D

(C) D > A > C > B

(D) A > C > D > B

26. Which of the following best ranks the average speed of the car in each region of the graph?

    (A) A > B > C > D
    (B) A > C > B > D
    (C) D > A > C > B
    (D) A > C > D > B

Multi-select: For questions 27–29, two of the suggested answers will be correct. Select the two best answers, and record them both on the answer sheet.

27. Which of the following are moving at a constant velocity?

    (A) A tetherball moving in a circle at a constant speed
    (B) A rolling ball constantly accelerating at -0.20 m/s^2
    (C) A jogger continuing to run at a speed of 2 m/s along a straight path
    (D) A box steadily sliding down an incline at a speed of 0.5 m/s

28. Which of the following are moving with a constant, nonzero acceleration?

    (A) A skydiver gaining speed as she falls through the air
    (B) A hammer falling near the surface of the moon
    (C) A truck moving in a circle as it gains 3 m/s each second
    (D) A cart moving in a straight line gaining 3 m/s each second

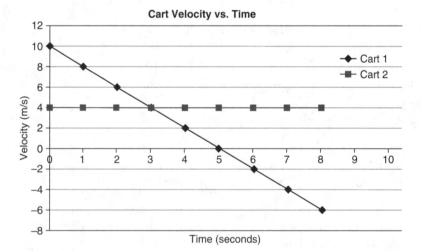

29. Which of the following are true about the motion of the carts in the graph above?

    (A) At the 7-second clock reading, Cart 1 is moving with the same speed as Cart 2.
    (B) Cart 1 moves at a constant speed in the negative direction.
    (C) Cart 1 moves in the negative direction over the entire 8-second trip.
    (D) At the 8-second clock reading, Cart 1 was moving faster than Cart 2.

30. An object is free-falling near the surface of the Earth. At a certain instant in time, it is falling downward at a rate 25 m/s. Two seconds later, what are its instantaneous speed and acceleration, respectively?
    (A) 25 m/s; 0 m/s²
    (B) 27 m/s, 2 m/s²
    (C) 10 m/s; 10 m/s²
    (D) 45 m/s; 10 m/s²

31. An object at the 35-m position of a one-dimensional coordinate system is moving in the negative direction at a constant speed of 25 m/s. Which function below best represents how the car's position (X) in meters on the coordinate system changes with time (t)?
    (A) $X = -25t + 35$
    (B) $X = -35t + 25$
    (C) $X = 10t^2 - 35t + 25$
    (D) $X = 10t^2 - 25t + 35$

32. At $t = 0$, an object is at a position of -12 meters of a one-dimensional coordinate system and is moving in the positive direction at 5 m/s. It constantly gains velocity at a rate of $+2$ m/s each and every second. Which function below best represents how the car's position (X) on the coordinate system changes with time (t)?
    (A) $X = 5t + -12$
    (B) $X = 2t^2 + 5t - 12$
    (C) $X = t^2 + 5t - 12$
    (D) $X = -12t^2 + 5t + 2$

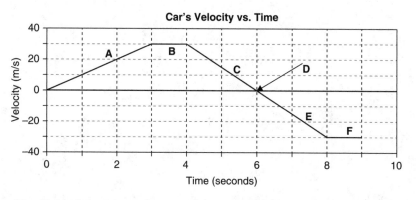

33. Rank the average velocities of the car in regions A, B, C, and E of the graph above.
    (A) $B > A = C > E$
    (B) $B = A > C = E$
    (C) $B > A = C = E$
    (D) $A > B > C = E$

34. A placekicker kicks a football at a velocity of 10.0 m/s from a tee on the ground at an angle of 30° from the horizontal. Approximately how long will the ball stay in the air?

(A) 0.0 s
(B) 0.6 s
(C) 0.8 s
(D) 1.0 s

35. A person drops a stone down a well and hears the echo 8.9 s later. If it takes 0.9 s for the echo to travel up the well, approximately how deep is the well?

(A) 40 m
(B) 320 m
(C) 405 m
(D) 640 m

36. An archer stands on a castle wall that is 45 m above the ground. He shoots an arrow with a velocity of 10.0 m/s at an angle of 45° relative to the horizontal. Determine the maximum range of the arrow.

(A) 3.8 m
(B) 14 m
(C) 27 m
(D) 52 m

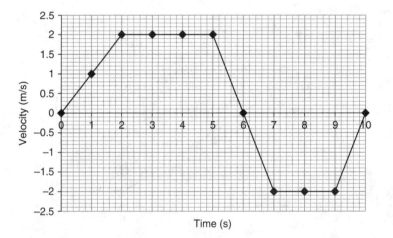

37. The velocity–time graph of an object's motion is shown in this graph. At 10 s, what is the object's displacement relative its position at t = 0?

(A) 3 m
(B) 6 m
(C) −3 m
(D) −6 m

38. A projectile is launched with an unknown velocity at an angle of 30° from the horizontal of level ground. Which of the following statements is true?

(A) The horizontal component of velocity is less than the vertical component of velocity.

(B) The horizontal component of velocity is greater than the vertical component of velocity.

(C) Both the horizontal and vertical components of velocity are equal.

(D) The horizontal component of velocity is used to calculate the time that the projectile is in the air.

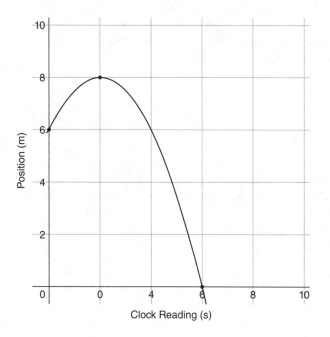

39. The graph above shows the position of an object versus clock reading. Which of the following best describes the motion of the object during the six seconds of elapsed time?

(A) The object speeds up for the first two seconds and slows down during the final four seconds.

(B) The object traveled 6 meters during the six seconds of elapsed time.

(C) The object slows down and then speeds up with a total displacement of −6 meters.

(D) The object's acceleration starts out negative and transitions to positive acceleration at the 2 second clock reading.

40. A bicycle moves at a constant velocity of v_o for 4 seconds and then uniformly slows down to rest through an additional 6 seconds of elapsed time. Which of the following expressions represents the distance the bicycle traveled throughout the entire 10-second trip?

(A) $5v_o$

(B) $7v_o$

(C) $10v_o$

(D) $12v_o$

41. A lacrosse ball is thrown across midfield at a 10-degree angle above the horizontal with negligible air drag. Which of the following best compares vertical acceleration of the ball immediately after it is released (a_i) to the acceleration at the peak of the trajectory (a_p)?

(A) $a_i = a_p \neq 0$

(B) $a_i > a_p$

(C) $a_i < a_p$

(D) $a_i = a_p = 0$

42. A stone is thrown straight upward into the air. Assuming up is the positive direction, which of the following best represents the direction of the velocity and acceleration of the ball, respectively, immediately after the object is released?

(A) ↓↓

(B) ↑↑

(C) ↓↑

(D) ↑↓

43. A dodge ball is thrown horizontally across a court. The ball hits the middle of the court, bounces up into the air, and continues on its way. Which of the following graphs represents possible horizontal and vertical components of velocity during the time immediately before and after the bounce?

(A)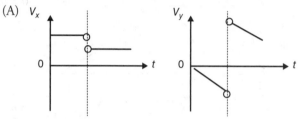

(B)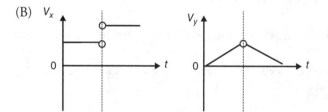

(C)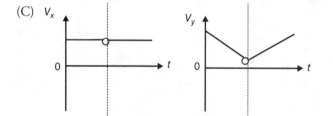

(D)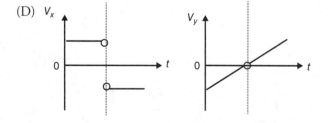

Free Response Questions 44–47:

A student conducts a lab and obtains the following velocity vs. time graph:

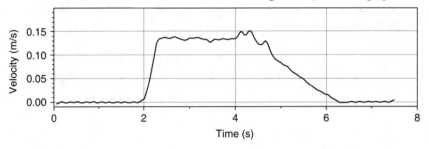

44. Provide a complete list of equipment commonly found in a physics lab that could be used to gather this data.

45. Describe and explain the motion of the object depicted on the graph.

46. Estimate a value for the displacement of the object during the first 7 seconds of the trip.

47. After "smoothing" out the fluctuations on the original graph, sketch the position vs. time and acceleration vs. time graphs that are quantitatively reasonable.

Free Response Questions 48–50:

The acceleration versus time of a bicycle rider is shown here:

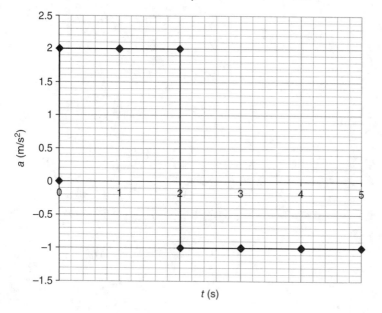

Assuming that the bicycle starts from the origin at an initial velocity of +4 m/s, complete the following questions

48. Sketch a scaled velocity–time graph for the 5-s motion.

49. Describe the motion of the bicyclist in detail during the 5 seconds, commenting on what's happening to the speed and the direction of motion throughout the trip.

50. Determine the total distance traveled during the 5 s of motion.

CHAPTER 2

Dynamics: Newton's Laws

Questions 51–65 are easier practice questions designed to allow the student to review specific AP learning objectives and essential knowledge of kinematics.

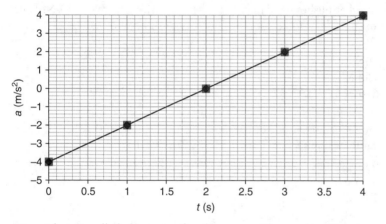

51. A box is pulled along a surface by a rope. The acceleration–time graph of an object's motion is shown in the figure above. At what time will the forces acting on the box be balanced?

 (A) 0 s
 (B) 1 s
 (C) 2 s
 (D) 3 s

Questions 52 and 53 refer to the 80-kg astronaut and her 40-kg daughter who are floating in deep space shown in the diagram below.

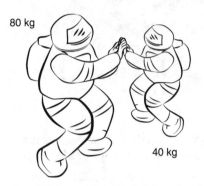

80 kg

40 kg

52. If the mother pushes her daughter to the right with a force of 160 N. With what magnitude of force does the daughter push her mother?

    (A) 0 N
    (B) 80N
    (C) 160 N
    (D) 640 N

53. Determine the magnitude of the mother's acceleration during her 160 N push on the daughter.

    (A) 0 m/s2
    (B) 0.5 m/s2
    (C) 1 m/s2
    (D) 2 m/s2

54. Object A, when acted upon by a force F, accelerates at a rate of 4.0 m/s/s. This same force accelerates object B at a rate of 8.0 m/s/s. Compared to the mass of object A, the mass of object B is:

    (A) Four times as great
    (B) Twice as great
    (C) The same
    (D) One-half as great

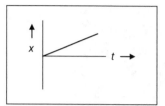

55. This position–time graph is typical of which type of motion?

(A) Motion of an object with an increasing net force acting upon it

(B) Motion of an object with constant positive net force acting upon it

(C) Motion of an object with no net force acting upon it

(D) Motion of an object with negative net force acting upon it

56. An object is supported by a vertical spring attached to the ceiling. What are the forces acting on the object?

(A) The mass of the object in the downward direction and the supporting force of the spring in the upward direction

(B) The mass of the object in the downward direction and the supporting force of the spring in the downward direction

(C) The weight of the object in the upward direction and the supporting force of the spring in the downward direction

(D) The gravitational force of the object in the downward direction and the supporting force of the spring in the upward direction

57. A girl pushes a 10-kg box from rest across a horizontal floor with a force of 50 N. The force of friction opposing her is 45 N. If the box uniformly accelerates from rest to a final velocity of 2.0 m/s, how much time did it take to get to that velocity?

(A) 1 s

(B) 2 s

(C) 3 s

(D) 4 s

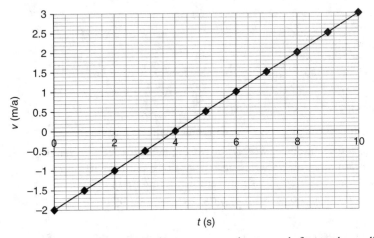

58. A boy is pushing a 50-kg crate across horizontal, frictionless rollers. The velocity is changing with time as shown in the graph above. What is the magnitude of the force that the boy applies to the crate?

    (A) 5 N
    (B) 10 N
    (C) 15 N
    (D) 25 N

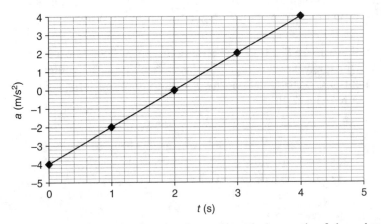

59. The acceleration of a 5-kg object through 4 seconds of elapsed time is shown in the graph above. What is the net force on the object at the 1-second clock reading?

    (A) −10 N
    (B) −5 N
    (C) −2.5 N
    (D) 5 N

60. Two students push a 5-kg box on a frictionless floor. Jamie pushes the box with a 10-N force to the right. Louis pushes the box with an 8-N force to the left. What is the magnitude and direction of the box's acceleration?

(A) 0.4 m/s² to the right
(B) 0.4 m/s² to the left
(C) 1.6 m/s² to the right
(D) 1.6 m/s² to the left

61. You pull straight down on one side of a vertical rope stretched around a pulley. Attached to the other side of the rope is a hanging 10-kg box. How much force must you pull down on the rope to get the box to accelerate upward at a rate of 10 m/s2?

(A) 10 N
(B) 20 N
(C) 100 N
(D) 200 N

62. A jet takes off at an angle of 60° above the horizontal. The jet flies against a wind that exerts a horizontal force of 1,000 N on it. The engines produce 20,000 N of thrust (60° above the horizontal), and the mass of the jet is 90,000 kg. What is the rate of the jet's acceleration in the horizontal direction?

(A) 0.1 m/s²
(B) 0.2 m/s²
(C) 1 m/s²
(D) 10 m/s²

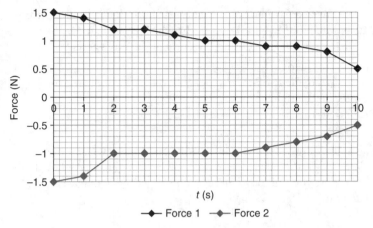

63. Only two forces act on a 0.1-kg object. This graph depicts the magnitudes and directions of those two forces. What is the acceleration of the object at the 2-second clock reading?

    (A) 0 m/s²
    (B) 0.2 m/s²
    (C) 1 m/s²
    (D) 2 m/s²

64. A girl pushes a 10-kg crate to the right across the floor with a constant force of 10 N against a force of friction. The box accelerates to the right at a rate of 0.1 m/s². What is the magnitude of the opposing frictional force?

    (A) 0 N
    (B) 1 N
    (C) 5 N
    (D) 9 N

65. A soldier fires a musket with a barrel that is 1 m in length. The gases from the exploding gunpowder exert a constant net force of 50 N on a 0.010-kg bullet as it travels through the musket barrel. What is the bullet's velocity as it leaves the musket barrel?

    (A) 10 m/s
    (B) 100 m/s
    (C) 1,000 m/s
    (D) 10,000 m/s

Questions 66–100 are higher-level, AP-style questions designed to test enduring understanding of AP content.

66. A car stalls and is rolling down and to the right on a sloped hill. Which of the following free body diagrams best represents the forces acting on the car?

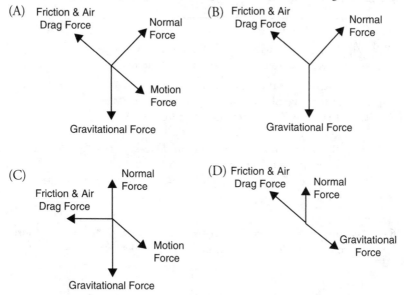

(A) Friction & Air Drag Force Normal Force Motion Force Gravitational Force

(B) Friction & Air Drag Force Normal Force Gravitational Force

(C) Normal Force Friction & Air Drag Force Motion Force Gravitational Force

(D) Friction & Air Drag Force Normal Force Gravitational Force

67. A cartoon dog sits at rest on a horizontal floor. Four AP physics students are debating about how the forces on the dog compare to one another. Which of the following arguments is correct?

(A) Fred claims that the magnitude of the normal force from the floor is equal to the gravitational force because they form an equal and opposite Newton's third law pair.

(B) Velma claims that the magnitude of the normal force from the floor is greater than the gravitational force, otherwise Newton's first law would predict that the dog would accelerate downward through the floor.

(C) Daphne claims that the magnitude of the normal force from the floor equals the gravitational force because Newton's second law requires that the net force on the dog is zero.

(D) Shaggy claims that the magnitude of the gravitational force is greater than the normal force, otherwise the dog would float off the table.

Problems 68 and 69 refer to the system of two boxes connected by a rope as shown above on the floor of an elevator. A force F is applied to the 6-kg box.

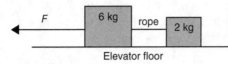

Elevator floor

68. Which of the following pair of forces ALWAYS have the same magnitude, regardless of the state of motion of the system?

    (A) The force of the rope pulling the 6-kg block to the right and the force of the 6-kg block pulling the rope to the left

    (B) The force F to the left and the force of the rope pulling the 6-kg box to the right

    (C) The normal force of the floor on the 6-kg block and the gravitational force on the 6-kg box

    (D) The force F to the left and the force of the rope on the 2-kg box to the left

69. Assuming negligible friction between the blocks and the horizontal surface, determine the value of the tension in the rope between the boxes if $F = 24$ N.

    (A) 2 N
    (B) 6 N
    (C) 8 N
    (D) 20 N

70. A car's wheels are locked as it skids to the right as shown above. The coefficient of friction between the road and the tires is 0.5. Which of the following free body diagrams best represents the relative size and direction of the relevant forces on the car?

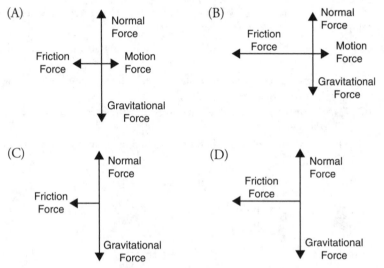

71. What force is responsible for accelerating a car along a horizontal road?
    (A) the normal force of the car on the road
    (B) the static friction force of the road on the car
    (C) the engine pulling the car
    (D) a component of the gravitations force

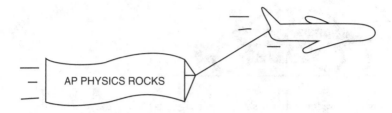

72. An airplane uses a cable to tow a large banner advertisement as shown in the figure above.

    When the airplane cruises at a constant velocity through the air, which of the following correctly compares forces?

    (A) The tension force in the cable equals the gravitational force on the banner.

    (B) The forward force on the airplane equals the air drag force on the airplane and banner.

    (C) The y-component of cable tension equals the aerodynamic lift force on the airplane.

    (D) The x-component of cable tension is greater than the air drag force on the banner.

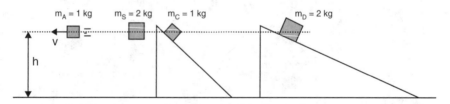

73. The four blocks shown in the figure above are released from the same height above the ground. Blocks B, C, and D are each released from rest, and block A is initially moving horizontally with a speed v. The mass of blocks A and C is 1 kg and the mass of blocks B and D is 2 kg. Assuming air drag and surface friction are negligible, rank the time it takes each block to reach the ground?

    (A) $t_A = t_C < t_B = t_D$

    (B) $t_A < t_B < t_C < t_D$

    (C) $t_A = t_B = t_C = t_D$

    (D) $t_A = t_B < t_C < t_D$

74. Rank the following scenarios from the smallest acceleration to the greatest acceleration:
   I. Net force F applied to a mass M
   II. Net force $2F$ applied to a mass M
   III. Net force F applied to a mass $2M$
   IV. Net force $2F$ applied to a mass $2M$
   (A) $II > I = IV > III$
   (B) $I > II > III > IV$
   (C) $III > IV = I > II$
   (D) $IV > II > III > I$

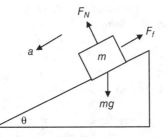

75. A box of unknown mass (m) slides down a plane inclined at an angle (θ) as shown in the diagram above. The plane has a coefficient of friction (μ). Which of the following expressions represents the rate of acceleration (a) of the box?
   (A) $a = g(\sin\theta - \mu g \cos\theta)/m$
   (B) $a = g(\cos\theta - \mu g \sin\theta)/m$
   (C) $a = g(\cos\theta - \mu\sin\theta)$
   (D) $a = g(\sin\theta - \mu\cos\theta)$

76. A tow truck is accelerating a car out of a ditch. Which of the following statements is true about the forces between the truck and the car?
   (A) The force of the truck on the car is greater than the force of the car on the truck.
   (B) The force of the truck on the car is less than the force of the car on the truck.
   (C) The force of the truck on the car is equal in magnitude to the force of the car on the truck.
   (D) The force of the truck on the car may be equal to the force of the car on the truck, but only when the system is in a state of constant velocity.

77. A box slides to the right along a horizontal surface. Which is true about the friction force?
    (A) It acts perpendicular to the surface and is directly proportional to the speed of the box.
    (B) It is a force in the direction of motion that allows the box to move.
    (C) It is a force that is proportional to the normal force that acts in opposition to the direction of motion.
    (D) It is a force that is proportional to the surface area of contact and acts in the direction of motion.

78. A box that is resting on an inclined plane has what forces acting on it?
    (A) The gravitational force on the box, the box's push on the plane, and the friction force along the surface of the incline plane beneath the box
    (B) The box's component forces perpendicular to and along the plane, the resultant force of the plane on the box, and the friction force along the surface of the plane beneath the box
    (C) The gravitational force on the box and the friction force along the surface of the plane beneath the box
    (D) The gravitational force on the box, the perpendicular force of the plane on the box, and the friction force along the surface of the plane beneath the box

79. A skier with mass m pushes off from the top of a ski slope with a force F directed the along the slope inclined 30° below the horizontal. What expression for F allows the skier to accelerate at a rate equivalent to the free fall acceleration g?

    (A) $F = \dfrac{mg}{2}$

    (B) $F = mg\left(\dfrac{2 - \sqrt{3}}{2}\right)$

    (C) $F = mg$

    (D) $F = 2mg$

80. A student claims that two spheres of different mass dropped from rest above the surface of the Moon will hit the ground at the same time, even though the less massive sphere has a larger radius. Which of the following is a correct assessment of this statement?

    (A) The more massive sphere will hit the surface first because it's heavier.
    (B) Neither sphere will hit the surface because there is no gravity on the Moon and they will both float.
    (C) The less massive sphere will hit the surface first because its larger profile will hit more air, which will slow down its motion.
    (D) They will hit the ground at approximately the same time because the net force-to-mass ratio is the same for both.

81. A rope is strung between two cliffs. A mountain climber weighing 100 kg is halfway across the rope when the rope forms an angle of 30° with the horizontal. The tension in the rope is closest to what value?

    (A) 1,000 N
    (B) 500 N
    (C) 250 N
    (D) 100 N

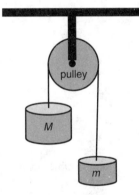

82. Two masses hang vertically by a rope strung through a pulley on a planet with a gravitational field g. The mass "M" is on the left of the pulley while the mass "m" on the right of the pulley as shown above. Derive an expression for the acceleration of the system assuming that the mass has negligible friction.

    (A) $a = g(M - m)$

    (B) $a = g\dfrac{(M - m)}{(M + m)}$

    (C) $a = g\dfrac{(M + m)}{(M - m)}$

    (D) $a = g$

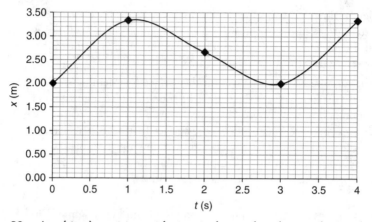

83. An object's position with time is depicted in this graph. At which time range will there be nearly no net force acting on the object?

(A) 0.5 to 1.0 s
(B) 1.0 to 1.5 s
(C) 1.8 to 2.2 s
(D) 2.5 to 3.5 s

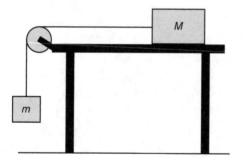

84. A block with a mass M is located on a horizontal, frictionless tabletop as shown above. This block is connected by a rope to less-massive block with a mass m. The rope is looped through a pulley on the table's edge so that the less massive block is hanging over the edge of the table. What is the magnitude of the acceleration of the system?

(A) $a = \dfrac{(M - m)g}{(m + M)}$

(B) $a = \dfrac{mg}{(M - m)}$

(C) $a = \dfrac{mg}{(m + M)}$

(D) $a = g$

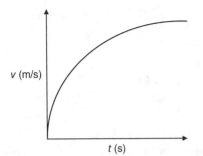

85. The graph above depicts the velocity of a skydiver over time during a free fall. Which of the following statements is true about the magnitude of the net force on the skydiver?

(A) It increases until the acceleration reaches its maximum and the velocity becomes constant.
(B) It decreases until the acceleration reaches zero and the velocity becomes constant.
(C) It has a value of zero throughout the skydiver's free fall.
(D) It increases until the acceleration reaches zero and the velocity becomes constant.

86. A car travels at a constant velocity of 30 m/s on a horizontal road. How does the total amount of backward force on the car (due to air drag and rolling friction) compare with the forward force of the road on the car?

(A) The forward force equals the backward force.
(B) The forward force is greater than the backward force.
(C) The forward force is less than the backward force.
(D) The forward force initially equals the backward force and continues to increase.

Multi-select: For questions 87–91, two of the suggested answers will be correct. Select the two best answers, and record them both on the answer sheet.

87. A 40-kg child stands in an elevator on a bathroom scale and notices that the scale reads 300 N. What are two possible states of motion of the elevator?

(A) The elevator is moving upward and slowing down.
(B) The elevator is moving upward and speeding up.
(C) The elevator is moving downward and slowing down.
(D) The elevator is moving downward and speeding up.

88. A book is resting on a table. Which two of the following forces act on the book?

(A) The gravitational force
(B) The force of the book on the table
(C) The supporting force of the table on the book
(D) The net downward force of air on the book

89. Consider the forces on a child standing in an elevator. When is the normal force from the elevator equal to the gravitational force?

(A) When the elevator moves up at a constant speed
(B) When the elevator accelerates upward
(C) When the elevator is at rest
(D) When the elevator accelerates downward at a uniform rate

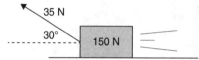

90. A rope applies 35 N force as shown in the figure above. As a result, the box accelerates to the left along the surface. In addition to the gravitational force, which two of the following forces act on the box?

(A) The downward force of the box on the table
(B) The frictional force of the surface on the box
(C) The upward force of the table on the box
(D) The force of motion to the left on the box

91. Which of the following are properties of mass?

(A) Mass is the ratio of weight to volume.
(B) Mass resists changes in motion.
(C) A mass experiences an attractive force with another mass.
(D) Mass is the amount of space something occupies.

Free Response questions 92–95:

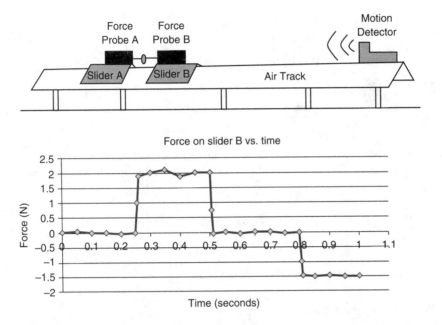

Force on slider B vs. time

Two air track sliders have force probes linked together as on a horizontal air track as shown in the diagram above. Slider A has a mass of 1000 grams and slider B has a mass of 500 kg. Someone grabs slider A and interacts with it for one second of time. Force Probe B is calibrated such that a pushing force to the right is positive and a pulling force to the left is negative. Force Probe B measures the force during that one second of time as shown in the graph.

92. The motion detector points to the left as show in the diagram above, and it is set up so the positive direction is to the left. Assuming the sliders started at rest, sketch a quantitative graph for velocity vs. time, supporting the values and signs of the velocity with explanations and/or calculations.

93. Sketch a quantitative graph of force on slider A vs. time, clearly indicating whether the sign of your force is to the right or to the left. Support the values and direction of the force with explanations and/or calculations.

94. Estimate the value of the displacement of the sliders during the one second of elapsed time, clearly showing your calculations.

95. What value and direction of a constant force in the time interval between 1.0 and 1.5 seconds would be measured by slider B's force probe in order to return the slider system to its starting position?

Free Response questions 96–100:

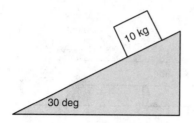

A 10-kg box starts from rest and slides down an inclined plane for 2.0 s as shown in the diagram above. The coefficient of friction between the box and the inclined plane is 0.1

96. Draw a free-body diagram of this situation, and label all the forces on the box.

97. Calculate the force of friction on the box.

98. Calculate the acceleration of the box.

99. Calculate the final velocity of the box.

100. Calculate the distance that the box moves down the plane in the given time interval.

CHAPTER 3

Circular Motion and the Universal Law of Gravitation

Questions 101–115 are easier practice questions designed to allow the student to review specific AP learning objectives and essential knowledge of circular motion and the universal gravitation.

101. A pendulum bob is attached to a string that is tied to the ceiling, and the bob is pulled back and released from different heights. As the bob moves through the bottom of the swing, how is its centripetal acceleration related to its speed?

(A) The centripetal acceleration is directly proportional to the speed of the pendulum.

(B) The centripetal acceleration is inversely proportional to the speed of the pendulum.

(C) The centripetal acceleration is directly proportional to the square of the speed of the pendulum.

(D) The centripetal acceleration is inversely proportional to the square of the speed of the pendulum.

Problems 102 and 103 refer to the following material.

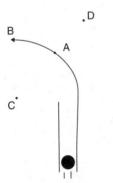

The diagram above shows a top view of a pinball moving on a horizontal plane after it is launched from a spring mechanism.

102. While the ball encounters the curved wall at position A, which of the following forces act on the ball?

   I. A force along the line pointed from A toward C
  II. A force along the line pointed from A toward D
 III. A force pointed up and to the left along a line tangent to the curve

(A) I only
(B) II only
(C) I & II
(D) II & III

103. Which of the following best represents the future path of the ball when it leaves the ball at point B?

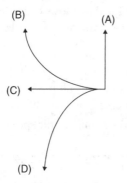

104. Two satellites orbit the Earth at the same speed in identical orbits. Satellite A is twice the mass of Satellite B. How does the centripetal acceleration of Satellite A compare with that of Satellite B?

(A) Four times as much
(B) Twice as much
(C) The same
(D) One-half as much

105. A car moves around a curve in a horizontal circle with a radius of 100 m. The tangential speed of the car is constant at a value of 30 m/s. What is the car's acceleration?

(A) 9 m/s^2 toward the center of the circle
(B) 9 m/s^2 away from the center of the circle
(C) 9 m/s^2 tangent to its circular path
(D) 0 m/s^2

106. If the car in the previous question has a mass of 1,000 kg, then what is the force of friction acting on the car?

(A) 3,000 N toward the center
(B) 3,000 N away from the center
(C) 9,000 N away from the center
(D) 9,000 N toward the center

107. A satellite orbits the Earth at a distance of 100 km. The mass of the satellite is 100 kg, while the mass of the Earth is approximately 6.0×10^{24} kg. The radius of the Earth is approximately 6.4×10^6 m. What is the approximate force of gravity acting on the satellite?

(A) 9.5×10^2 N
(B) 6.2×10^6 N
(C) 9.5×10^8 N
(D) 6.2×10^9 N

108. A 70-kg astronaut floats at a distance of 10 m from a 50,000-kg spacecraft. What is the force of attraction between the astronaut and spacecraft?

(A) 2.3×10^{-6} N
(B) 2.3×10^{-5} N
(C) 2.3×10^5 N
(D) 2.3×10^6 N

109. The centripetal acceleration on a 1,000-kg car in a turn is 1×10^5 m/s². The radius of the turn is 40 m. What is the car's speed?

(A) 2×10^1 m/s
(B) 2×10^2 m/s
(C) 2×10^3 m/s
(D) 2×10^4 m/s

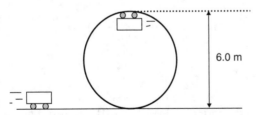

6.0 m

110. An empty 150-kg rollercoaster cart is approaching a 6.0-meter-tall circular-shaped loop-the-loop as shown in the figure above. What is the minimum speed of the cart when it is upside-down at the top of the loop?

(A) 5.5 m/s
(B) 7.7 m/s
(C) 10 m/s
(D) 12 m/s

111. A warrior spins a slingshot in a horizontal circle above their head at a constant speed. The sling is 1.5 m long, and the stone has a mass of 50 g. The tension in the string is 3.3 N. What is the stone's speed as it is released?

(A) 5 m/s
(B) 10 m/s
(C) 25 m/s
(D) 30 m/s

112. A satellite orbits the Earth at a distance of 200. km. If the mass of the Earth is 6.0×10^{24} kg and the Earth's radius is 6.4×10^6 m, what is the satellite's speed?

(A) 1.0×10^3 m/s
(B) 3.5×10^3 m/s
(C) 7.8×10^3 m/s
(D) 5.0×10^6 m/s

113. A tetherball swings in a horizontal circle. If the radius of the swing is tripled but the tangential speed remains the same, by what factor does the centripetal force change?

(A) Nine times greater
(B) Three times greater
(C) One-third as much
(D) One-ninth as much

114. A turntable has three coins at different distances from the center of rotation. Coin A is 1 cm away, Coin B is 2 cm away, and Coin C is 3 cm away. If the turntable is spinning 45 rotations/min, what coin has the greatest tangential speed?

(A) Coin A
(B) Coin B
(C) Coin C
(D) All the coins have the same tangential velocity

115. Mars orbits the Sun at a distance of 2.3×10^{11} m. The mass of the Sun is 2×10^{30} kg, and the mass of Mars is 6.4×10^{23} kg. How much greater is the gravitational force that the Sun exerts on Mars compared to the gravitational force that Mars exerts on the Sun?

(A) 2.5×10^3 N
(B) 1.6×10^{21} N
(C) 2.5×10^{21} N
(D) 0

Questions 116–150 are higher-level, AP-style questions designed to test enduring understanding of AP content.

116. A car is moving over the top of a hill at a constant speed. Which of the following may be said about the vertical forces on the car in this scenario?

(A) The normal force of the road is greater than the gravitational force from the Earth.

(B) The normal force of the road is less than the gravitational force from the Earth.

(C) The normal force of the road equals the gravitational force from the Earth.

(D) The centrifugal force equals the gravitational force from the Earth.

Problems 117 and 118 refer to the following material.

Vernier Software and Technology's Centripetal Force Apparatus, shown in the figure below, consists of a horizontal arm that may be rotated at a variety of speeds. Resting on the arm is a variable-mass wheeled carriage that may be moved to different distances from the center of the apparatus by adjusting the length of a string that pulls the cart toward the center of the apparatus. A force probe measures the tension in that string and a photogate measures the orbital period of the rotating arm.

117. Which equation correctly calculates the tangential speed of the carriage?

(A) $v = \dfrac{\text{Diameter of Orbit}}{\text{Orbital Period}}$

(B) $v = \dfrac{\pi * \text{Diameter of Orbit}}{\text{Orbital Period}}$

(C) $v = \dfrac{\text{\# of Revolutions}}{\text{Orbital Period}}$

(D) $v = \text{gravitational field strength} * \text{Orbital Period}$

118. The slope of which of the following graphs may be used to determine the value of the mass of the carriage? (Note: D is the diameter of orbit, v is the tangential speed, and F_T is the tension in the string.)

(A) F_T versus $\dfrac{vD}{2}$

(B) F_T versus $\dfrac{2v^2}{D}$

(C) $\dfrac{v^2}{D}$ versus F_T

(D) $\dfrac{v^2 D}{2}$ versus F_T

119. In 1798, Henry Cavendish experimentally determined the value of the universal gravitational constant, G, which, in turn, enabled him to calculate the mass of the Earth. Given the Earth's surface gravitational field strength (g), the radius of the Earth (R_E) and G, which of the following expressions may be used to calculate the mass of the Earth?

(A) $M_E = \dfrac{gR_E^2}{G}$

(B) $M_E = GgR_E^2$

(C) $M_E = \dfrac{G}{gR_E^2}$

(D) $M_E = \dfrac{gR_E}{G}$

120. If the Earth were a gaseous planet with twice the radius and half the mass, determine gravitational field strength at the surface of the gaseous planet.

(A) 2 m/s^2
(B) 5 m/s^2
(C) 10 m/s^2
(D) 20 m/s^2

121. Four planets, A through D, orbit the same star. The relative masses and distances from the star for each planet are shown in the table. For example, Planet A has twice the mass of Planet B, and Planet D has three times the orbital radius of Planet A. Which planet has the highest gravitational attraction to the star?

Planet	Relative mass	Relative distance to star
A	2 m	r
B	m	0.1 r
C	0.5 m	2 r
D	4 m	3 r

(A) Planet A
(B) Planet B
(C) Planet C
(D) Planet D

122. A tetherball is whirled in a horizontal circle above your head. If the string breaks, the ball will follow what type of path if it is observed from above?

(A) Straight outward from the center
(B) Straight toward the center
(C) An expanding spiral
(D) Tangent to the original circular path

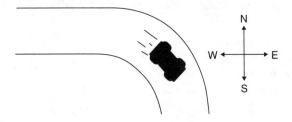

123. The driver of a race car takes a turn on a horizontal track and is moving southeast at a particular instant as shown in the diagram above. If the car is gaining speed, which of the following best describes the direction of acceleration of the car at instant shown in the diagram?

    (A) southwest toward the center of the turn
    (B) southeast in the direction of motion
    (C) south on the diagram
    (D) northeast away from the center of the turn

124. A pendulum bob is attached to a string that is tied to the ceiling, and the bob is pulled back and released. As the bob moves through the bottom of the swing, how does the magnitude of the tension force from the string compare to the gravitational force on the bob?

    (A) The tension force is less than the gravitational force.
    (B) The tension force is greater than the gravitational force.
    (C) The tension force is equal to the gravitational force.
    (D) The mass of the ball and release height are needed in order to compare these forces.

125. When climbing from sea level to the top of Mount Everest, a hiker changes elevation by 8,848 m. By what percentage will the gravitational field of the Earth change during the climb? (The Earth's mass is 6.0×10^{24} kg, and its radius is 6.4×10^6 m.)

    (A) It will increase by approximately 0.3%.
    (B) It will decrease by approximately 0.3%.
    (C) It will increase by approximately 12%.
    (D) It will decrease by approximately 12%.

Multi-select: For questions 126–130, two of the suggested answers will be correct. Select the two best answers, and record them both on the answer sheet.

126. What can be said about the Moon as it orbits the Earth at a constant speed?

    (A) The Moon's velocity is constant.
    (B) The Moon experiences acceleration toward the Earth.
    (C) There is a net force on the Moon.
    (D) The Moon's acceleration is constant.

127. Two masses, M_1 and M_2, are separated a distance d. What changes in the variables will result in NO CHANGE in the gravitational force between the masses?

   (A) M_1 is doubled, and d is doubled.
   (B) M_2 is tripled, and d is quadrupled.
   (C) Both M_1 and M_2 are tripled, and d is tripled.
   (D) M_2 is quadrupled, and d is doubled.

128. The planet Jupiter orbits the Sun at a nearly constant speed. Which of the following statements are true?

   (A) There is a force on Jupiter toward the center of the orbit.
   (B) There is a force on Jupiter pulling it out from the center of the orbit.
   (C) There is a force on Jupiter in the direction of its motion.
   (D) Jupiter is accelerating toward the center of the orbit.

129. A child swings from the end of a rope tied to the branch of a tree. As she swings through the bottom of the arc, which forces act on her?

   (A) The forward force of motion
   (B) A downward centrifugal force
   (C) The gravitational force
   (D) The upward tension from the rope

130. An object rests on the surface of a planet. Which of the following affect the strength of the gravitational field on the surface of a planet?

   (A) The mass of the object at the surface
   (B) The mass of the planet
   (C) The radius of the planet
   (D) The presence of air at the surface of the planet

131. Two identical cars are moving at the same constant speed as they take different exit ramps from the highway. Ramp 1 is a circular arc with a radius of 25 m. Ramp 2 is a circular arc with a radius of 50 m. How does the centripetal force on the car taking Ramp 2 compare with that for the car taking Ramp 1?

   (A) Ramp 2 requires four times the centripetal force.
   (B) Ramp 2 requires two times the centripetal force.
   (C) Ramp 2 requires one-half the centripetal force.
   (D) Ramp 2 requires one-fourth the centripetal force.

Questions 132 and 133 are based on the following graph:

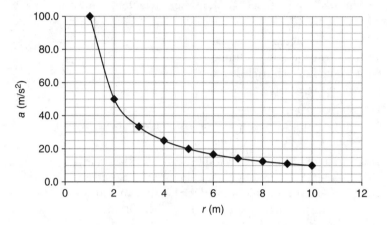

132. Engineers have designed a centrifuge for studying the effects of high gravity environments on plants and animals. The graph above shows the results of the relationship between the radius and the centripetal acceleration. If the scientists want to simulate a "3-g environment" where the gravitational field strength is three times the value at the surface of Earth. To do this, what should the radius of the centrifuge be?

(A) 1 m
(B) 2 m
(C) 3 m
(D) 5 m

133. If an astronaut with a mass of 70 kg were placed in that same centrifuge with a radius of 5 m, what would be the centripetal force acting on them?

(A) 300 N
(B) 700 N
(C) 1400 N
(D) 2100 N

134. A bicycle wheel has a radius, R, and has a pebble with a mass m wedged in the treads. Develop an expression for the force needed to keep the pebble attached to the wheel when the wheel completes N turns in t seconds.

(A) $\dfrac{4\pi^2 mRN^2}{t^2}$

(B) $\dfrac{4\pi^2 RN^2}{t^2}$

(C) $\dfrac{2\pi mRN}{t}$

(D) $2\pi mRNt$

135. A physics teacher tests a new spool of string by hanging masses from the end of the string. The string consistently snapped when masses more than 12 kg were hung vertically from it. Next, the teacher ties the string to the handle of a bucket, fills the bucket with water, and whirls the water-filled bucket around in a 3.0-m-tall vertical circle. What is the maximum speed of the bucket/water system if its mass is 8.0 kg?

(A) 2.7 m/s
(B) 3.9 m/s
(C) 4.7 m/s
(D) 7.5 m/s

136. Friction allows a car to make a turn at a speed of 10 miles per hour. By what factor will the friction have to change to allow the driver to make the same turn at 20 miles per hour?

(A) Four times the friction
(B) Twice the friction
(C) One-half the friction
(D) One-fourth the friction

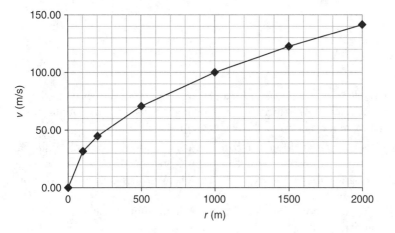

137. The graph above depicts the tangential velocities of several circular space stations with different radii. All the stations are spinning. Which of the following statements is true?

(A) The centripetal accelerations of the three shorter radii space stations are greater than 10 m/s²; those of the larger ones are less than 10 m/s².
(B) The centripetal accelerations of the three shorter radii space stations are greater than 5 m/s²; those of the larger ones are less than 5 m/s².
(C) The centripetal accelerations of all the stations are all nearly 5 m/s².
(D) The centripetal accelerations of all the stations are all nearly 10 m/s².

138. The Earth is at an average distance of 1 AU from the Sun and has an orbital period of 1 year. Jupiter orbits the Sun at approximately 5 AU. About how long is the orbital period of Jupiter?

(A) 1 year
(B) 2 years
(C) 5 years
(D) 11 years

139. An ice skater with mass m skates around a flat, circular rink with a diameter D on a planet with a gravitation field g. If it takes her a period T to go around the rink once, develop an expression for the coefficient of friction between the ice and the skater.

(A) $\mu = \dfrac{\pi D}{gT}$

(B) $\mu = \dfrac{2\pi^2 D}{gT^2}$

(C) $\mu = \dfrac{2\pi}{gT}$

(D) $\mu = \dfrac{\pi^2 D^2}{gT^2}$

140. Two satellites of equal mass orbit a planet. Satellite B orbits at twice the radius of Satellite A. Which of the following statements is true about the gravitational force between the planet and its satellites?

(A) The gravitational force on Satellite A is one-fourth that on Satellite B.
(B) The gravitational force on Satellite A is one-half that on Satellite B.
(C) The gravitational force on Satellite A is two times greater than that on Satellite B.
(D) The gravitational force on Satellite A is four times greater than that on Satellite B.

141. Assign the acceleration of the Moon the symbol a_m and the mass of the Moon M_m. If a satellite with a mass M_s were placed in the same orbit at the same speed, what is the gravitational field strength at the satellite's orbital position?

(A) a_m
(B) $(M_s/M_m)\, a_m$
(C) $(M_m/M_s)\, a_m$
(D) $(M_s + M_m)\, a_m/M_s$

142. The mass, turn radius, and speed of each car in the table below are shown relative to Car A. Which of the following best ranks the centripetal force on the cars?

Car	Mass	Radius	Speed
A	M	R	V
B	$2M$	R	V
C	M	$2R$	V
D	M	$2R$	$2V$

(A) $D > A = B > C$
(B) $D > C = B > A$
(C) $D = A = B > C$
(D) $D = B > A > C$

143. The coefficient of friction between the rubber tires of a car and dry concrete is $\mu = 0.64$. If a car enters a horizontal turn with a radius of 10.0 m, what is the maximum speed that the car can have and still maintain contact with the road?

(A) 4 m/s
(B) 8 m/s
(C) 32 m/s
(D) 64 m/s

Free Response Questions 144–147:
Two satellites orbit a 1×10^{24}–kg planet as shown in the diagram below. The 400-kg satellite moves in a circular orbit at as distance of 3 planet radii from the center of the planet while the 100-kg satellite moves in a circular orbit at a distance of 2 planet radii from the center of the planet.

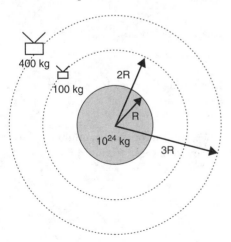

144. Compare the gravitational field strength at the surface of the planet with the gravitational field strength at each satellite's location, clearly justifying your comparison.

145. Derive an expression from basic principles that allows you to compare the speed of the 400-kg satellite with the speed of the 100-kg satellite and describe how the speeds compare.

146. If $R = 2 \times 10^6$ m, calculate how many hours it takes the 400-kg satellite to complete one orbit.

147. At the instant the satellites are aligned radially (as shown in the original diagram), rank the magnitude of the following forces from greatest to least, clearly justifying your reasoning:

    I. Gravitational force of the 400-kg satellite on the 100-kg satellite
    II. Gravitational force of the 100-kg satellite on the 400-kg satellite
    III. Gravitational force of the planet on the 100-kg satellite
    IV. Gravitational force of the planet on the 400-kg satellite

Free Response Questions 148–150:

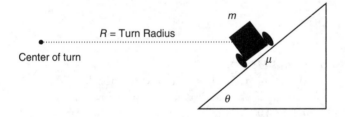

R = Turn Radius

Center of turn

A race car makes a turn on a banked track as shown above.

148. Draw a free-body diagram of this situation, clearly labeling all the forces on the car.

149. Calculate the car's maximum speed, assuming the track is frictionless. Use $m = 1,000$ kg, R = 300 m, and $\theta = 30°$.

150. Using a bank angle $\theta = 0$o, derive an expression for the minimum friction coefficient, μ, required for the car to move at a speed v around the turn with radius R.

CHAPTER 4

Simple Harmonic Motion

Questions 151–165 are easier practice questions designed to allow the student to review specific AP learning objectives and essential knowledge of simple harmonic motion.

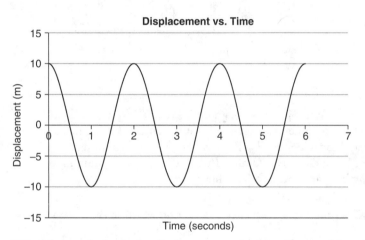

151. The graph shows the displacement versus time for an object. Which equation best describes its displacement in meters?

    (A) $\Delta x = 20 \cos(0.5t)$
    (B) $\Delta x = 10 \cos(2t)$
    (C) $\Delta x = 10 \cos(\pi t)$
    (D) $\Delta x = 20 \sin(\pi t)$

152. A meter stick is held at one end by a frictionless pivot and is held horizontally at the other end. Neglecting air resistance, how far will the meter stick swing when released?

(A) It will swing in a circle around the pivot and back to the starting point.

(B) It will swing just short of horizontal on the other side of the pivot.

(C) It will swing just beyond horizontal on the other side of the pivot.

(D) It will swing to horizontal on the other side of the pivot.

Questions 153 & 154 refer to the following material:

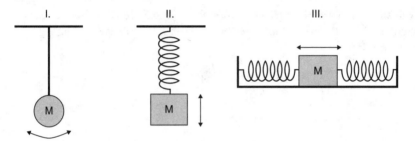

The three systems above are vibrating along the directions shown by the double-headed arrows. The first system is a small mass at the end of a string that's swinging back and forth in a small arc. The second system is a spring-mass system vibrating up and down vertically. The third system is a spring-mass system vibrating back and forth horizontally.

153. The mass, M, affects the frequency of vibration which of the systems above?

(A) I only

(B) II & III

(C) I, II, & III

(D) None of the systems

154. Assuming the vibrations are small, the amplitude of vibration (represented by the length of the double-headed arrows) significantly affects the frequency of which of the oscillating systems above?

(A) I only

(B) II & III

(C) I, II, & III

(D) None of the systems

155. A 2.0-m pendulum on a particular planet has a period of 4.6 s. What is the gravitational field strength on that planet?

(A) 1.6 N/kg
(B) 3.7 N/kg
(C) 4.9 N/kg
(D) 9.8 N/kg

156. Which choice below best explains why a pendulum does not oscillate in zero gravity?

(A) The pendulum has no mass in zero gravity.
(B) A pendulum requires gravity to create the restoring force.
(C) The pendulum is in orbit and considered weightless.
(D) The pendulum only oscillates in a rotating frame of reference like the Earth.

157. A spring-mass oscillator with negligible friction has a 10-kg mass and a spring constant of 20 N/m. When set in motion, what is the period of vibration when the system is vertical and horizontal, respectively.

(A) 4 s and 9 s
(B) 9 s for both
(C) 9 s and 18 s
(D) 4 s for both

158. Some large oil tankers have an antiroll water tank inside the hull that matches the resonant frequency of the ship's hull. When ocean waves hit the ship at the resonant frequency, how does the water tank prevent the ship from capsizing in the waves?

(A) The water in the tank is in phase with the ship's hull.
(B) The waves enter the tank and are dampened.
(C) The water tank is 180° out of phase with the ship's hull.
(D) The water tank is 90° out of phase with the ship's hull.

159. The displacement (in centimeters) of the vibrating cone of a large loudspeaker is represented by the equation $\Delta x = 2.0 \cos(150t)$. What is the frequency of the vibration of the tip of the cone?

(A) 24 Hz
(B) 0.042 Hz
(C) 150 Hz
(D) 2.0 Hz

160. A Foucault pendulum is a large pendulum often used to demonstrate that the Earth rotates relative to the stars. A Foucault pendulum at a children's museum has a 28-kg bob that is 38 cm in diameter, and it is hung on a wire that is 67 m long. What are its period and frequency, respectively?

    (A) 0.061 s and 16 cycles/s
    (B) 16 s and 0.061 cycle/s
    (C) 11 s and 0.094 cycle/s
    (D) 0.094 s and 11 cycles/s

161. An air conditioner compressor that has a mass of 8 kg is fixed to parallel springs on the refrigerator frame. The effective spring constant of the springs is 60 N/m. What is the natural frequency of the compressor system?

    (A) 0.01 cycle/s
    (B) 0.3 cycle/s
    (C) 0.4 cycle/s
    (D) 2 cycles/s

162. A mass is attached to a spring and allowed to oscillate vertically. Which of the following would NOT change the period of the oscillation?

    (A) Double the mass and double the spring constant
    (B) Double the amplitude of vibration and double the mass
    (C) Double the gravitational field strength and double the mass
    (D) Double the gravitational field strength and double the spring constant

163. A 0.40-kg mass hangs on a spring with a spring constant of 12 N/m. The system oscillates with a constant amplitude of 12 cm. What is the maximum acceleration of the system?

    (A) 0.62 m/s^2
    (B) 1.4 m/s^2
    (C) 1.6 m/s^2
    (D) 3.6 m/s^2

164. The pendulum on an old mechanical, weight-driven clock has a period of 3.0 s. What is the length of the clock's pendulum?

    (A) 2.3 m
    (B) 3.5 m
    (C) 22 cm
    (D) 35 cm

165. A blue light wave vibrates at 6.98×10^{14} Hz. What is its period of vibration?

    (A) 6.98×10^{14} s
    (B) 1.43×10^{-15} s
    (C) 9.0×10^{-15} s
    (D) 2.3×10^{-16} s

Questions 166–200 are higher-level, AP-style questions designed to test enduring understanding of AP content.

Questions 166 and 167 refer to the following material:

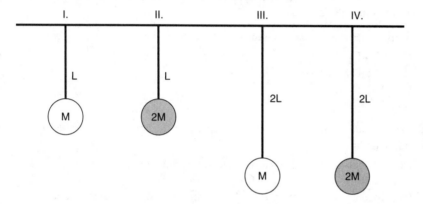

Pendulums II and IV have twice the mass of pendulums I and III. Pendulums III and IV have twice the length of Pendulums I and II. All four of the pendulums are set into motion with a displacement angle of 10 degrees.

166. Rank the vibration period of each simple pendulum.

    (A) IV > III > II > I
    (B) III > IV > I > II
    (C) IV = III > II = I
    (D) I = II > III = IV

167. Rank the frequency of vibration of each simple pendulum.

    (A) IV > III > II > I
    (B) III > IV > I > II
    (C) IV = III > II = I
    (D) I = II > III = IV

Questions 168 and 169 refer to the following material:

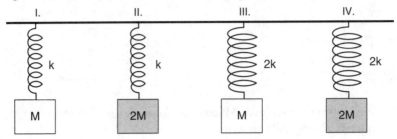

The spring-mass systems above are set into oscillation. Systems I & III have the twice the mass of systems II & IV. Systems III & IV have twice the spring constant of systems I & II.

168. Rank the period of each system's oscillation.

    (A) II > I > IV > III

    (B) II > I = IV > III

    (C) I = II > III = IV

    (D) IV > III > II > I

169. Which the following statements is true about the spring-mass oscillators in the diagram?

    (A) Increasing the gravitational field strength will increase the period of oscillation.

    (B) Increasing the gravitational field strength will decrease the period of oscillation.

    (C) An increase in air density will decrease the period of oscillation.

    (D) An increase the amplitude of vibration will have no effect on the period of oscillation.

Questions 170 and 171 refer to the following material:

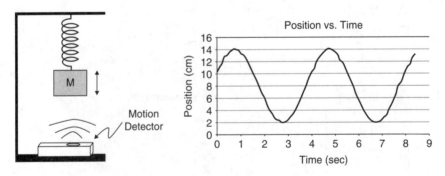

A motion detector is set up underneath an spring-mass system as shown in the diagram. The postion versus time graphs diplays the data produced by the motion detector as the system oscillates.

170. Which of the following graphs best represents how the **speed** of the oscillating system changes with time? (Note: for clarity, the slight fluctuations in the motion detector data have been smoothed in order to produce the following graphs.)

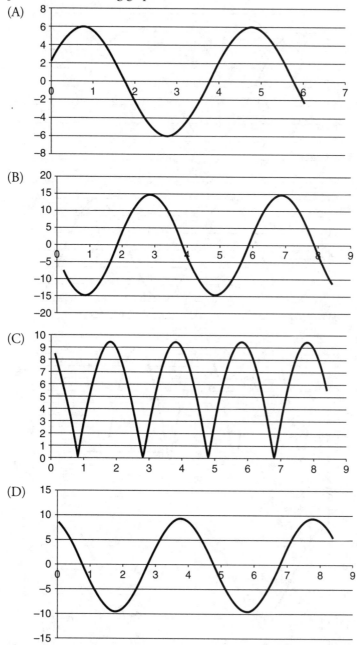

171. Which of the following graphs best represents how the **acceleration** of the oscillating system changes with time? (Note: for clarity, the slight fluctuations in the motion detector data have been smoothed in order to produce the following graphs.)

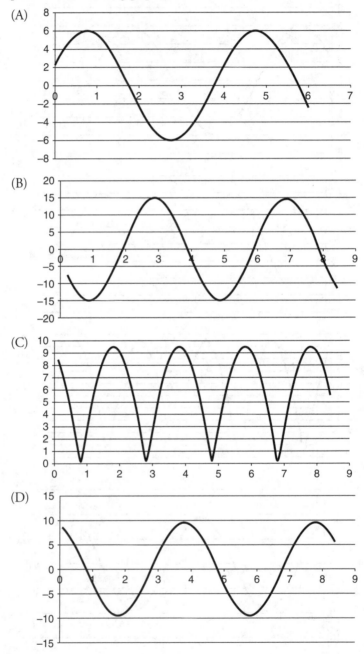

172. A mass of 12 kg is hung onto a spring attached to the ceiling. The spring's constant is 190 N/m. How far will the spring stretch when the weight is hung, and what will be the system's period when activated?

    (A) 0.42 m and 0.26 s
    (B) 0.42 m and 1.6 s
    (C) 0.63 m and 0.26 s
    (D) 0.63 m and 1.6 s

173. A bell is rung when the dangling clapper within it makes contact with the bell. A poorly designed bell has a clapper that swings with the same period as the bell. How can this design be improved?

    (A) Use a clapper with a smaller mass on the end so it is out of period with the bell.
    (B) Use a clapper with a bigger mass on the end so it is out of period with the bell.
    (C) Force the bell to swing with greater amplitude.
    (D) Use a longer clapper so it is out of period with the bell.

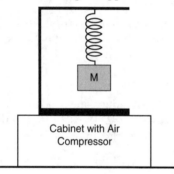

174. A spring-mass system hangs on a ring stand that rests on top of a cabinet as shown in the diagram above. The cabinet houses the air compressor for a physics lab. The compressor shakes the ring stand 0.2 centimeters up and down at a rate of 6 vibrations per second. Which of the following is a true statement?

    (A) The maximum vibration amplitude of the spring-mass system is 0.2 cm.
    (B) The spring mass system will only vibrate for very high values of the spring constant.
    (C) The spring-mass system may vibrate with an amplitude considerable greater than 0.2cm.
    (D) The spring-mass system will vibrate wildly if it has a natural frequency of 12 vibrations per second.

175. A steel ball with a mass of 100 g is dropped onto a steel plate. The collision is perfectly elastic. From what height must the ball be dropped for the vibrating system to have a bounce period of 2.0 s?

(A) 0.5 m
(B) 2 m
(C) 5 m
(D) 10 m

176. A pendulum on the surface of the Moon has a period of 1.0 s. If the length of the pendulum is quadrupled, what is the value of the new period?

(A) 0.25 s
(B) 0.50 s
(C) 1.0 s
(D) 2.0 s

177. A particle oscillates with simple harmonic motion with no damping. Which one of the following statements about the acceleration of the oscillating particle is true?

(A) It has a value of 10 m/s^2 when the oscillation is vertical.
(B) It is zero when the speed is the minimum.
(C) It is proportional to the frequency.
(D) It is zero when the speed is the maximum.

178. The displacement (in centimeters) of the vibrating cone of a large loudspeaker is represented by the equation $\Delta x = 2.0 \cos(150t)$, where t is the time in seconds. What total distance does the tip of the cone move in half a period of oscillation?

(A) 0.007 cm
(B) 1.0 cm
(C) 2.0 cm
(D) 4.0 cm

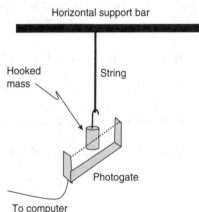

179. In the physics lab, a hooked mass is hung from a string as shown above. A photogate is set up at the bottom of the swing that provides a signal to the computer when and infrared beam (represented by the dashed line on the diagram) is blocked or unblocked by the hooked mass. How can the photogate signal be used to measure the oscillation period of the swing of the hooked mass?

(A) Divide the diameter of the hooked mass by the elapsed time between when the beam is blocked and subsequently unblocked.

(B) Measure the elapsed time between when the beam is blocked and subsequently unblocked.

(C) Measure the elapsed time between when the beam is blocked and subsequently blocked again.

(D) Double the elapsed time between when the beam is blocked and subsequently blocked again.

Questions 180–183 are based on the following figure of a mass-spring system. Assume the mass is pulled back to position +A and released, and it slides back and forth without friction.

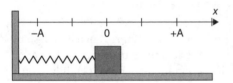

180. When the mass reaches position −A, what can be said about its speed?

(A) It is a minimum.

(B) It is a maximum.

(C) It is zero.

(D) It is decreasing.

181. When the mass reaches position 0, what can be said about its speed?

(A) It is at its minimum.

(B) It is at its maximum.

(C) It is zero.

(D) It is decreasing.

182. At what position does the mass have the greatest acceleration?

(A) −A

(B) −A/2

(C) 0

(D) +A/2

183. The mass is released from the −A position at time $t = 0$, and it oscillates with period T, measured in seconds. Which equation best represents the displacement?

(A) $\Delta x = -A \cos\left(\dfrac{T}{2\pi}t\right)$

(B) $\Delta x = -(A/2) \cos\left(2\pi T t\right)$

(C) $\Delta x = -A \cos\left(\dfrac{2\pi}{T}t\right)$

(D) $\Delta x = (A/2) \cos\left(T t\right)$

184. A mass is suspended from a spring and allowed to oscillate freely. When the amplitude of vibration is doubled, what happens to the frequency of vibration?

(A) It quadruples.
(B) It doubles.
(C) It stays the same.
(D) It reduces to one-half of what it was.

185. The Moon has a gravitational field strength that is approximately one-sixth of the gravitational field on the Earth. What is the ratio between the period of a pendulum on the Moon and the period of an identical pendulum on the Earth?

(A) 6
(B) $\sqrt{6}$
(C) $\dfrac{1}{6}$
(D) $\dfrac{1}{\sqrt{6}}$

Multi-select: For questions 186–190, two of the suggested answers will be correct. Select the two best answers, and record them both on the answer sheet.

186. Which of the following are the best examples of simple harmonic motion?

(A) A tennis ball bouncing on the ground
(B) A child swinging freely back and forth in a toddler swing
(C) A ball rolling back and forth in a bowl
(D) A child who continues to jump up and down

187. Which of the following best represent periodic motion?
    (A) A skydiver who has reached terminal velocity
    (B) The Moon in orbit about the Earth
    (C) A car driving to each state in the United States
    (D) A pendulum swinging over a 30-min time span

188. Which of the following significantly affect the period of a simple pendulum?
    (A) The length of the pendulum
    (B) The mass of the pendulum bob
    (C) The amplitude of swing
    (D) The gravitational field strength

189. A mass is suspended from a vertical spring attached to a support. Which of the following significantly affect the period of oscillation of this system?
    (A) The spring constant
    (B) The gravitational field strength
    (C) The value of the mass
    (D) Friction between the mass and the spring

190. A mass oscillates from the end of a vertical spring. What may be done to increase the frequency of oscillation?
    (A) Increase the amplitude of vibration
    (B) Decrease the mass
    (C) Increase the spring constant
    (D) Increase the strength of the gravitational field

Free Response Questions 191–195:

A system consists of a 2.0-kg mass hanging from a vertical spring that has a spring constant of 8.0 N/m. The system is displaced 20.0 cm and continues to vibrate with no damping.

191. Determine the amplitude, and calculate the period and frequency of the oscillation.

192. Write an equation for the displacement (in centimeters) of the mass as a function of time.

193. Sketch two oscillations of the displacement versus time graph.

194. Calculate the maximum values of spring force, acceleration, and velocity of the mass.

195. During one full oscillation, explain when the points of maximum acceleration and maximum velocity occur.

Free Response Questions 196–200:

A student group is conducting a lab to determine the variables that affect the period of a pendulum motion. The group identified three variables to test: the length of the pendulum, the mass of the pendulum bob, and the displacement angle of the swing. Answer the following questions about this experiment.

196. Explain how the period of the pendulum is measured. Identify the instruments that may be used to measure period, and comment on uncertainties in measurement.

197. The group first conducts an experiment to test the effect of the length of the pendulum. Identify the independent variable, the dependent variable, and the controlled (constant) variables in this experiment.

198. Sketch the expected shape of the period versus length graph.

199. Next, the group tests the effect of the mass of the bob on the period. Based on your knowledge of the pendulum, make all the necessary calculations to predict the missing data in this table:

Mass of Bob (g)	Period (s)
10.	
20.	
30.	0.76
40.	
50.	

Angle of swing = 20°, and the length of the pendulum = _____ m

200. Because of budgeting issues, the students did not test the effect of the gravitational field on the period of the pendulum. Based on your knowledge of a pendulum, sketch the shape of the graph of period versus the square root of the gravitational field. No numbers are required on your graph axes.

CHAPTER 5

Impulse, Linear Momentum, Conservation of Linear Momentum, and Collisions

Questions 201–215 are easier practice questions designed to allow the student to review specific AP learning objectives and essential knowledge of momentum and impulse.

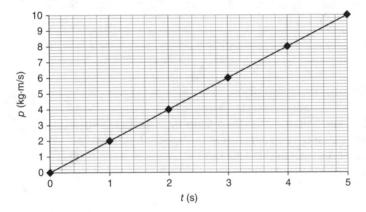

201. This graph depicts the motion of a box pushed across the floor. Which of the following statements describes the force upon the box?

(A) The force on the box is a constant 0.5 N.
(B) The force on the box is a constant 1 N.
(C) The force on the box is a constant 2 N.
(D) The force on the box is 2 N and increasing.

202. The momentum change of an object exactly equals which of the following?

(A) The force acting on the object
(B) The velocity change of the object
(C) The product of average force and the time the force acts
(D) The product of force and the change in velocity

203. A 1.0×10^3-kg car moving at a velocity of +11.0 m/s strikes a concrete barrier and comes to a complete stop in 2.0 s. What is the average force acting on the car?

(A) −5,500 N
(B) −180 N
(C) 180 N
(D) +5,500 N

204. A 2.0-kg ball moving at +10 m/s strikes a wall and bounces back. The collision is perfectly elastic. What is the ball's momentum immediately after the collision?

(A) −10 kg×m/s
(B) −20 kg×m/s
(C) +10 kg×m/s
(D) +20 kg×m/s

205. A 10-kg box is sliding across an ice rink at 10 m/s. A skater exerts a constant force of 10 N against it. How long will it take for the box to come to a complete stop?

(A) 0.5 s
(B) 1.0 s
(C) 10 s
(D) 100 s

206. Two balls of equal mass collide. Ball A moves to the right with a velocity of +10 m/s. Ball B moves to the left with a speed of 5 m/s. After the collision, Ball B moves to the right at 8 m/s. What is the velocity of Ball A immediately after the collision?

(A) −8 m/s
(B) −3 m/s
(C) +3 m/s
(D) +8 m/s

207. A 140-kg fullback is running in the positive direction with the football at a speed of 10 m/s. A 70-kg defender runs at him in the opposite direction at 5 m/s. The defender wraps his arms around the fullback. What is the velocity of the two players immediately after the collision?

(A) −10 m/s
(B) −5 m/s
(C) 0 m/s
(D) +5 m/s

208. A firework shell reaches the top of its parabolic trajectory and explodes. What happens to the center of mass of the system of all the shell fragments?

(A) It moves toward the largest fragment.
(B) It moves toward the smallest fragment.
(C) It continues to move in its original parabolic trajectory.
(D) It curves upward before falling back down.

209. A batter applies a constant force of 10.0 N over a period of 5.00 milliseconds when she strikes a softball. The mass of the baseball is 145 g. What is the magnitude of the velocity change of the baseball?

(A) 0.100 m/s
(B) 0.345 m/s
(C) 0.500 m/s
(D) 2.93 m/s

210. A 10-kg cart moving to the right at 5 m/s has a head-on collision with a 5-kg cart moving to the left at 7 m/s. If the carts stick together, what is the velocity of the combination?

(A) 1 m/s to the right
(B) 1 m/s to the left
(C) 9 m/s to the right
(D) 9 m/s to the left

211. A 750-kg aircraft is flying level at 100 m/s. A tailwind blows for 2 min, and the aircraft's speed increases to 120 m/s. What was the average force of the tailwind?

(A) 125 N
(B) 250 N
(C) 2,500 N
(D) 5,000 N

212. A 70.0-kg stunt person free-falls from a building for 2.5 s and hits an airbag. The airbag exerts a force over a time period of 2.0 s, and they comes to a complete stop. What was the magnitude of the average force exerted by the airbag on the person?

(A) 100 N
(B) 280 N
(C) 480 N
(D) 880 N

213. A rifle fires a 4.0-g bullet at a velocity of 950 m/s. If the bullet is in the rifle barrel for only 0.1 s, what average force does the rifle exert on the bullet?

    (A) 18 N
    (B) 28 N
    (C) 38 N
    (D) 48 N

214. A 1,000-kg cannon fires a 15-kg cannonball. The cannon is mounted on a low-friction carriage that allows it to recoil at −1.5 m/s. What is the speed of the cannonball?

    (A) 10 m/s
    (B) 50 m/s
    (C) 100 m/s
    (D) 200 m/s

215. A 5-kg cart moving with a kinetic energy of 8 joules has an elastic collision with a 10-kg cart moving to the left with 10 Joules of kinetic energy. What is the kinetic energy of the system of both carts after the collision?

    (A) 2 J
    (B) 14 J
    (C) 18 J
    (D) 60 J

Questions 216–250 are higher-level, AP-style questions designed to test enduring understanding of AP content.

216. A 1800-kg truck moving North at 15 m/s has a head-on collision with a 900-kg car moving south at 22 m/s. During the collision, compare the magnitudes of the following quantities for the car versus the truck during the collision.

	Force	Acceleration	Momentum Change
(A)	Same	Same	Same
(B)	Same	Different	Same
(C)	Different	Same	Different
(D)	Different	Different	Different

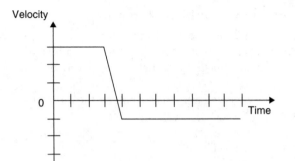

217. A 1-kg cart and a 2-kg cart have a head-on collision on a low friction track. The 1-kg cart experiences the velocity vs. time graphs shown above. Which of the following is a possible velocity vs. time graph for the 2-kg cart, assuming the axes have an identical scale to the given graph?

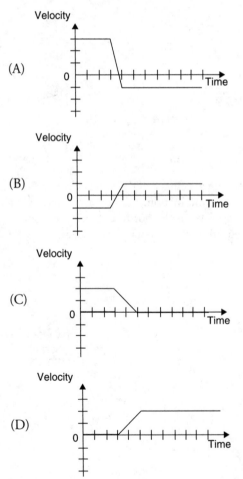

218. The following objects strike a stationary lab cart horizontally.

    I. A 50-gram ball moving at 2 m/s and bouncing back at 1m/s
    II. A 100-gram ball moving at 1 m/s and bouncing back at 0.5 m/s
    III. A 50-gram lump of clay moving at 2 m/s sticking to the cart and slowing to 1 m/s.
    IV. A 100-gram lump of clay moving at 2 m/s sticking to the cart and slowing to 1 m/s.

Rank the final speed of the cart after each collision.

    (A) I = II > IV > III
    (B) I = II > III = IV
    (C) I = III > IV > II
    (D) IV > II > I = III

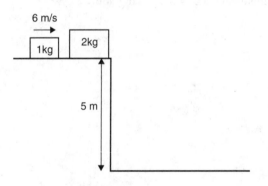

219. A 1-kg block of dry ice moving at 6 m/s collides and sticks to a 2-kg block of dry ice initially at rest. The combination slides off a 20-meter-tall cliff as shown in the diagram above. What is the horizontal distance from the base of the cliff to the landing location of the block combination?

    (A) 1 m
    (B) 2 m
    (C) 4 m
    (D) 5 m

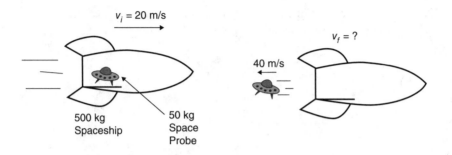

$v_i = 20$ m/s

$v_f = ?$

40 m/s

500 kg
Spaceship

50 kg
Space
Probe

220. A 500 kg spaceship in deep space is holding a 50 kg space probe, and the pair is initially drifting to the right at 20 m/s as shown in the first diagram above. If the spaceship fires the probe to the left at 40 m/s, what is the new speed of the spaceship?

(A) 9 m/s
(B) 13 m/s
(C) 18 m/s
(D) 26 m/s

Questions 221 and 222 refer to the following material:

Two railroad cars, each with of mass m, are traveling in the same direction along a track. Before the collision, Car A is initially traveling with speed v and Car B moving at half of Car A's speed. When Car A catches up with Car B, the two cars link together.

221. What is the speed of the combined cars after the collision?

(A) $\frac{1}{4}v$

(B) $\frac{1}{2}v$

(C) $\frac{2}{3}v$

(D) $\frac{3}{4}v$

222. What is the amount of energy transferred to internal energy in the system, including thermal and sound energy?

(A) $\dfrac{1}{16}mv^2$

(B) $\dfrac{5}{8}mv^2$

(C) $\dfrac{9}{16}mv^2$

(D) $\dfrac{3}{4}mv^2$

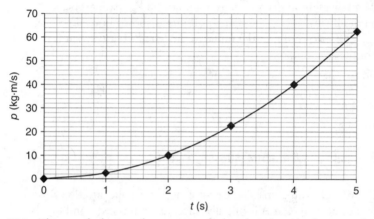

223. This graph depicts the motion of a box being pushed across a horizontal floor with negligible friction. Which of the following statements describes the force upon the box?

(A) The force on the box is constant.
(B) The force on the box is decreasing.
(C) The force on the box is increasing.
(D) More information is needed to describe the force on the box.

Questions 224 and 225 refer to the following material:

Two skaters are initially at rest on an ice rink. The first skater is a teenager with mass m and the second skater is a child with one-third of the mass of the teenager. The skaters push on each other and the child moves off with a speed v_C.

224. What is the speed of the teenager immediately after the push?

(A) $\dfrac{v_C}{3}$

(B) $\dfrac{v_C}{2}$

(C) $\dfrac{2v_C}{3}$

(D) $3v_C$

225. If the time of contact during the push is Δt, compare the magnitudes of the average forces on the teenager and the child.

(A) The child feels a force of $2mv_C\Delta t$ and the teenager's force is $mv_C\Delta t$

(B) The child feels a force of $3mv_C\Delta t$ and the teenager's force is $mv_C\Delta t$

(C) The child feels a force of $\dfrac{3mv_C}{\Delta t}$ and the teenager's force is $\dfrac{mv_C}{\Delta t}$

(D) Both forces are $\dfrac{mv_C}{3\Delta t}$

226. A cue ball with a mass of 250 g travels at 1.0 m/s and hits a numbered ball with a mass of 170 g at rest. The numbered ball moves off at an angle of 45°, while the cue ball moves off at an angle of −45°. At what speeds do the balls move?

(A) The cue ball and the numbered ball move at 1.0 m/s.

(B) The cue ball moves at 1.0 m/s, and the numbered ball moves at −1.0 m/s.

(C) The cue ball moves at 0.71 m/s, and the numbered ball moves at 0.71 m/s.

(D) The cue ball moves at 0.71 m/s, and the numbered ball moves at 1.04 m/s.

227. A 7.5-g bullet is fired from a loosely held 1.2-kg handgun. The bullet travels away at +365 m/s. At what velocity does the handgun recoil?

(A) −2.3 m/s
(B) −1.2 m/s
(C) +1.2 m/s
(D) +2.3 m/s

228. Rank the momenta of the following objects.

   I. A 90,000,000-kg aircraft carrier moving at 2 cm/s
  II. A 30,000-kg dump truck at rest
 III. A 1,000-kg SUV moving at 25 m/s
 IV. A proton moving at 90 percent of the speed of light

(A) IV > I > III > II
(B) I > III > IV > II
(C) I > II > III > IV
(D) IV > III > I > II

229. In a particular crash safety test, engineers study what happens when cars hit solid walls. Which of the following observations best indicates that LESS force is exerted on the car?

(A) The car hits the wall and bounces back.
(B) The car crushes during the collision.
(C) The crash dummy flies through the windshield.
(D) The front seat airbags are deployed.

230. A 4-kg cart moving to the right with 18 J of kinetic energy has a head-on collision with a 2-kg cart moving to the left with 1 J of kinetic energy. After the collision, the 4-kg cart continues moving to the right, but its kinetic energy decreases to 2 J. The 2-kg cart is driven to the right, but its kinetic energy increases to 9 J. Which of the following is true about this collision?

(A) This is an inelastic collision that demonstrates momentum conservation.
(B) This is an elastic collision that demonstrates momentum conservation.
(C) This is an inelastic collision where momentum is not conserved.
(D) This is an elastic collision where momentum is not conserved.

231. A cannonball is shot out of the barrel of a horizontal cannon. Which of the following results in the cannonball leaving a cannon with the least speed?

(A) Increase the strength of the gravitational field
(B) Decrease the length of the cannon barrel
(C) Decrease the friction in the barrel
(D) Decrease the mass of the ball while keeping its size the same

Questions 232 and 233 refer to the following material:

A 50.0-gram ball moving to the left strikes a wall and bounces back to the right. Slow motion video analysis produces the following horizontal position versus time graph.

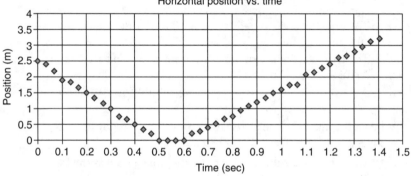

232. Determine the momentum change of the bouncing ball.

(A) +0.05 kg·m/s
(B) +0.45 kg·m/s
(C) −0.45 kg·m/s
(D) −0.05 kg·m/s

233. The video camera used in the experiment has a frame rate of 30 pictures per second. In the video, the ball makes contact with the floor for three frames. What is the magnitude and direction of the average force that the ball exerts on the wall?

(A) 7.2 N to the right
(B) 4.5 N to the right
(C) 4.5 N to the left
(D) 7.2 N to the left

Multi-select: For questions 234–238, two of the suggested answers will be correct. Select the two best answers, and record them both on the answer sheet.

234. Which of the following may be modeled as an elastic collision?
   (A) A ball bounces as high as it's dropped.
   (B) Two cars experience a head-on collision.
   (C) A piece of soft clay hits a wall and sticks.
   (D) A moving cart stops as it hits and pushes a resting cart away at the same speed.

235. Which of the following two statements are true for an isolated system of two colliding objects?
   (A) The system's momentum is the same before and after inelastic and elastic collisions.
   (B) The velocity of the system's center of mass is the same before and after the collision.
   (C) The system's kinetic energy is the same before and after an inelastic collision.
   (D) A system's thermal energy will change during an elastic collision.

236. When a bat hits a tee-ball at rest, which two of the following will increase the magnitude of the tee-ball's momentum?
   (A) The bat contacts the ball for twice the time with half the force.
   (B) The bat contacts the ball for the same amount of time but exerts twice the force on the ball.
   (C) The bat hits the ball with the same force but contacts it for a greater time.
   (D) The bat hits the ball with the same force and contacts it for half the time.

237. Which of the two following quantities are needed to determine the momentum of an object at a particular instant?
   (A) Its acceleration
   (B) Its speed
   (C) Its direction of motion
   (D) The net force on the object

238. The momentum of a system is conserved in which of the following two scenarios?

    (A) The center of mass of a system accelerates
    (B) A net force acts on the system
    (C) An inelastic collision occurs within a two-cart system
    (D) An explosion occurs within a system

Questions 239–241 refer to the following material:

A 800.0-kg car is traveling along a wet road at a velocity of 25.5 m/s. A 1,000.0-kg car is traveling along the same road in the same direction at 34.7 m/s. The two cars collide and lock together.

239. The two interlocked cars proceed at what velocity immediately after the collision?

    (A) 30.6 m/s
    (B) 34.7 m/s
    (C) 35.3 m/s
    (D) 60.2 m/s

240. Which of the following statements best describes the collision?

    (A) An elastic collision with no energy transferred to thermal energy
    (B) An inelastic collision with no energy transferred to thermal energy
    (C) An inelastic collision with 1.9×10^4 J transferred to thermal energy
    (D) An inelastic collision with 8.4×10^5 J transferred to thermal energy

241. If the coefficient of kinetic friction between the tires of the cars and the wet pavement is 0.70, how much time does it take for the two interlocked cars to come to a complete stop on the wet pavement?

    (A) 1.2 s
    (B) 2.2 s
    (C) 4.4 s
    (D) 6.3 s

Free Response questions 242–245:

A 2.0-kg box is initially moving at +3.0 m/s and is pushed along a horizontal, frictionless surface with a force that varies with time according to the following graph:

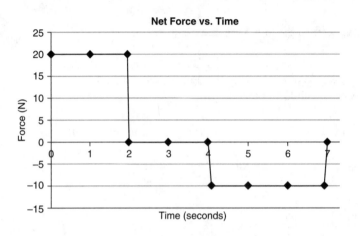

242. Qualitatively describe what happens to the motion of the box in the following time intervals: 0–2 s, 2–4 s, and 4–7 s.

243. Calculate the momentum change of the box during each second of elapsed time.

244. Plot the velocity versus time graph for this motion.

245. At the 7-second clock reading, the box collides with a wall and bounces backward at 6 m/s. Given that the box is in contact with the wall for 0.20 s, calculate the average force that the wall exerts on the box.

Free Response Questions 246–250:

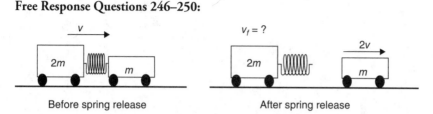

Before spring release   After spring release

The carts with masses $2m$ and m initially moving with a speed v on a low friction track as shown in the diagram. The carts are initially connected by a compressed, negligible-mass spring that is fixed to the more massive car. After the spring is released, the less-massive cart moves to the right with a speed $2v$.

246. Derive an expression for more-massive cart's velocity, v_f, in terms of m and v.

247. Find the ratio between the kinetic energy of the 2-cart system after the spring release to the system's kinetic energy before the release. Based on this ratio, explain whether this scenario is physically possible.

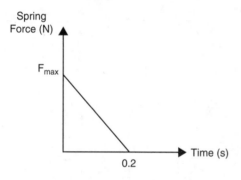

248. The force vs. time graph models the positive force that the less massive cart experiences during the release period of 0.2 seconds. Using the values $m = 500$ g and $v = 1.2$ m/s, calculate the maximum spring force, F_{max}.

249. Sketch a quantitative force vs. time graph for the system that includes the spring and the more-massive cart. Justify the signs and numbers on your graph using at least one physics principle.

250. How does the velocity of the center of mass of the 2-cart system after the spring release compare to the initial velocity, v, of the same system? Explain your reasoning and/or provide calculations.

CHAPTER 6

Work, Energy, and Conservation of Energy

Questions 251–265 are easier practice questions designed to allow the student to review specific AP learning objectives and essential knowledge of work and energy.

Questions 251–253 refer to the material below.

A roller coaster is initially moving to the right as it approaches point A in the figure below. Assume that air drag and friction are negligible.

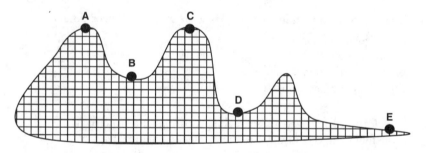

251. At which locations will a roller-coaster car have the same gravitational potential energy?
    (A) A and E
    (B) B and C
    (C) C and D
    (D) A and C

252. At which location will the roller-coaster car move at the greatest speed?
    (A) E
    (B) B
    (C) C
    (D) D

253. At which point is the total mechanical energy of the coaster-earth system the greatest?
    (A) A
    (B) D
    (C) E
    (D) It is the same at all points

254. A 5-kg box is pushed with a horizontal force of 100 N across a floor. What power output is needed to push the box a distance of 60 meters in 2 minutes?
    (A) 10 W
    (B) 25 W
    (C) 30 W
    (D) 50 W

255. What happens to the kinetic energy of a car if the car's speed doubles?
    (A) K quadruples.
    (B) K doubles.
    (C) K stays the same.
    (D) K is one-half as much.

256. A net force is applied to a system along a particular axis. Which of the following is equivalent to the change in kinetic energy of the system?
    (A) The slope of the F_{net} vs. time graph
    (B) The area of the F_{net} vs. time graph
    (C) The slope of the F_{net} vs. displacement graph
    (D) The area of the F_{net} vs. displacement graph

257. A 10-kg box is pulled across an ice rink for a distance of 50 m. It is pulled with a constant force of 10 N on a rope angled at 60° to the horizontal. How much work is done on the box?

(A) 50 J
(B) 100 J
(C) 250 J
(D) 500 J

258. Starting from rest, a 5-kg box slides all the way down a frictionless incline from a vertical height of 10 m. It travels a diagonal distance of 15 m. What is the box's velocity at the bottom of the hill?

(A) 5 m/s
(B) 10 m/s
(C) 14 m/s
(D) 17 m/s

259. An archer pulls a bowstring back a distance of 20 cm with an average force of 75 N. The arrow has a mass of 20.0 g. When the string is released, what is the velocity of the arrow when it leaves the bow?

(A) 1.2 m/s
(B) 22 m/s
(C) 32 m/s
(D) 39 m/s

260. A 1,000-kg car traveling at 30 m/s skids 10 m before it stops. What magnitude of force is the frictional force on the car?

(A) 1.5×10^3 N
(B) 3.0×10^3 N
(C) 4.5×10^3 N
(D) 4.5×10^4 N

261. A 9.0-kg box is attached to a horizontal spring with a spring constant of 2,500 N/m. If the box is pulled 12 cm horizontally from the equilibrium position, what is its maximum kinetic energy?

(A) 9.0 J
(B) 18 J
(C) 25 J
(D) 50 J

262. A 1-kg block is attached to a spring with a constant of 100 N/m. The spring is displaced 0.2 m from equilibrium. When the block is let go, what is its velocity as it passes the equilibrium point?

(A) 0.4 m/s
(B) 1.4 m/s
(C) 1.6 m/s
(D) 2.0 m/s

263. A 750-kg glider is flying level at 100.0 m/s. A tailwind blows constantly for 1,200 m, and the glider's speed increases to 120.0 m/s. What is the approximate force of the tailwind?

(A) 125 N
(B) 250 N
(C) 1,400 N
(D) 5,000 N

264. A worker pushes a lawn mower with the handle at an angle of 60° to the horizontal. A constant 20-N force is applied along the axis of the handle and moves the lawn mower a horizontal distance of 100 m in 5 min. What is the worker's power output?

(A) 3 W
(B) 7 W
(C) 10 W
(D) 17 W

265. A proposed "space elevator" lifts a 1,000-kg payload 150 km above the Earth's surface. The radius of the Earth is 6.4×10^6 m, and the Earth's mass is 6×10^{24} kg. By how much does the gravitational potential energy of the payload *change* as it is lifted from the earth's surface to the 150-km position?

(A) $+1.5 \times 10^9$ J
(B) -1.5×10^9 J
(C) $+1.4 \times 10^9$ J
(D) -1.4×10^9 J

Questions 266–300 are higher-level, AP-style questions designed to test enduring understanding of AP content.

266. A pendulum bob is pulled back and released. As it arrives to the lowest point of the swing, the bob collides with and sticks to a lump of clay and continues to swing. Assuming that air drag and pivot friction are negligible, which of the following is a correct statement about the energy in the bob/clay/earth system?

   (A) The mechanical energy remains the same throughout the swing.
   (B) Some of the initial gravitational potential energy transfers to internal energy.
   (C) The kinetic energy of the bob immediately before the collision equals the kinetic energy of the bob/clay immediately after the collision.
   (D) The gravitational energy increases throughout the swing.

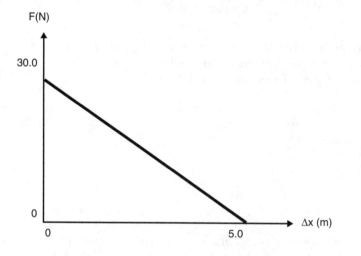

267. A 3.0-kg object, initially moving to the right with a velocity of +4.0 m/s experiences a positive net force that decreases linearly throughout the displacement as shown on the graph above. What is the kinetic energy of the object at the instant the net force is zero?

   (A) 24 J
   (B) 75 J
   (C) 99 J
   (D) 174 J

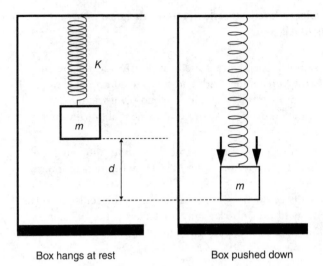

Box hangs at rest   Box pushed down

268. A box (mass m) is initially hangs at rest from a spring (spring constant k). The box is pushed down a distance d and held at rest. Find the *change* in mechanical energy of the mass-spring-earth system.

(A) $\frac{1}{2}kd^2 - mgd$

(B) $\frac{1}{2}kd^2 + mgd$

(C) $\frac{1}{2}kd^2$

(D) $2mgd$

269. The gravitational potential energy of a box sliding down an incline decreases by 25 J while the kinetic energy increases by 23 J. Which of the following best describes this scenario?

(A) The law of conservation of energy is violated in this situation.
(B) 2 J of energy is transferred to thermal energy.
(C) The momentum of the box system must remain the same.
(D) The total energy of the system must remain at 48 J.

270. A 70.0-kg stunt person freefalls from rest from a 125-m-tall building and hits an oversized airbag. The airbag compresses 5.0 as the person comes to a complete stop. What is the average force exerted by the airbag on the person?

(A) 1.0×10^2 N
(B) 2.8×10^2 N
(C) 1.8×10^4 N
(D) 2.8×10^4 N

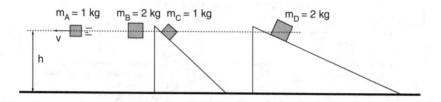

271. The four blocks shown in the figure above are released from the same height. Blocks B, C, and D are each released from rest, and block A is initially moving horizontally with a speed v. Blocks A and C each have a mass of 1 kg and blocks B and D are each 2 kg. Assuming air drag and incline friction are negligible, rank the speed of each block as it reaches the ground.

(A) $v_A = v_B > v_C > v_D$
(B) $v_A > v_B = v_C = v_D$
(C) $v_A = v_B = v_C = v_D$
(D) $v_B = v_D > v_A > v_C$

Questions 272–274 refer to the following material.

An experiment was conducted with a hoop spring attached to a force probe, both of which were mounted to a low friction dynamics cart. The compression of a hoop spring may be modeled as a Hookean spring. The system was placed on a horizontal track with a motion encoder to measure the displacement of the cart. The following graph shows the experimental force vs. displacement for a black hoop (steeper line) and a white hoop, each tested separately. The white hoop/probe/cart mass is 0.500-kg cart and the black hoop/probe/cart mass is 1.000-kg.

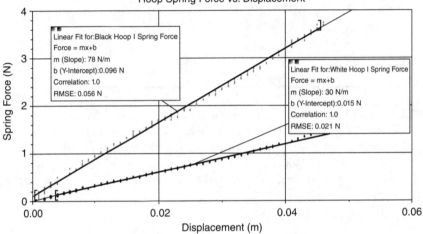

272. The carts experience a head-on collision. If the white hoop compresses a total distance of 5.0 cm, what is the compression distance of the black hoop?

   (A) 1.9 cm
   (B) 4.0 cm
   (C) 5.0 cm
   (D) 5.3 cm

273. If the cart with the black hoop is pushed against a wall and compresses the spring 5.0 cm, how fast will it be released?

   (A) 0.22 m/s
   (B) 0.44 m/s
   (C) 0.53 m/s
   (D) 0.55 m/s

274. How far must the white cart's hoop be compressed against the wall for it to leave at the same speed as the black-hoop cart moved in the previous question?

(A) 5.0 cm
(B) 5.7 cm
(C) 6.2 cm
(D) 8.1 cm

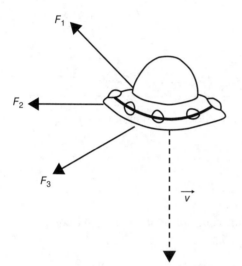

275. A spacecraft in deep space is isolated from its surroundings and is initially moving with the velocity v shown in the diagram above. It has thrusters on a swivel that fire such that the spacecraft experiences three possible forces that act at fixed angles relative the velocity vector of the spacecraft. With each of the forces separately with a steady magnitude, what initially happens to the kinetic energy, K, of the spacecraft?

	F_1	F_2	F_3
(A)	K decreases	K constant	K increases
(B)	K increases	K increases	K increases
(C)	K decreases	K constant	K decreases
(D)	K increases	K decreases	K decreases

Questions 276–277 refer to the following material:

A 5-kg box slides 10 m diagonally down a frictionless ramp inclined at 45°. At the bottom of the ramp, it slides on a rough horizontal concrete floor with a coefficient of friction of 0.6.

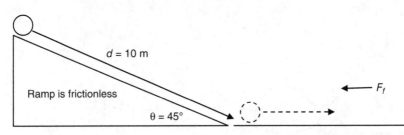

276. What is the speed of the box as it reaches the bottom of the ramp?
    (A) 6 m/s
    (B) 10 m/s
    (C) 12 m/s
    (D) 14 m/s

277. How far does the box travel on the concrete before coming to a complete stop?
    (A) 6 m
    (B) 8 m
    (C) 10 m
    (D) 12 m

278. Two cannons fire identical cannonballs with the same amount of powder. The barrel of Cannon 2 is twice as long as the barrel of Cannon 1. How does the velocity of a cannonball fired from Cannon 2 compare with that of the ball fired from Cannon 1?
    (A) Four times that of Cannon 1
    (B) Twice that of Cannon 1
    (C) 1.4 times that of Cannon 1
    (D) One-half that of Cannon 1

279. A tire hangs at rest from a rope in a gravitational field g. The tire has a mass m and a child has a mass equivalent to the mass of two tires. A child runs and jumps on the swing. How fast must the child run in order for the swing to raise a vertical distance d?

(A) $\sqrt{gd}$

(B) $\sqrt{2gd}$

(C) $\frac{3}{2}\sqrt{2gd}$

(D) $2\sqrt{gd}$

280. Two 500-g carts are on a frictionless track. Cart A is moving at 0.2 m/s when it collides into Cart B, which is at rest. Both cars move away at 0.1 m/s. Compared to the total energy of the system before the collision, what percentage of energy is transferred to thermal energy in the collision?

(A) 10 percent
(B) 20 percent
(C) 25 percent
(D) 50 percent

281. Spring 1 is stretched and stores 2 J of elastic potential energy. An identical spring, Spring 2, is stretched and stores 18 J of elastic potential energy. What is the ratio of the displacement of Spring 2 to the displacement of Spring 1?

(A) 9:1
(B) 3:1
(C) 1:1
(D) 1:3

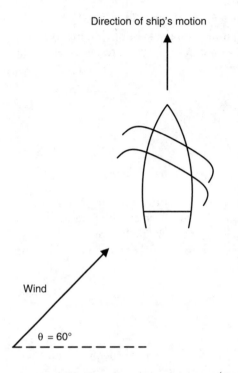

Direction of ship's motion

Wind

$\theta = 60°$

282. A tall sailing ship (m $= 1.43 \times 10^4$ kg) is initially at rest. A steady wind blows at the 60.0° angle shown in the diagram and moves the ship forward a distance of 850 m. The ship's final speed is 9.0 m/s.

What is the force of the wind on the boat?
(A) 200 N
(B) 390 N
(C) 680 N
(D) 790 N

283. A car and a pickup truck are moving down the highway. The truck is twice as massive as the car, but it is only moving at half the speed. How does the kinetic energy of the truck compare with that of the car?
(A) Four times as much
(B) Twice as much
(C) The same
(D) One-half as much

284. 50 J of gravitational potential energy is stored in a box-earth system when the box is 10 m off the ground and it's moving at 4 m/s. If a twice-as-massive box is released from rest 20 m off the ground, how much kinetic energy will it have as it arrives at the ground?

(A) 50 J

(B) 150 J

(C) 200 J

(D) 400 J

285. Rank the gravitational potential energy of the object in each of the four scenarios below:

I. A 2-kg object held at rest 3 m above the ground

II. A 2-kg object moving at 5 m/s at the instant it's 3 m off the ground

III. A 1-kg object moving at 10 m/s at the instant it's 3 m off the ground

IV. A 3-kg object held at rest 2 m above the ground

(A) I = II = IV > III

(B) II > III > I = IV

(C) III > II > I > IV

(D) I = II = III = IV

286. A spring is stretched 5 cm. What happens to its elastic potential energy if it is stretched 20 cm?

(A) It doubles.

(B) It quadruples.

(C) It increases by a factor of 8.

(D) It increases by a factor of 16.

287. Two cars skid to a stop. How does the skid distance of a 100-kg car initially moving at 30 miles per hour compare to the skid distance of a 50-kg car initially moving at 15 miles per hour?

(A) Four times as much

(B) Twice as much

(C) The same

(D) Half as much

288. Which of the following forces could be responsible for a loss of total mechanical energy in a spring-mass-earth system? Select two answers.

(A) Spring force

(B) Gravitational forces

(C) Friction force

(D) Air drag force

289. A box is pushed all the way up an incline at a constant speed of 3 m/s. An identical box is pushed all the way up the same incline at a constant speed of 6 m/s. What quantities are the SAME for these two scenarios? Select two answers.

(A) The power required to push the objects
(B) The change in gravitational potential energy
(C) The time it takes to push the box up the incline
(D) The work done on the object by the pushing force

290. A stone is propelled vertically off the ground at a speed small enough that air drag is negligible. After it is released, which of the following are true about the stone-earth system? Select two answers.

(A) Its kinetic energy decreases.
(B) Its total mechanical energy increases.
(C) Its gravitational potential energy increases.
(D) Its speed decreases linearly with its distance off the ground.

291. Which of the following scenarios result in NO work done on the underlined object? Select two answers.

(A) The gravitational force from the Earth acts on the <u>Moon</u> throughout its circular orbit.
(B) A compressed spring pushes a <u>rock</u> upward.
(C) A child pushes a <u>box</u> across a rough horizontal surface.
(D) A football player pushes on a stationary <u>wall</u> with all his might.

292. A child stands on the floor of an elevator that's initially at rest and begins to uniformly accelerate upward. Which of the following statements are true about the child-earth system throughout the acceleration? Select two answers.

(A) The total mechanical energy is constant.
(B) The gravitational potential energy increases and the kinetic energy increases.
(C) Work is done to change the total mechanical energy of the system.
(D) The net force on the system is increasing.

Free Response Questions 293–296 refer to the following material:

In her backyard, Gretchen has a swing set with a rope hanging from it. She fantasizes about running fast enough toward a rope so that she can grab the rope and swing around in a full circle.

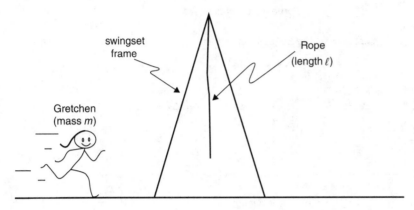

293. List at least three simplifying assumptions that need to be made in order to use basic physics models to predict the minimum speed Gretchen must run to make a full circle on the rope. Justify your assumptions.

294. Derive an expression for the minimum speed Gretchen needs at the **top** of her circular path in order to complete the full circular path.

295. Derive an expression for Gretchen's minimum running speed in order to complete a full circle swing. Pick reasonable values for the variables and use your expression to estimate a value for the minimum running speed. Comment on whether or not this speed is a realistic value for Gretchen.

296. As the child swings in the full circle at the minimum speed condition, at what position will the tension in the rope be the greatest? What is the value of tension there?

Free Response Questions 297–300:

The graph below shows the external force applied to a 15-kg object throughout a displacement of 8.0 m.

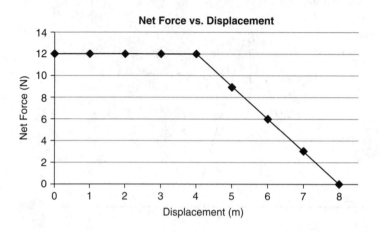

297. How much work was done on the object throughout the 8.0-m displacement?

298. If the object was initially moving with a velocity of +4.0 m/s (before the force was applied), calculate the object's kinetic energy after the work was done on it.

299. Calculate the speed of the object after the work was done on it.

300. Next, the object hits a compressional spring with a spring constant of 650 N/m. Calculate the maximum compression of the spring.

CHAPTER 7

Torque and Rotational Motion

Questions 301–315 are easier practice questions designed to allow the student to review specific AP learning objectives and essential knowledge of torque and rotational motion.

301. What happens to the rotational kinetic energy of an object if its rotational speed is tripled?

(A) The rotational kinetic energy is nine times as much.
(B) The rotational kinetic energy triples.
(C) The rotational kinetic energy stays the same.
(D) The rotational kinetic energy is one-third as much.

302. As an ice skater is spinning, she extends her arms away from her body. Assuming the friction on the ice is negligible, her angular velocity _____, and her angular momentum _____.

(A) Decreases; increases
(B) Increases; decreases
(C) Decreases; decreases
(D) Decreases; remains the same

303. At $t = 0$, a circular disk is initially rotating with a positive angular velocity of 6 radians per second. The rotation slows down at a uniform rate of 2 radians per second each and every second. What are the signs of the angular velocity, angular acceleration, and net torque at the 4-second clock reading?

	Angular velocity	Angular Acceleration	Net torque
(A)	Positive	Positive	Positive
(B)	Negative	Negative	Negative
(C)	Positive	Negative	Negative
(D)	Negative	Positive	Negative

304. A crane is used to pick up a 50.0-m-long steel beam to place in a building. The beam is uniform and horizontal, but the crane cable is placed 2.0 m off the center of the beam. How much vertical force must be placed on the guide rope to keep the beam level? The beam has a mass per meter of length is 5.0 kg/m, and the guide rope is placed on the end of the shorter side of the beam.

(A) 220 N
(B) 50 N
(C) 22 N
(D) 5 N

305. When a skater performs a spin on ice with his arms outstretched, what happens when he brings his arms close to his body?

(A) His angular acceleration decreases because his rotational inertia decreases.
(B) His angular acceleration increases because his rotational inertia decreases.
(C) His angular velocity decreases because his rotational inertia decreases.
(D) His angular velocity increases because his rotational inertia decreases.

306. A dry ice puck tethered to a string revolves in a horizontal circle on a smooth surface. If the string breaks, what happens to the angular momentum of the puck relative to center of its initial orbit? Assume friction and air drag are negligible.

(A) It increases.
(B) It decreases.
(C) It immediately increases when the string breaks, then decreases.
(D) It remains constant.

307. The rotational inertia of a thin-walled cylinder around its central axis is given by mR^2. What expression best represents the angular momentum of this cylinder if it spins about the central axis at a rate of 12 revolutions per second?

(A) $(24\,\pi)mR^2$
(B) $(12\,\pi)mR^2$
(C) $12mR^2$
(D) $\left(\dfrac{1}{12}\right)mR^2$

308. The Moon orbits the Earth once every 27.3 days with an orbital radius of 385,000 km. What is the orbital speed of the Moon in units of meters per second?

(A) 0.163 m/s
(B) 27.3 m/s
(C) 163 m/s
(D) 1,030 m/s

309. A boy and girl are on a rotating merry-go-round. The girl is on the outer edge, while the boy is halfway between the center and the girl. How does the **angular speed** of the girl compare to that of the boy?

(A) The girl's rotational speed is four times as much.
(B) The girl's rotational speed is twice as much.
(C) The girl's rotational speed is the same.
(D) The girl's rotational speed is half as much.

310. A boy and girl are still on the rotating merry-go-round. The girl is on the outer edge, while the boy is halfway between the center and the girl. How does the **linear speed** of the girl compare to that of the boy?

(A) The girl's linear speed is four times as much.
(B) The girl's linear speed is twice as much.
(C) The girl's linear speed is the same.
(D) The girl's linear speed is half as much.

311. A propeller, initially at rest, rotates about its midpoint with an angular acceleration of 12 radians/sec^2. How much time will it take to rotate through a 90.0° angle?

(A) 0.51 s
(B) 0.72 s
(C) 1.2 s
(D) 3.9 s

312. A disk, initially rotating at +11 rad/s, slows down at a constant rate of 1.5 rad/s^2. What is the angular displacement of the disk through an elapsed time of 6.0 s of time?

(A) 9.0 rad
(B) 27 rad
(C) 39 rad
(D) 66 rad

313. A car tire is initially spinning with an angular speed of 150 radians per second. As the brakes are applied, the tire slows down at a rate of 25 rad/s². How much time does it take the car to stop?

(A) 2.0 s

(B) 2.5 s

(C) 3.0 s

(D) 6.0 s

314. Two children make a seesaw out of a 5.0-m wooden plank. They balance it on a fulcrum located 2.0 m from the left end. The 42.0-kg child sits at the end of the plank on the left side. What distance (measured from the fulcrum) can the 35-kg child sit on the right side of the plank to keep it balanced?

(A) 1.0 m

(B) 1.5 m

(C) 2.0 m

(D) 2.4 m

315. An object, initially rotating with an angular speed of +15 rad/s, is subjected to a torque of +55 Nm that accelerates it constantly at +5.0 rad/s². What is the rotational inertia of the object?

(A) $3.0 \ kg \cdot m^2$

(B) $3.5 \ kg \cdot m^2$

(C) $5.5 \ kg \cdot m^2$

(D) $11 \ kg \cdot m^2$

Questions 316–350 are higher-level, AP-style questions designed to test enduring understanding of AP content.

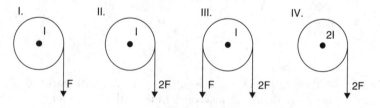

316. The figure above shows four identically-shaped discs, each with a fixed axis of rotation at their centers. Disk IV has twice the rotational inertia of disks I, II & III. The disks are subjected to a variety of forces as shown. Rank the magnitude of the angular acceleration of the disks.

(A) III > II = IV > I

(B) I = II = III = IV

(C) II = IV > I = III

(D) II > I = III = IV

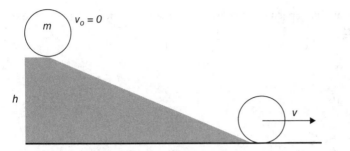

317. As shown in the figure above, a wheel (mass m) starts at rest at the top of an incline (height h) and rolls without slipping to the bottom of the incline with a speed v. Assuming the effect of air drag is negligible, which of the following is a true statement?

(A) $mgh > \frac{1}{2}mv^2$

(B) $mgh < \frac{1}{2}mv^2$

(C) $mgh = \frac{1}{2}mv^2$

(D) Additional information is needed to compare these quantities.

Questions 318–319 refer to the following information:

At a carnival, one of the booths has a shooting gallery with spring-loaded guns that fire 12-g suction-cup darts with a muzzle velocity of 2.5 m/s. The 95-g targets are 25 cm tall and hinged at the bottom and may be modeled as a plank pinned at one end ($I = \frac{1}{3}ML^2$). Assume the dart is moving horizontally when it hits the target 5 cm from the top edge and that the hinge has negligible friction.

318. Determine the magnitude of the angular momentum of the dart/target system immediately after the target is hit if angular momentum is measured relative to the hinge of the target.

(A) $0.0015\dfrac{\text{kg m}^2}{\text{s}}$

(B) $0.0030\dfrac{\text{kg m}^2}{\text{s}}$

(C) $0.0060\dfrac{\text{kg m}^2}{\text{s}}$

(D) $0.0120\dfrac{\text{kg m}^2}{\text{s}}$

319. What is the angular speed of the dart/target system immediately after the target is hit?

(A) 2.4 rad/s
(B) 3.0 rad/s
(C) 6.0 rad/s
(D) 12.5 rad/s

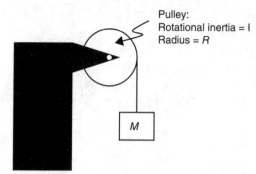

Pulley:
Rotational inertia = I
Radius = R

M

320. Taken by itself, a pulley has a rotational inertia I and radius R. A string is wrapped around the pulley and a mass M is hung from the end of it as shown in the diagram above. Which of the following is true about the magnitude of the angular acceleration of the pulley?

(A) $|\alpha| < \dfrac{MgR}{I}$

(B) $|\alpha| > \dfrac{MgR}{I}$

(C) $|\alpha| = \dfrac{MgR}{I}$

(D) More information is needed.

321. A door rotates about its hinges with negligible friction. A piece of putty is thrown at the door and sticks above the door handle. Is angular momentum conserved during the collision?

(A) Yes, but only if the door is considered as the system.
(B) Yes, it is conserved for the door/putty system.
(C) Not necessarily; the angle that the putty strikes the door must be known.
(D) No, because the putty exerts a net torque about the axis of rotation.

Questions 322–323 refer to the following information.

The diagram below shows a top-view of a rod that is free to rotate about its center and is initially rotating with a positive counterclockwise angular velocity ω_0. Two forces are applied to the rod that are steady in magnitude and will continue to act perpendicular to the rod, even after it rotates.

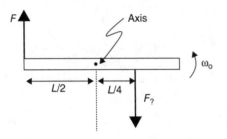

322. What value of the unknown downward force will result in a constant angular velocity of the rod?

   (A) F
   (B) $F/2$
   (C) $2F$
   (D) $4F$

323. If both forces in the diagram are equal in magnitude, which of the following graphs best represent the angular velocity verses time?

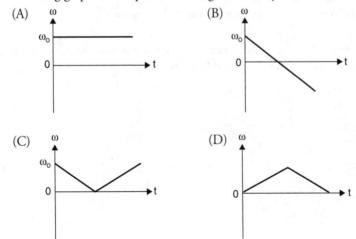

324. A body with a rotational inertia $4 \text{ kg} \cdot \text{m}^2$ accelerates constantly from rest with an angular acceleration of 5 rad/s^2. How much time does it take to obtain a rotational kinetic energy of 800 J?

(A) 1 s

(B) 2 s

(C) 4 s

(D) 8 s

325. Object 1 has a rotational inertia of $8 \text{ kg} \cdot \text{m}^2$, and Object 2 has a rotational inertia of $2 \text{ kg} \cdot \text{m}^2$. If Object 1 is rotating with an angular velocity of 1 rad/s, what angular velocity would give Object 2 the same rotational kinetic energy?

(A) 0.25 rad/s

(B) 0.5 rad/s

(C) 1.0 rad/s

(D) 2 rad/s

326. A disk spins at a rate of 4 rad/sec. Later, mass is added to the disk so that its rotational inertia doubles and it is spun up to a rate of 8 rad/sec. How does the magnitude of the new disk's angular momentum compare to the original disk?

(A) The angular momentum doubles.

(B) The angular momentum quadruples.

(C) The angular momentum stays the same.

(D) The angular momentum is one-half as much.

327. A cylinder has a rotational inertia, I. How much time does it take a torque, τ, to increase its angular speed from ω_1 to ω_2?

(A) $\dfrac{I(\omega_2 - \omega_1)}{\tau}$

(B) $\dfrac{\tau}{I\omega_2 - I\omega_1}$

(C) $\dfrac{(I\omega_2 - I\omega_1)\tau}{\tau}$

(D) $\dfrac{\tau}{\frac{1}{2}I\omega_2^2 - \frac{1}{2}I\omega_1^2}$

328. A car wheel has a rotational inertia of $1.5 \text{ kg} \cdot \text{m}^2$. A brake is applied, which decreases its rotational velocity from 25 revolutions per second to zero. How much energy is transferred to thermal energy in the braking process?

(A) 470 J
(B) 940 J
(C) 1,900 J
(D) 19,000 J

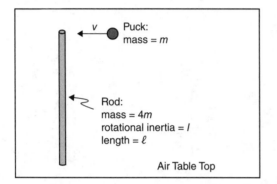

329. The diagram above shows a top view of a long rod (length $= \ell$, mass $= 4m$, rotational inertia $= I$) that sits at rest on its side on a frictionless air table. A puck (mass $= m$) initially slides to the left with a speed v, strikes the rod, and bounces back to the right, moving at half its initial speed. Develop expressions for the linear speed (v_{rod}) and rotational speed (ω_{rod}) of the rod immediately after the collision.

(A) $v_{rod} = \dfrac{v}{4}$ and $\omega_{rod} = \dfrac{mv\ell}{2I}$

(B) $v_{rod} = \dfrac{3v}{4}$ and $\omega_{rod} = \dfrac{3mv\ell}{2I}$

(C) $v_{rod} = \dfrac{v}{8}$ and $\omega_{rod} = \dfrac{mv\ell}{4I}$

(D) $v_{rod} = \dfrac{3v}{8}$ and $\omega_{rod} = \dfrac{3mv\ell}{4I}$

330. A barbell consists of a long, uniform rod with the center of 3.0-kg masses attached to each end. The rod is 2.2 m long and has a rotational inertia about its center of mass of 1.5 kg·m². Calculate the rotational momentum of the barbell when it rotates at 0.50 rad/s about the center of the rod.

(A) $1.1\dfrac{\text{kg} \cdot \text{m}^2}{\text{s}}$

(B) $2.2\dfrac{\text{kg} \cdot \text{m}^2}{\text{s}}$

(C) $3.0\dfrac{\text{kg} \cdot \text{m}^2}{\text{s}}$

(D) $4.4\dfrac{\text{kg} \cdot \text{m}^2}{\text{s}}$

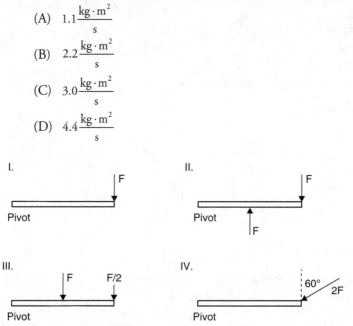

331. Four identical rods shown above experience the forces as shown. Rank the magnitude of the torques about the pivot point on the left end of the rod.

(A) III > I = IV > II

(B) II > IV > III > I

(C) I = III = IV > II

(D) III > II > I > IV

332. Starting from rest, a spinning disk accelerates uniformly to a final rotational speed, ω, in a period of time, Δt. What expression best represents the revolutions the disk has turned through during this time?

(A) $\dfrac{\omega \Delta t}{2\pi}$

(B) $\dfrac{\omega \Delta t}{4\pi}$

(C) $\dfrac{\omega \Delta t^2}{2}$

(D) $\dfrac{\omega}{\Delta t}$

333. A baton of length L rotates with a constant angular speed, ω, measured in radians per second. What is the period of the baton's rotation?

(A) $\dfrac{2\pi L}{\omega}$

(B) $\dfrac{\omega}{2\pi}$

(C) $\dfrac{1}{\omega}$

(D) $\dfrac{2\pi}{\omega}$

334. A sphere (mass $= m$, radius $= R$, moment of inertia $= \dfrac{2}{5}mR^2$) is sliding on a frictionless table with linear speed v and does not rotate. An identical sphere is spinning on the same table (not sliding) about its center with an angular velocity, ω. What is the ratio between the kinetic energy of the sliding sphere and the kinetic energy of the rotating sphere?

(A) $\dfrac{5v^2}{2R^2\omega^2}$

(B) $\dfrac{5v^2}{2\omega^2}$

(C) $\dfrac{v^2}{\omega^2}$

(D) 1

Questions 335–336 refer to the following diagram:

A comet orbits the Sun in a periodic elliptical orbit as shown below:

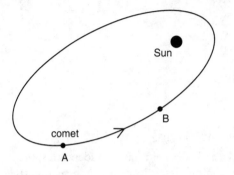

335. As the comet moves from point A to point B, what happens to the comet's angular momentum about the Sun?
    (A) increases linearly
    (B) increases proportionally to the square of the distance from the Sun
    (C) decreases
    (D) stays constant

336. What happens to the gravitational potential energy and the kinetic energy, respectively, of the comet/sun system as the comet moves from point A to point B?

	U_g	K
(A)	increases	increases
(B)	decreases	decreases
(C)	increases	decreases
(D)	decreases	increases

Multi-select: For questions 337–341, two of the suggested answers will be correct. Select the two best answers, and record them both on the answer sheet.

337. A torque is applied about the axis of rotation in which two of the following scenarios?
    (A) A force is applied parallel to the lever arm and acts through the axis of rotation.
    (B) A force is applied perpendicular to the lever arm and acts through the axis of rotation.
    (C) A force is applied perpendicular to the lever arm but not through the axis of rotation.
    (D) A force is applied at a 45° angle but not through the axis of rotation.

338. Which two methods provide enough information to determine a value for the rotational inertia of a car tire about its center axis?
    (A) Apply a known, uniform torque to the tire. Use a rotary motion sensor to graph its angular velocity vs. time.
    (B) Measure the tire's mass and radius and use the formula for a solid disk's rotational inertia.
    (C) Measure its mass and radius of the tire and let it roll from rest without slipping down an incline of known height. Use a motion detector to measure its speed at the bottom.
    (D) Paint a circle on the edge of the tire, mount it on the axle car of a car. Video the car wheel as the car accelerates from rest to a speed of 20 m/s.

339. If a child sits on the edge a rotating merry-go-round, which two accelerations are possible for the child?
    (A) Linear acceleration toward the center
    (B) Angular acceleration
    (C) Zero acceleration
    (D) Linear acceleration outward from the center

340. When a solid object rotates with a uniform angular acceleration, which two of the following are true?
    (A) The net torque on the object is zero.
    (B) The net torque on the object is constant and nonzero.
    (C) The net torque on the object must increase.
    (D) The object's angular velocity changes at a steady rate.

341. The rotational inertia of a body depends on which two of the following?
    (A) The angular acceleration of the body
    (B) The distribution of mass in the body
    (C) The angular velocity of the body
    (D) The axis of rotation of the body

Free response questions 342–346 refer to the following material:

A 3.0-m-long uniform rod with a mass of 12 kg rotates about an axis through its center. There are two applied forces as shown in the diagram below that always keep the same angle relative to the rod. The rotational inertia for a rod rotating about its center is given by $I = \dfrac{1}{12}ML^2$.

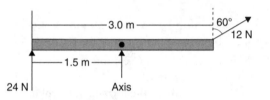

342. Assuming a counterclockwise rotation is positive, calculate the net torque on the rod.

343. Calculate the rotational inertia of the rod.

344. Calculate the angular acceleration of the rod.

345. If the rod accelerates from rest, determine the time it takes the rod to rotate through a 90° angle.

346. How many revolutions does the rod make in 5.0 s?

Free response questions 347–350 refer to the following material:

As shown in the diagram above, a child (mass = m) initially sits at on top of a tree branch at height h above an empty merry-go-round (radius = R, mass = $10m$) that is initially rotating with an angular velocity ω_0. The child jumps off the branch and lands on the merry-go-round, a distance $R/2$ from the axis of rotation. Later, the child walks to the outer edge and sits, pushing her feet against the ground.

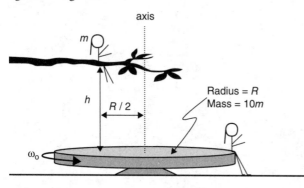

347. Without solving for the angular velocity, state and discuss the main physics principle needed determine the angular velocity of child/merry-go-round system after the child lands and walks to the outer edge of the merry-go-round (and before she pushes her feet against the ground). Also, discuss and justify assumptions which must be made to apply this principle.

348. By what percentage does the angular velocity of the merry-go-round change from before child lands compared to immediately after the child lands? Note: The rotational inertia of a point particle is the product of its mass and the square of the distance from the axis of rotation. The rotational inertia of a solid disk is the product of half its mass and the square of its radius.

349. Determine the system's angular velocity at the instant the child reaches the outer edge of the merry-go-round as a fraction of the post-drop angular velocity of the child/merry-go-round system, ω_{drop}.

350. The child now sits at the edge of the merry-go-round and pushes her shoes against the pavement with a steady force with a vertical component F_y. Using the symbol ω_R for the starting angular velocity of the child/merry-go-round system immediately before the force is applied, the symbol μ for the coefficient of friction between the shoes and the pavement, and other symbols provided in the figure, develop an expression for the time it takes the system to stop rotating.

CHAPTER 8

Electric Charge and Electric Force

Questions 351–365 are easier practice questions designed to allow the student to review specific AP learning objectives and essential knowledge of Electric Charge and Electric Force.

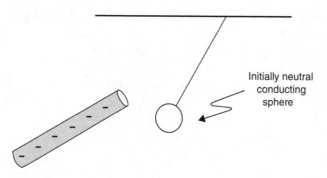

Initially neutral
conducting
sphere

351. A negatively charged rod is placed near an initially neutral conducting sphere hanging from a string. As a result, the two objects attract one another, but never touch. Which of the following occurs?

   (A) The sphere gains positive charge to become positively charged.
   (B) The sphere loses positive charges to become negatively charged.
   (C) Positive charges flow to the left side of the sphere.
   (D) Negative charges flow to the right side of the sphere.

352. An initially neutral conductor is touched with a positively charged glass rod. Which of the following best describes what happens?

   (A) Electrons flow from the conductor to the glass rod.
   (B) Electrons flow from the glass rod to the conductor.
   (C) Protons flow from the conductor to the glass rod.
   (D) Protons flow from the glass rod to the conductor.

353. An object consists of subatomic particles. It has a net charge of $+8.0 \times 10^{-19}$ C. Which of the following statements best describes this object?

(A) The object has eight more protons than electrons.
(B) The object has eight fewer protons than electrons.
(C) The object has five more protons than electrons.
(D) The object has five fewer protons than electrons.

354. Two protons are 1.0 μm apart. What is the electric force between them?

(A) 2.3×10^{-22} N attractive
(B) 2.3×10^{-16} N attractive
(C) 2.3×10^{-16} N repulsive
(D) 2.3×10^{-22} N repulsive

355. A rubber comb is rubbed on hair and then attracts paper bits off the table. Which of the following best compares the forces on the paper bits?

(A) The gravitational force is stronger than the electric force.
(B) The electric force is stronger than the gravitational force.
(C) The strong nuclear force dominates all other forces.
(D) The normal force is stronger than the electric force.

356. What is the smallest magnitude of electric charge?

(A) 9.11×10^{-31} C
(B) 8.0×10^{-20} C
(C) 1.6×10^{-19} C
(D) 9.0×10^{9} C

357. Two electric objects experience a repulsive force. What happens to that force if the distance between the objects is doubled?

(A) It decreases to one-fourth its value.
(B) It decreases to one-half its value.
(C) It stays the same.
(D) It doubles.

358. Two electric charges experience an attractive force. Assuming the distance between the objects stays the same, what happens to that force if the charge of one of the objects is tripled and the charge of the other object is doubled?

(A) The force doubles.
(B) The force triples.
(C) The force is five times greater.
(D) The force is six times greater.

359. Two pith balls each hang from a thread and are suspended from the same hook. If each pith ball is charged -6.4×10^{-8} C and they are separated by a distance of 0.56 cm, what is the force between them?

(A) 1.3×10^{-10} C

(B) 6.6×10^{-3} C

(C) 0.60 N

(D) 1.2 N

360. How many electrons are responsible for a charging an initially neutral object to $-8 \, \mu C$?

(A) 5×10^{13} electrons

(B) 8×10^{19} electrons

(C) 8 electrons

(D) 5 electrons

361. A 2-C charge and a –4-C charge attract each other with 100 N of force when placed a certain distance apart. With how much force will a 4-C and a –4-C charge attract each other when placed the same distance apart?

(A) 25 N

(B) 50 N

(C) 100 N

(D) 200 N

362. Which of the following may be said about an object that is a good electrical conductor?

(A) The protons are free to move within the object.

(B) The electrons are free to move within the object.

(C) The electrons are bound to their individual atom.

(D) The object cannot maintain its electric charge.

363. Glass becomes positively charged when it is rubbed with silk. Which of the following is the best description of what's happening?

(A) Electrons are rubbed off the glass onto the silk.

(B) Electrons are rubbed off the silk onto the glass.

(C) Protons are rubbed off the glass onto the silk.

(D) Protons are rubbed off the silk onto the glass.

364. A helium atom has two protons in its nucleus. If the attractive force between an orbital electron and the nucleus is 4.8×10^{-7} N, what is the atomic radius of a helium atom?

(A) 31 pm
(B) 53 pm
(C) 62 pm
(D) 110 pm

365. In an electrostatics experiment, two pieces of transparent tape attract each other. What is the best conclusion one can draw from this observation?

(A) At least one of the pieces of tape is charged.
(B) One of the pieces of tape is neutral.
(C) The two pieces of tape are oppositely charged.
(D) The two pieces of tape have the same charge.

Questions 366–400 are higher-level, AP-style questions designed to test enduring understanding of AP content.

366. An alpha particle consists of two protons and two neutrons bound together. If an alpha particle and a proton are held a certain distance apart, rank the magnitude of the following forces:

$F_{e_{\alpha \text{ on } p}}$ = The magnitude of the electric force of the alpha particle on the proton

$F_{e_{p \text{ on } \alpha}}$ = The magnitude of the electric force of the proton on the alpha particle

$F_{g_{\alpha \text{ on } p}}$ = The magnitude of the gravitational force of the alpha particle on the proton

$F_{g_{p \text{ on } \alpha}}$ = The magnitude of the gravitational force of the proton on the alpha particle

(A) $F_{e_{\alpha \text{ on } p}} = F_{e_{p \text{ on } \alpha}} > F_{g_{\alpha \text{ on } p}} = F_{g_{p \text{ on } \alpha}}$

(B) $F_{e_{\alpha \text{ on } p}} > F_{e_{p \text{ on } \alpha}} > F_{g_{\alpha \text{ on } p}} > F_{g_{p \text{ on } \alpha}}$

(C) $F_{e_{\alpha \text{ on } p}} = F_{e_{p \text{ on } \alpha}} = F_{g_{\alpha \text{ on } p}} = F_{g_{p \text{ on } \alpha}}$

(D) $F_{g_{\alpha \text{ on } p}} > F_{g_{p \text{ on } \alpha}} > F_{e_{\alpha \text{ on } p}} > F_{e_{p \text{ on } \alpha}}$

367. A physics student seeks to replicate a famous experiment originally conducted by Robert Millikan in 1909. In this experiment, the weight of tiny charged oil droplets is balanced by the electric force, and the charge of each droplet is calculated from an analysis of the data. The results from five of the student's initial trials are as follows:

	Trial 1	Trial 2	Trial 3	Trial 4	Trial 5
Charge (10^{-19} C)	6.25	11.30	0.86	1.65	3.41

Based on your knowledge of electric charge, which of the following is the best analysis of errors in the experiment.

(A) All the values are within 5% of the expected values.

(B) The wide range of data in the trials indicates the presence of both systematic and random errors; the experimental procedure must be revamped.

(C) The order of magnitude of the data is incorrect, indicating a significant systematic error in the experimental calculations.

(D) There appears to be a flaw in Trial 3's results, but the other trials are all within 7% of the expected values.

368. Consider an isolated, neutral system consisting of wool fabric and a rubber rod. If the rubber rod is rubbed with wool to become negatively charged, what can be said about the wool fabric?

(A) It becomes equally negatively charged.

(B) It becomes equally positively charged.

(C) It becomes negatively charged but not equally.

(D) It becomes positively charged but not equally.

369. Paper is considered an insulator. How does a positively charged piece of tape pick up a neutral paper bit?

(A) The tape makes the protons flow to the opposite end of the paper, causing an attraction between the electrons left behind and the tape.

(B) The tape polarizes the paper atoms, attracting the electrons to the side of the atoms closest to the tape.

(C) The tape forces electrons at the opposite end of the paper to flow through the paper toward the tape.

(D) The tape polarizes the paper atoms, moving the protons within the atoms to the side of the atom farthest from the tape.

370. Which of the following statements is NOT correct?

(A) Negatively charged objects have an excess of electrons.

(B) Protons easily move from atom to atom in a solid.

(C) Negatively charged objects typically have the same number of protons as before they were charged.

(D) Positively charged objects have fewer electrons than protons.

Questions 371–373 refer to an electroscope. An electroscope is a device used in electrostatics experiments and consists of a metal ball connected by a metal stem to two thin gold leaves that can freely rotate. The following picture shows the parts of an electroscope:

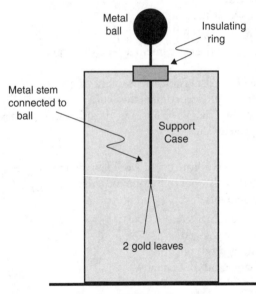

Electroscope

371. A student observes that the gold leaves of the electroscope are standing apart and nothing is interacting with the electroscope. Which of the following best explains this observation?

(A) One leaf is neutral, and the other leaf is negative.

(B) One leaf is neutral, and the other leaf is positive.

(C) The leaves both have opposite charges.

(D) The leaves both have the same charge.

372. Why do the two leaves of a neutral electroscope go apart when a positive rod is brought near the metal ball (but not touching it)?

(A) Protons in the electroscope flow up toward the rod, leaving the leaves negative.

(B) Protons in the electroscope flow away from the rod, giving the leaves a positive charge.

(C) Electrons in the electroscope flow up toward the rod, making the positive leaves repel.

(D) The leaves will actually come together because neutral objects are attracted to charged objects.

373. When a rod is brought near (but not touching) the metal ball of a positively charged electroscope, the leaves initially move closer together. Which of the following best explains this observation?

(A) The rod is negative and attracts the positive leaves toward each other because opposite charges attract.

(B) The rod is negative and pushes electrons from the ball into the leaves and begins to neutralizes them.

(C) The rod is neutral and the leaves attract because neutral objects attract charged objects.

(D) The rod is positive and pulls protons up to the ball of the electroscope allowing them to approach a neutral state.

374. An electron and a proton are separated by 1.50×10^{-10} m. If they are released, which one will accelerate at a greater rate, and what is the magnitude of that initial acceleration?

(A) The electron; 1.12×10^{22} m/s^2

(B) The proton; 1.12×10^{22} m/s^2

(C) The electron; 6.13×10^{18} m/s^2

(D) The proton; 6.13×10^{18} m/s^2

375. Three particles are located on a coordinate system. An electron is located at the origin, a proton is located at (0, 1), and an electron is located at (1, 0). What is the direction of the net electrostatic force on the electron located at the origin?

(A) To the right on the coordinate plane

(B) At an angle of 45° (up and to the right on the coordinate plane)

(C) Up on the coordinate plane

(D) At an angle of 135° (up and to the left on the coordinate plane)

376. Calculate the ratio of the electric force to the gravitational force between an electron and a proton.

(A) 4.41×10^{-40}

(B) 1

(C) 1.35×10^{20}

(D) 2.27×10^{39}

377. What can be said about a sphere that has a net charge of $+4.0 \times 10^{-15}$ C?

(A) The sphere has 50,000 more electrons than protons.

(B) The sphere has 50,000 more protons than electrons.

(C) The sphere has 25,000 more electrons than protons.

(D) The sphere has 25,000 more protons than electrons.

378. There are four charged objects: A, B, C, and D. Object A is charged positively. Object A is attracted to Object B. Object B is repelled from Object C. Object C is attracted to Object D. What are the charges on Objects B, C, and D?

(A) B is negative, and C and D are positive.

(B) B and C are positive, and D is negative or neutral.

(C) B, C, and D are positive.

(D) B and C are negative, and D is positive or neutral.

379. Conducting Sphere A has a charge of –8 μC, and identical Sphere B has a charge of +12 μC. If the spheres are touched and then separated, what is the charge on each sphere?

(A) Sphere A is +12 μC, and Sphere B is –8 μC.

(B) Sphere A is –8 μC, and Sphere B is +12 μC.

(C) Sphere A is +10 μC, and Sphere B is +10 μC.

(D) Sphere A is +2 μC, and Sphere B is +2 μC.

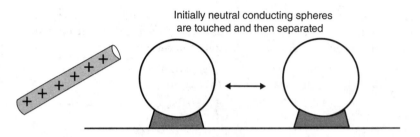

Initially neutral conducting spheres
are touched and then separated

380. The diagram above three objects: a positive glass rod and two initially neutral, identical conducting spheres. If the spheres are touched and then separated, what can be said about each sphere, assuming the glass rod never makes contact with either sphere?

(A) Each sphere is negatively charged.
(B) Each sphere is positively charged.
(C) The sphere on the left is positively charged, and the sphere on the right is negatively charged.
(D) The sphere on the left is negatively charged, and the sphere on the right is positively charged.

381. A negatively charged balloon is observed to attract a piece of aluminum foil. What can be concluded about the foil?

(A) The foil must be positively charged.
(B) The foil must be neutral.
(C) The foil must be negatively charged.
(D) The foil is neutral or positively charged.

382. A rubber balloon becomes negatively charged when it is rubbed with a wool cloth. What can be said about the subsequent charge distribution on the balloon?

(A) Excess protons are on the balloon in the region where it was rubbed on the wool.
(B) Excess electrons are on the balloon in the region where it was rubbed on the wool.
(C) Excess protons are spread evenly throughout the balloon.
(D) Excess electrons are spread evenly throughout the balloon.

383. A negative object is brought near the left side of a conducting sphere but does not touch it. Meanwhile, a person briefly touches the right-hand side of the sphere. What happens to the sphere in this process?

(A) The sphere gains electrons from the person.
(B) The sphere gains protons from the person.
(C) The sphere loses electrons to the person.
(D) The sphere loses protons to the person.

384. A carbon nucleus has 6 protons. What can be said about the electrostatic force between an orbital electron and the carbon nucleus?

(A) The attractive force of the nucleus on the electron is greater than the force of the electron on the nucleus.
(B) The attractive force of the nucleus on the electron is less than the force of the electron on the nucleus.
(C) The attractive force of the nucleus on the electron is equal to the force of the electron on the nucleus.
(D) The repulsive force of the nucleus on the electron is equal to the force of the electron on the nucleus.

385. Two identical spheres are initially neutral. Sphere A obtains a charge of -1.28×10^{-13} C by induction and grounding, while Sphere B remains neutral. How does the mass of Sphere A compare with that of Sphere B?

(A) Sphere A has 7.29×10^{-25} kg more mass than Sphere B.
(B) Sphere B has 7.29×10^{-25} kg more mass than Sphere A.
(C) Sphere A has 1.34×10^{-21} kg more mass than Sphere B.
(D) Sphere B has 1.35×10^{-21} kg more mass than Sphere A.

386. A hydrogen nucleus (charge $+e$) and a beryllium nucleus (charge $+4e$) experience a force, F. Given k as the Coulomb's law constant, which of the following is the distance between the nuclei?

(A) $e\sqrt{\dfrac{5k}{F}}$

(B) $2e\sqrt{\dfrac{k}{F}}$

(C) $\dfrac{4ke^2}{F}$

(D) $6Fe^2$

387. Three identical conducting spheres are on insulated stands and are not touching one another initially. Sphere A has a charge of +10 μC, Sphere B has a charge of –6 μC, and Sphere C has a charge of –4 μC. Sphere A contacts Sphere B, and they are separated. Next, Sphere B contacts Sphere C, and they are separated. What is the final charge on Sphere C?

(A) –1 μC
(B) –2 μC
(C) 0 μC
(D) +2 μC

388. A helium nucleus (charge +2e) and a hydrogen nucleus (charge +e) are initially separated a certain distance. If the helium nucleus is held in place, describe the motion of the hydrogen nucleus.

(A) It moves away from the helium nucleus with a decreasing acceleration rate.
(B) It moves away from the helium nucleus with an increasing acceleration rate.
(C) It moves away from the helium nucleus with a uniform acceleration rate.
(D) It moves toward the helium nucleus with a constant acceleration rate.

Multi-select: For questions 389–393, two of the suggested answers will be correct. Select the two best answers, and record them both on the answer sheet.

389. Which of the two following are valid quantities for the net electric charge on an object?

(A) 1.6×10^{-20} C
(B) 3.2×10^{-19} C
(C) 2.4×10^{-19} C
(D) 2.4×10^{-18} C

390. The magnitude of the electric force between two charges depend on which two of the following?
    (A) The charge of the each object
    (B) The sign of the charges
    (C) The distance between the objects
    (D) The mass of each object

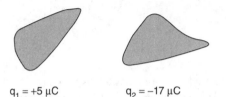

$q_1 = +5\,\mu C$ $q_2 = -17\,\mu C$

391. The diagram above shows the initial charges of two metallic objects of different sizes and shapes. If they are isolated from their surroundings, touched, and then separated, what are two possible final charge states for the spheres?
    (A) $q_1 = -4\,\mu C$ and $q_2 = -8\,\mu C$
    (B) $q_1 = +17\,\mu C$ and $q_2 = -5\,\mu C$
    (C) $q_1 = -6\,\mu C$ and $q_2 = -6\,\mu C$
    (D) $q_1 = +11\,\mu C$ and $q_2 = -11\,\mu C$

392. A balloon is attracted to the wall. Which of the following can explain this observation?
    (A) The wall is positive, and the balloon is negative.
    (B) The wall is neutral, and the balloon is negative.
    (C) The balloon and the wall are negative.
    (D) The balloon and the wall are neutral.

393. Two electrons repel each other with a certain force. Which of the following changes will keep the magnitude of the electric force the same?
    (A) Each electron is replaced with a proton.
    (B) Each electron is replaced with two electrons, and the distance between them is doubled.
    (C) One electron is replaced with two electrons, and the distance between them is doubled.
    (D) Each electron is replaced with two electrons, and the distance between them is quadrupled.

Free response questions 394–396 refer to the following diagram:

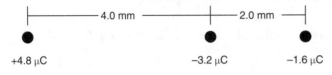

394. Construct a diagram showing arrows that represent the forces on the −3.2 μC charge.

395. Calculate the net force on the −3.2 μC charge.

396. If the −3.2 μC charge has a mass of 75 grams, calculate its initial acceleration when released.

Free response questions 397–400 refer to the following material:

A pith ball consists of a small foam sphere sprayed with metallic paint. One 24-g conducting pith ball has −6.4 μC of charge and touches an identical pith ball that is initially neutral. The diagram below (not to scale) shows the final configuration of the two pith balls as they hang from threads:

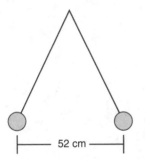

397. Explain the value of the charge on each pith ball after they are separated.

398. Construct a free-body diagram with symbols representing all the forces on the pith ball on the right.

399. Calculate the value of all the forces on the pith ball in your free-body diagram.

400. Determine the angle between the threads in the diagram above.

CHAPTER 9

DC Circuits

Questions 401–415 are easier practice questions designed to allow the student to review specific AP learning objectives and essential knowledge of DC Circuits.

Questions 401–403 refer to the following figure:

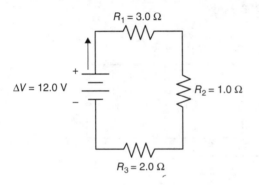

401. What is the current flowing through the circuit shown in the diagram?

    (A) 1 A

    (B) 2 A

    (C) 4 A

    (D) 6 A

402. Which of the following statements is true about the circuit shown in the diagram?

    (A) The voltage drop is greatest across R_1, but R_1 has the least amount of current flowing through it.

    (B) The voltage drop is greatest across R_2, but R_2 has the least amount of current flowing through it.

    (C) The voltage drop is greatest across R_3, but R_3 has the least amount of current flowing through it.

    (D) The voltage drop is greatest across R_1, and the current is equal at all points in the circuit.

403. What is the power dissipated by all of the resistors in the circuit?

    (A) 2 W

    (B) 6 W

    (C) 12 W

    (D) 24 W

404. As the temperature increases, what happens to the current-carrying ability of a wire?

    (A) The current increases.

    (B) The current decreases.

    (C) The current stays the same.

    (D) The current increases and then decreases.

Questions 405–406 use the following figure:

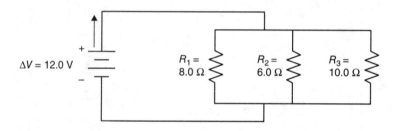

405. For the circuit shown in the diagram, rank the potential difference across each resistor.

    (A) $\Delta V_1 = \Delta V_2 = \Delta V_3$

    (B) $\Delta V_1 > \Delta V_2 > \Delta V_3$

    (C) $\Delta V_3 > \Delta V_2 > \Delta V_1$

    (D) $\Delta V_1 = \Delta V_2 > \Delta V_3$

406. For the circuit in the diagram, which of the following expressions will describe the amount of current flowing through the resistors?

    (A) $I_1 = I_2 = I_3$

    (B) $I_3 > I_2 > I_1$

    (C) $I_1 > I_2 < I_3$

    (D) $I_2 > I_1 > I_3$

407. In a circuit, 40 C of charge passes through a 10-Ω resistor in 80 s. What is the voltage that drives the current?

(A) 0.5 V

(B) 1 V

(C) 5 V

(D) 10 V

408. A resistor dissipates 100 kW of power when a 5-A current passes through it. What is the value of its resistance?

(A) 1 kΩ

(B) 2 kΩ

(C) 4 kΩ

(D) 5 kΩ

Questions 409–411 use the following figure:

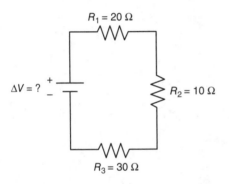

409. For the circuit shown in the figure, what is the voltage of the battery if the current flowing out of the battery is 2.0 A?

(A) 40 V

(B) 50 V

(C) 60 V

(D) 120 V

410. For the circuit shown in the figure, what is the voltage drop across the 30-Ω resistor if the current flowing out the battery is 5.0 A?

(A) 0 V

(B) 50 V

(C) 100 V

(D) 150 V

411. For the circuit shown in the figure, what must be the sum of the voltages around the complete circuit if the current is 10 A?

(A) 0 V

(B) 200 V

(C) 100 V

(D) 300 V

412. A 3-Ω headlight in a car is attached to the 12-V battery. How much energy transfers from the battery for every coulomb of electric charge that flows through this simple circuit?

(A) 3 J

(B) 4 J

(C) 12 J

(D) 24 J

Questions 413 and 414 use the following figure:

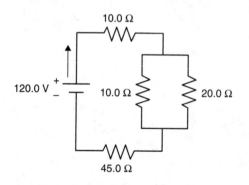

413. For the circuit shown in the figure, what is the value of the current leaving the parallel branch of the circuit?

(A) 1.0 A

(B) 1.9 A

(C) 5 A

(D) 10 A

414. In a basic circuit consisting of a battery and a thermal resistor, what happens when the potential difference across it is doubled?

(A) The current doubles.

(B) The resistance doubles.

(C) The power doubles.

(D) The current is one-half its previous value.

415. Under certain conditions, the resistivity of copper is 1.7×10^{-8} Ωm. What is the resistance of a 1.5-m-long copper wire with a cross-sectional area of 4.0 mm²?

(A) 1.6×10^{-3} Ω

(B) 6.4×10^{-3} Ω

(C) 6.4×10^{-6} Ω

(D) 3.2×10^{-6} Ω

Questions 416–450 are higher-level, AP-style questions designed to test enduring understanding of AP content.

Questions 416 and 417 refer to the following figure:

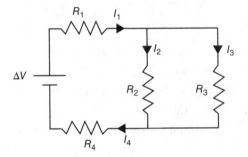

416. Which of the following equations correctly represents the relationship between the currents I_1, I_2, I_3 and I_4?

(A) $I_1 = I_2 = I_3 = I_4$

(B) $I_1 = I_4 = I_2 + I_3$

(C) $I_1 > I_4 > I_2 > I_3$

(D) The values of the resistances must be known to predict this relationship.

417. Which of the following equations correctly represents the total potential difference in a complete loop in the circuit diagram above?

(A) $\Delta V - I_1 R_1 - I_2 R_2 - I_3 R_3 - I_4 R_4 = 0$

(B) $\Delta V - I_1 R_1 + I_2 R_2 - I_3 R_3 + I_4 R_4 = 0$

(C) $\Delta V - I_1 (R_1 + R_4) - I_2 R_2 - I_3 R_3 = 0$

(D) $\Delta V - I_1 (R_1 + R_4) - I_2 R_2 = 0$

Questions 418–420 refer to the following circuit with a battery, three identical bulbs, and a switch that is initially open.

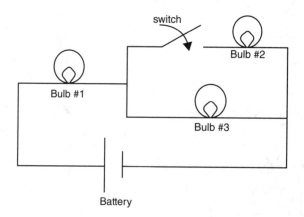

switch

Bulb #2

Bulb #1

Bulb #3

Battery

418. Before the switch is closed, describe the brightness of the three bulbs.

(A) All three bulbs have the same brightness.

(B) Bulb #1 is the brightest, and bulb #2 and #3 are equally, but dimly lit.

(C) Bulb #2 is not lit, and bulb #1 is brighter than bulb #3.

(D) Bulb #2 is not lit, and bulb #1 and bulb #3 have the same brightness.

419. After the switch is closed in the circuit above, bulb #1 has a power output P. What is the power output of bulb #2?

(A) $2P$

(B) P

(C) $P/2$

(D) $P/4$

420. At the instant the switch is closed, what happens to the current running through bulb #1 and what happens to the potential difference across it?

(A) I increases and ΔV increases

(B) I decreases and ΔV decreases

(C) I increases and ΔV decreases

(D) I decreases and ΔV increases

Questions 421–423 refer to a lab experiment that studies resistance and resistivity of nichrome wire.

421. A physics lab group studies the relationship between the cross-sectional area of nichrome wire and its resistance. Which of the following best describes the relationship found when they graphed resistance versus cross-sectional area?

(A) direct proportion

(B) linear relationship with a significant y-intercept

(C) inverse relationship

(D) inverse-squared relationship

422. Now, the physics lab group studies the relationship between the length of nichrome wire and its resistance. They produce a graph the wire resistance versus length. How can they calculate the resistivity of their sample of nichrome wire?

(A) Multiply the graph slope by the cross-sectional area of the wire.

(B) Divide the graph slope by the cross-sectional area of the wire.

(C) Divide the voltage applied to the wire by the current running through it.

(D) Multiply the slope by the length of the wire.

423. Now, another physics lab group also studies the relationship between the length of nichrome wire and its resistance. To calculate the resistance, they use a voltmeter to measure the applied potential difference across the wire and an ammeter to measure current flowing through the wire. When they analyze their results, they find that inconsistent results. Which of the following is a possible explanation for their poor results?

(A) They did not apply the same voltage across the wire in each trial.

(B) The temperature in the room fluctuated during the experiment.

(C) They did not change the length of the wire in equal increments.

(D) They measured current by placing the ammeter in series with the wire.

424. Rank the following in regard to the voltage across just one resistor in the circuit. Assume all resistors are identical.

    I. A circuit with a battery of voltage V connected across a resistor

    II. A circuit with a battery of voltage V connected across two resistors in series

    III. A circuit with a battery of voltage V connected across two resistors in parallel

    IV. A circuit with a battery of voltage 2V connected across two resistors in series

    (A) $IV > II = III > I$

    (B) $I = III = IV > II$

    (C) $I > III > IV = II$

    (D) $II = III > IV = I$

425. For a series circuit with three different resistances, the voltage drops across each resistor are _____, and the currents through each resistor are _____.

    (A) the same; the same

    (B) different; different

    (C) different; the same

    (D) the same; different

426. A certain current is initially flowing through a wire. If the voltage across the wire remains the same, what happens to the current in the wire when its cross-sectional area is doubled and its length is doubled?

    (A) Quadruples

    (B) Doubles

    (C) Stays the same

    (D) Reduced to one-half

427. Which of the following increases the resistance of a wire?

    (A) Increasing the temperature of the wire

    (B) Increasing the cross-sectional area of the wire

    (C) Decreasing the length of the wire

    (D) Decreasing the current in the wire

428. A space heater with a resistance of 12 Ω is connected to a 120-V power supply. How much energy is transferred to thermal energy as this device operates for 2 hours?

(A) 1.2×10^3 J

(B) 2.4×10^3 J

(C) 8.6×10^6 J

(D) 2.4×10^6 J

429. Two 40-Ω resistors wired in parallel are connected in series with a 20-Ω resistor and a power supply. The current in each of the parallel resistors is 1.5 A. What is the current flowing through the 20-Ω resistor and the power supply, respectively?

(A) 1.5 A, 1.5 A

(B) 3.0 A, 1.5 A

(C) 1.5 A, 3.0 A

(D) 3.0 A, 3.0 A

430. Two identical resistors with resistance R are connected in series with a power supply with a potential difference of ΔV. Which expression represents the power output of the entire circuit?

(A) $\dfrac{\Delta V^2}{4R}$

(B) $\dfrac{\Delta V^2}{2R}$

(C) $\dfrac{\Delta V^2}{2R}$

(D) $\dfrac{2(\Delta V)^2}{R}$

431. Two identical resistors with resistance R are connected in series with a power supply with a potential difference of ΔV. Which expression represents the rate that the circuit transfers energy to a single resistor?

(A) $\dfrac{\Delta V^2}{4R}$

(B) $\dfrac{\Delta V^2}{2R}$

(C) $\dfrac{\Delta V^2}{R}$

(D) $\dfrac{2(\Delta V)^2}{R}$

432. Two identical resistors with resistance R are connected in parallel with a power supply with a potential difference of ΔV. Which expression represents the rate that the circuit transfers energy to a single resistor?

(A) $\dfrac{\Delta V^2}{4R}$

(B) $\dfrac{\Delta V^2}{2R}$

(C) $\dfrac{\Delta V^2}{R}$

(D) $\dfrac{2(\Delta V)^2}{R}$

433. What happens to the resistance of a wire if its length is cut in half and its cross-sectional area is doubled?

(A) It doubles.

(B) It stays the same.

(C) It is reduced to one-half

(D) It is reduced to one-fourth.

434. The flow of current throughout a circuit on based on _____. The potential differences across each device in a complete loop of a circuit is based on _____.

(A) Conservation of energy; Conservation of charge

(B) Conservation of charge; Conservation of energy

(C) Coulomb's law; Newton's laws

(D) Conservation of momentum; Conservation of mass

Questions 435–437 refer to the following circuits. All batteries and all bulbs are identical, and the battery has negligible internal resistance.

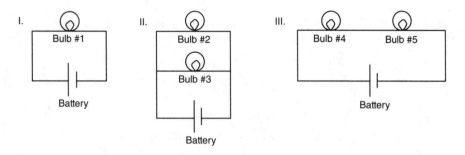

435. Rank the current flowing through the battery in each of the circuits above.
    (A) $I_I > I_{II} > I_{III}$
    (B) $I_{II} > I_I > I_{III}$
    (C) $I_I = I_{II} > I_{III}$
    (D) $I_{III} > I_{II} > I_I$

436. Compare the brightness, B, of the five bulbs in the three circuits.
    (A) $B_2 = B_3 > B_4 = B_5 > B_1$
    (B) $B_1 = B_2 = B_3 = B_4 > B_5$
    (C) $B_1 = B_2 = B_3 = B_4 = B_5$
    (D) $B_1 = B_2 = B_3 > B_4 = B_5$

437. Given that each bulb has the same resistance R and each battery has the same potential difference ΔV, find the total power output of the three circuits?
    (A) $\dfrac{7\Delta V^2}{2R}$

    (B) $\dfrac{\Delta V^2}{2R}$

    (C) $\dfrac{\Delta V^2}{R}$

    (D) $\dfrac{5\Delta V^2}{R}$

Multi-select: For questions 438–442, two of the suggested answers will be correct. Select the two best answers, and record them both on the answer sheet.

438. Which of the following can be said about a series circuit of two or more resistors with a power supply?
    (A) The current is the same through all the elements.
    (B) The current through each element adds up to the current through the power supply.
    (C) The voltage is the same across each element.
    (D) The resistance increases as devices are added.

439. The resistance of a wire depends on which two of the following quantities?
    (A) Current
    (B) Cross-sectional area
    (C) Voltage
    (D) The length of the wire

440. What is true about a basic circuit consisting of a battery and a resistor?
    (A) The battery provides all the charge for the circuit.
    (B) The circuit's electrons stay in the circuit throughout its operation.
    (C) More electrons flow into the resistor than out of it.
    (D) The electrons flow at the same rate in and out of the battery.

441. Which of the following are true about the power output of a circuit?
    (A) Power decreases as devices are added in a parallel circuit.
    (B) Power is the product of current and voltage.
    (C) Power is the rate at which energy is transferred to or from a device.
    (D) Power is inversely proportional to the square of current.

442. What is true about the energy in a basic circuit consisting of a battery and a resistor?
    (A) The chemical energy in the battery transfers to thermal energy in the resistor.
    (B) Energy moves from the battery to the resistor and back to the battery.
    (C) The electrons are turned into energy as the resistor consumes them.
    (D) The circuit does not create or destroy energy.

Free response questions 443–446 refer to the following circuit:

Two identical thermal resistors are wired in series. The series combination is placed in parallel across a resistor with a resistance less than the sum of the series resistors. A battery is placed across the circuit as shown in the following diagram:

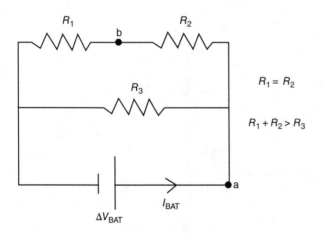

$R_1 = R_2$

$R_1 + R_2 > R_3$

443. Let I_1, I_2, I_3 and I_{BAT} represent the current through R_1, R_2, R_3 and the battery, respectively. Rank the currents in each device in the circuit. Briefly explain your reasoning.

444. A student uses a voltmeter and reads a value of $4V$ when it is connected across points "a" and "b". Determine values of the voltmeter readings across each device in the circuit, $\Delta V_1, \Delta V_2, \Delta V_3$ and ΔV_{BAT}. Briefly explain your reasoning.

445. If $R_1 = R_2 = R_3 = R$, develop an expression for the power output of the circuit in terms of the symbols R and ΔV_{BAT}.

446. A wire is added connecting both sides of resistor R_2 as shown in the diagram below.

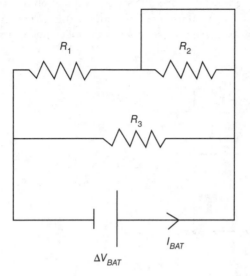

How does the current in this new circuit compare with the current in the original circuit? Briefly explain your reasoning without using values.

Free response questions 447–450 refer to the following material:

An experiment is conducted with a 12-V battery and four 1-Ω resistors.

Experiment 1:

1. Wire the battery to a resistor, calculate the equivalent resistance, measure the total current, and calculate the power dissipated by the resistor in the circuit.

2. Add the second resistor in series, and repeat the measurements and calculations.

3. Add the third resistor in series, and repeat the measurements and calculations.

4. Add the fourth resistor in series, and repeat the measurements and calculations.

5. Graph the results.

Experiment 2:

Follow the same procedure for Experiment 1, but wire the resistors in parallel for this second experiment.

The following graphs were obtained from the two experiments:

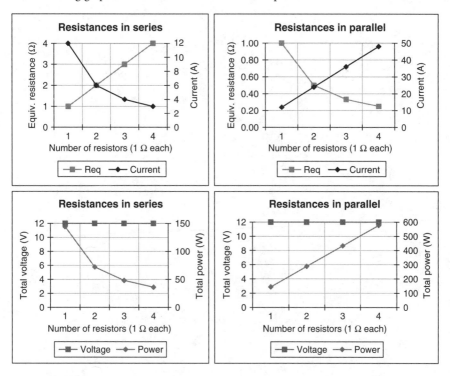

Using the graphs, answer the following questions:

447. Describe the behavior of the equivalent resistance of the circuit as you add resistors in series versus parallel.

448. Describe and explain the behavior of the current through the power supply as you add resistors in series versus parallel.

449. Describe and explain the behavior of the power demanded of the power supply as you add resistors in series versus parallel.

450. If the resistors were lightbulbs in strings of holiday lights, one wired in series and one in parallel, what can be said about the brightness of an individual bulb as you increase the number of bulbs? Explain your reasoning.

CHAPTER 10

Mechanical Waves and Sound

Questions 451–500 are easier practice questions designed to allow the student to review specific AP learning objectives and essential knowledge of mechanical waves and sound.

451. Which of the following best describes a mechanical wave?

(A) A pattern resembling a sine wave

(B) An object that oscillates back and forth at a characteristic frequency

(C) A disturbance that carries energy and momentum from one place to another with the transfer of mass

(D) A disturbance that carries energy and momentum from one place to another without the transfer of mass

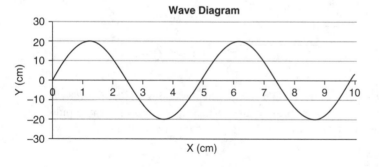

452. What are the approximate amplitude and wavelength, respectively, of the wave shown in the diagram?

(A) 40 cm; 10 cm

(B) 20 cm; 5 cm

(C) 40 cm; 5 cm

(D) 20 cm; 10 cm

453. Which of the following best describes the role of the medium for a transverse mechanical wave?

(A) The medium vibrates back and forth parallel to the motion of the wave.

(B) The medium vibrates back and forth perpendicular to the motion of the wave.

(C) The medium oscillates between parallel and perpendicular vibrations.

(D) The particles in the medium travel in the direction that the wave travels.

454. The highest sound pitch that a human can hear has a frequency of 20.0 kHz. On a day when the speed of sound is 340 m/s, what is the distance between adjacent rarefactions of the sound wave?

(A) 0.0085 m

(B) 0.017 m

(C) 6.8 m

(D) 13.6 m

Questions 455 and 456 use the following figure:

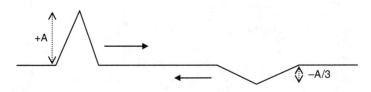

455. Two wave pulses travel on a string. The directions and amplitude of each wave are shown in the figure. When the centers of the two pulses completely overlap, what is the amplitude of the resulting wave?

(A) −2A/3

(B) 0

(C) +2A/3

(D) +4A/3

456. What happens after the pulses overlap?

(A) One pulse (2A/3) travels to the right.

(B) One pulse (+A) travels to the left, while another pulse (−A/3) travels to the right.

(C) One pulse (+A) travels to the right, while another pulse (−A/3) travels to the left.

(D) One pulse (−A) travels to the right, while another pulse (+A/3) travels to the left.

457. A vertical, 0.50-meter-long tube is partially submerged in a bucket of water. The tube can be moved up and down to vary the length of the air column inside the tube. The temperature of the air is 20°C which corresponds to a sound speed of 343 m/s. A 440-Hz tuning fork is struck and placed over the open end of the tube. The tube is moved up and down until the lowest frequency resonance is heard. What is the length of the column of air inside the tube when only one displacement antinode and one displacement node form in the tube?

(A) 0.09 m

(B) 0.19 m

(C) 0.27 m

(D) 0.38 m

458. A favorite radio station is located on the dial at 100 MHz. What is the wavelength of the radio waves emitted from the radio station if the speed of these waves is 3.00×10^8 m/s?

(A) 3 m

(B) 30 m

(C) 300 m

(D) 3 km

459. A girl sitting on a beach counts six waves passing a buoy in 3.0 s. She measures a 1.5-meter distance between the wave crests. What is the speed of the waves the girl observed?

(A) 3.0 m/s

(B) 9.0 m/s

(C) 0.75 m/s

(D) 1.3 m/s

460. If a wave disturbance travels 16 m each second and the distance between adjacent troughs is 4 m, determine the frequency of the disturbance.

(A) 0.25 Hz

(B) 2 Hz

(C) 4 Hz

(D) 64 Hz

461. Which of the following will cause the phenomenon of sound beats to occur?

(A) Two slightly different frequencies played simultaneously

(B) The frequency of one object matches the natural frequency of another

(C) A sound wave reflects off a boundary back onto itself

(D) A sound source varies its amplitude at regular intervals

462. An observer notices a 2.00-s delay between seeing fireworks and hearing them. How far away are the fireworks from the observer if the speed of sound is 344 m/s?

(A) 86 m

(B) 172 m

(C) 344 m

(D) 688 m

463. A tuning fork vibrates 256 times each second. What is the distance between compressions if the speed of the sound waves is 345 m/s?

(A) 0.742 m

(B) 1.35 m

(C) 1.48 m

(D) 88.3 km

464. A dolphin swimming at the surface of the sea emits an ultrasonic sound wave. It takes 0.15s for the sound to go from the dolphin to the ocean floor and back. Determine the depth of the ocean if the speed of sound in the water is 1,400 m/s.

(A) 93 m

(B) 105 m

(C) 186 m

(D) 210 m

465. A 0.500-meter-long tube is open at both ends, and the speed of sound in the air within the tube is 343 m/s. What frequency of air vibration results in pressure nodes forming at the two open ends of the tube and one pressure antinode forming at its center?

(A) 86 Hz

(B) 172 Hz

(C) 343 Hz

(D) 686 Hz

Questions 466–500 are higher-level, AP-style questions designed to test enduring understanding of AP content.

Questions 466 and 467 refer to the following material.

A microphone probe is interfaced with a computer and graphs the following pressure vs. time graph when a particular sound is measured.

466. What does an observer hear when they listen to this sound wave.?

(A) A sound that pulsates from loud to soft two times every second.

(B) A high-pitched note and a low-pitched note with half the frequency sounding simultaneously.

(C) Six clicks are heard in every three seconds of time.

(D) A sound often referred to as "white noise."

467. The observer is listening to two trumpet players play a note. One player is vibrating their lips at 256 Hz. To get a pressure pattern similar to the graph above, what can be said about the other trumpet players note?

(A) The other trumpet play is playing a 2 Hz note.

(B) The other trumpet could be playing a 258 Hz note.

(C) The other trumpet play is playing a 258.5 Hz note.

(D) The other trumpet could be playing a 259 Hz note.

Questions 468 and 469 refer to the following material.

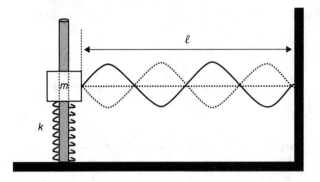

The diagram above shows a block (mass = m) that can slide freely on a vertical pole through its center. The block is supported by a vertical spring (spring constant = k) wrapped around the pole. As the mass oscillates vertically up and down, a standing wave form on a horizontal cord (length = ℓ) attached to the block.

468. What is the speed of the wave on the cord?

(A) $4\pi\ell\sqrt{\dfrac{m}{k}}$

(B) $\dfrac{\ell}{8\pi}\sqrt{\dfrac{k}{m}}$

(C) $\dfrac{\ell}{2\pi}\sqrt{\dfrac{k}{m}}$

(D) $\dfrac{\ell}{4\pi}\sqrt{\dfrac{k}{m}}$

469. Imagine that string is cut in half (length = $\ell/2$) and the mass/spring system is moved to the right such that the tension in the string remains the same as before. Compared to the wave speed in the full-length string, what happens to the speed on the half-length cord if the distance of the vertical vibration doubles?

(A) doubles
(B) quadruples
(C) halves
(D) no change

470. Two transverse wave pulses on a spring are moving toward one another. One wave has an amplitude of 10 cm and another wave has an amplitude of 15 cm. What are possible amplitudes when they completely overlap? Select two answers.

(A) 5 cm
(B) 10 cm
(C) 15 cm
(D) 25 cm

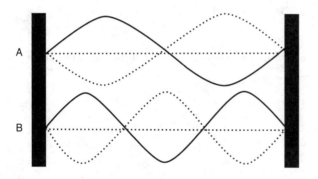

471. Two identical guitar strings of equal length and tension are vibrating as shown in the diagram above. How do the speeds of the wave on the strings compare? How do the wavelengths of the waves compare?

(A) $v_A = v_B$ and $\lambda_A = \dfrac{3}{2}\lambda_B$

(B) $v_A < v_B$ and $\lambda_A = \dfrac{3}{2}\lambda_B$

(C) $v_A = v_B$ and $\lambda_A = \dfrac{2}{3}\lambda_B$

(D) $v_A < v_B$ and $\lambda_A = \dfrac{2}{3}\lambda_B$

472. Which of the following is observed at the moment of time a constantly moving source of sound passes a receiver who is at rest?

(A) The frequency and the wave speed both increase.
(B) The frequency decreases, and the wave speed increases.
(C) The frequency decreases, and the wave speed stays the same.
(D) The frequency increases, and the wave speed decreases.

Questions 473 and 474 refer to the information below:

The figure below shows a full wave pulse at a certain instant in time moving to the right on a rope. Tape has been wrapped around the rope at points A, B, and C.

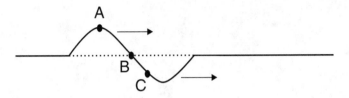

473. What is the direction of the instantaneous velocity of the tape at each point? If it has no velocity, choose $\vec{v} = 0$.

(A) $\vec{v}_A = 0$ $\vec{v}_B = $ up $\vec{v}_C = $ up

(B) $\vec{v}_A = $ right $\vec{v}_B = 0$ $\vec{v}_C = $ right

(C) $\vec{v}_A = $ down $\vec{v}_B = 0$ $\vec{v}_C = $ up

(D) $\vec{v}_A = $ right $\vec{v}_B = $ right $\vec{v}_C = $ right

474. What is the direction of the instantaneous acceleration of the tape at each point? If it has no acceleration, choose $\vec{a} = 0$.

(A) $\vec{a}_A = 0$ $\vec{a}_B = $ up $\vec{a}_C = $ up

(B) $\vec{a}_A = $ left $\vec{a}_B = 0$ $\vec{a}_C = $ left

(C) $\vec{a}_A = $ down $\vec{a}_B = 0$ $\vec{a}_C = $ up

(D) $\vec{a}_A = 0$ $\vec{a}_B = $ right $\vec{a}_C = $ left

475. An ambulance emits a siren with a steady frequency. When the ambulance is at rest, the time between wave compressions is T_{rest}. When the ambulance is moving down the highway, three observers separately measure the time between the compressions. Observer 1 is in the passenger seat of the ambulance. Observer 2 measures the sound as the ambulance approaches her. Observer 3 measures the sound as the ambulance drives away from him. Rank the observed times.

(A) $T_2 > T_{rest} = T_1 > T_3$

(B) $T_3 > T_{rest} = T_1 > T_2$

(C) $T_{rest} = T_1 = T_2 = T_3$

(D) $T_{rest} = T_1 > T_2 = T_3$

Questions 476–478 refer to the following material

When the diaphragm on a microphone vibrates it sends an electrical signal to an oscilloscope which displays the amount of vibration on the vertical axis and the time on the horizontal axis. The traces from two separate sounds striking the microphone are detected and displayed on the oscilloscope as follows:

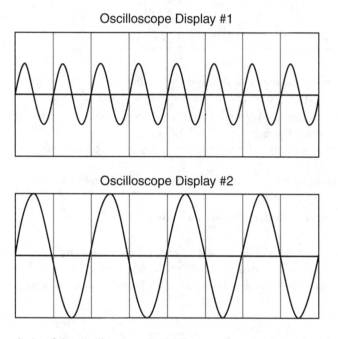

Oscilloscope Display #1

Oscilloscope Display #2

476. If the oscilloscope display has the same horizontal and vertical scale in both diagrams, how would a human perceive sound #2 compared with sound #1?

(A) Sound # 2 is a softer sound with a higher pitch.
(B) Sound # 2 is a softer sound with a lower pitch.
(C) Sound # 2 is a louder sound with a higher pitch.
(D) Sound # 2 is louder sound with a lower pitch.

477. Assuming the air conditions remain the same, how does the speed of the sound #2 compare with the speed of sound #1 as each travels from the source to the microphone?

(A) $v_2 > v_1$
(B) $v_2 < v_1$
(C) $v_2 = v_1$
(D) More information is needed to compare the speed of sound from the two sources.

Oscilloscope Display #3

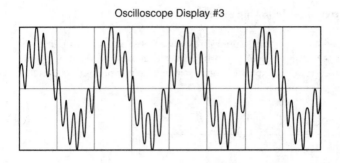

478. The microphone detects a new sound, and the oscilloscope trace is shown above. What is a possible description of the new sound source?

(A) High-pitched and low-pitched notes played simultaneously.
(B) A single note is played with varying loudness.
(C) A single note is played with varying pitch, sometimes called a vibrato in music.
(D) Two notes of almost the same frequency are played simultaneously.

Questions 479 and 480 refer to the information below:

The figure below shows a function generator which sends an amplified signal to a speaker. The speaker is placed at the open end of a tube that is closed on the opposite end. The frequency of the signal is adjusted and certain resonances are heard.

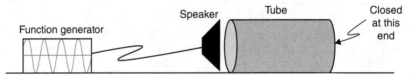

479. The lowest frequency that speaker produces a resonance is 170 Hz. If the speed of sound in air is 340 m/s, what is the approximate length of the tube?

(A) 0.5 m
(B) 1.0 m
(C) 1.5 m
(D) 2.0 m

480. The frequency is gradually increased from 170 Hz until the next resonance is obtained. What is the value of this new frequency?

(A) 255 Hz
(B) 340 Hz
(C) 510 Hz
(D) 680 Hz

481. Two waves are traveling on a string. The directions and amplitude of each wave are shown in the figure. When the two waves meet, what is the amplitude of the resulting wave?

(A) A/2
(B) A
(C) 3A/2
(D) 2A

482. In a physics demonstration, a 2-meter-long coiled spring is connected to a spring of the same length but with thicker wire and a smaller diameter. If a transverse wave pulse is made at one end of the series combination, which of the following quantities remains constant as a pulse travels from one spring into another?

(A) Frequency
(B) Wavelength
(C) Speed
(D) Amplitude

Questions 483 and 484 refer to the following material:

Bats emit ultrasonic sounds in order to echolocate. A particular bat emits a 25-kHz ultrasonic sound to navigate in a cave in which the speed of sound is 343 m/s.

483. Determine the distance between compressions of the bat's sound signal.

(A) 0.014 m
(B) 0.086 m
(C) 8.6 m
(D) 14 m

484. As the bat hovers 3.5 m from the wall of the cave, it emits a signal in an attempt to echo-locate. Calculate the amount of time it takes the sound to travel to the wall and back again.

(A) 0.010 s
(B) 0.020 s
(C) 0.49 s
(D) 0.98 s

485. What is true about a loud sound with a low pitch?

(A) It travels faster than a soft sound.
(B) It travels slower than a high-pitch sound.
(C) It has large amplitude and low frequency.
(D) It has small amplitude and high frequency.

486. In a lab experiment, one end of a horizontal cord is attached to an oscillator and the other end of the cord is attached to a fixed support. The frequency of the oscillator is adjusted until standing waves are formed, and the wavelength of each wave is measured. Which of the following is the best description of the graph of wavelength versus frequency?

(A) The graph shows a directly proportional relationship between the variables with the slope equal to wave speed on the cord.
(B) The graph shows the variables are linearly related with a y-intercept equal to the distance between nodes on the cord.
(C) The graph shows an inversely proportional relationship between wavelength and frequency.
(D) The graph shows the wavelength is directly proportional to the square of the frequency.

487. What is observed when sound beats occur?

(A) A rhythmic change in the pitch of the sound
(B) A regular increase and decrease in the speed of the sound
(C) An increase in frequency of the sound
(D) A sound that gets louder and softer at regular intervals

488. A child dips her finger repeatedly into the water to make waves. If she dips her finger more frequently, the wavelength _____ and the speed _____.

(A) Increases; decreases
(B) Decreases; increases
(C) Increases; stays the same
(D) Decreases; stays the same

489. Which of the following best describes the air particles as sound travels through air?

(A) The air particles vibrate along lines perpendicular to the motion of the wave.
(B) The air particles vibrate along lines parallel to the motion of the wave.
(C) The air particles move from the source of the wave to the receiver.
(D) The air particles remain stationary as the wave travels through them.

Multi-select: For questions 490–494, two of the suggested answers are correct. Select the two best answers, and record them both on the answer sheet.

490. Which of the following are true about sound waves?
   (A) Their speed increases slightly with higher temperature air.
   (B) They can travel in the vacuum of space.
   (C) Their speed increases as the pitch of the sound increases.
   (D) They travel faster in steel than air.

491. Which of the following are necessary for a standing wave to form?
   (A) A vibration at a natural frequency of the medium
   (B) Reflection off a boundary
   (C) At least two different vibration frequencies
   (D) The source must move faster than the speed of the wave

492. The speed of a sound wave depends on which of the following?
   (A) The loudness and pitch of the sound
   (B) The intensity of the vibration
   (C) The characteristics of the medium
   (D) The type of medium

493. Which of the following may occur when a single wave hits a boundary between one medium and another?
   (A) It reflects back into the original medium.
   (B) Its frequency changes.
   (C) It transmits into the new medium.
   (D) It gains energy.

494. Which of the following are examples of resonance?
   (A) A low frequency beat is detected when two tuning forks are played together.
   (B) Two waves combine to form a wave with a larger amplitude.
   (C) A tuning fork starts vibrating when an identical tuning fork vibrates next to it.
   (D) A wineglass vibrates dramatically and shatters when a certain pitch is played on a nearby speaker.

Free response questions 495–497 refer to the following material:

The end of a 2.5-meter-long spring is attached to a wall. A student vibrates the end of a spring with 5.0 vibrations each second. The following standing wave forms:

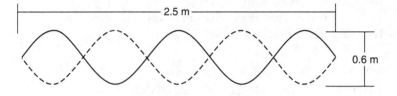

495. What is the speed of the wave as it travels along the spring?

496. How much time does it take a disturbance to travel from the hand to the wall and back again?

497. Explain what happens to the speed and wavelength of the wave if the frequency is doubled.

Free response questions 498–500 refer to the following information:

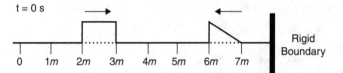

At t = 0 seconds, two wave pulses with the same height are moving toward each other as shown in the in the diagram above. The square pulse moves to the right at a speed of 0.5 *m/s*. When a wave hits a rigid boundary, assume that it does not lose energy, and that the wave inverts such that crests become troughs upon reflection.

498. Sketch the wave pattern at t = 4 seconds on the diagram below. Briefly explain your reasoning.

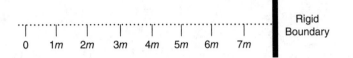

499. Sketch the wave pattern at t = 11 seconds on the diagram below. Briefly explain your reasoning.

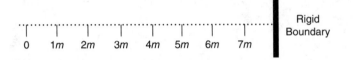

500. At the 11-second clock reading, at what positions is energy stored along the medium?

ANSWERS

Chapter 1: Kinematics

1. (B) Acceleration is the slope of the velocity versus clock reading graph (it is not the value of velocity at the 5-second clock reading!). To find the slope at the 6-second clock reading, one may examine the constant slope from $t = 4$ s to $t = 8$ s:

2. (D) The position in the graph is increasing linearly in the positive direction. This is consistent with motion with a constant positive velocity and, hence, zero acceleration.

3. (B) The height $= 125$ m, the initial velocity $= 0$ m/s, and the acceleration due to gravity $= 10$ m/s². Solve this equation for t:

$$\Delta x = v_0 t + \frac{1}{2}at^2 \rightarrow (125 \text{ m}) = (0 \text{ m/s})t + \frac{1}{2}(10 \text{ m/s}^2)t^2 \rightarrow 125 = 5t^2 \rightarrow \boxed{t = 5.0 \text{ s}}$$

4. (D) The distance the car traveled is 500 m, the initial velocity is 0 m/s, and the final velocity is 50 m/s. Solve this equation for a:

$$v_f^2 = v_0^2 + 2a\,\Delta x$$

$$(50 \text{ m/s})^2 = (0 \text{ m/s})^2 + 2a\,(500 \text{ m}) \rightarrow \boxed{a = 2.5 \text{ m/s}^2}$$

5. (C) The horizontal velocity of the package is the same as that of the plane (50.0 m/s). The height of the plane is 125.0 m. First, find the time it takes for the package to reach the ground, and use that time to calculate the horizontal distance that the package travels.

1. Solve for time:

$$\Delta y = v_0 t - \frac{1}{2}gt^2 \rightarrow (-125 \text{ m}) = (0 \text{ m/s}) - \frac{1}{2}(10 \text{ m/s}^2)t^2 \rightarrow t = 5.0 \text{ s}$$

2. Solve for horizontal distance:

$$\Delta x = v_x t \rightarrow \Delta x = (50.0 \text{ m/s})(5.0 \text{ s}) \rightarrow \boxed{\Delta x = 250 \text{ m}}$$

6. (C) The object is at rest during the time interval of 3–4 s when the object's position does not change.

7. (D) Knowing the car's final velocity (30 m/s), the rate of acceleration (3.0 m/s²), and the time interval over which it accelerated (5.0 s), calculate the initial velocity as follows:

$$v_t = v_0 + at \rightarrow v_0 = v_f - at$$

$$v_0 = (30 \text{ m/s}) - (3.0 \text{ m/s}^2)(5 \text{ s}) \rightarrow \boxed{v_0 = 15 \text{ m/s}}$$

8. **(C)** The airplane's initial velocity was 0 m/s, and it accelerated at 1.0 m/s² for 5 min (300 s). Calculate the distance as follows:

$$\Delta x = v_0 t + \frac{1}{2} at^2 \rightarrow \Delta x = 0 + \frac{1}{2}(1.0 \text{ m/s}^2)(300 \text{ s})^2$$

$$\Delta x = 45{,}000 \text{ m} \rightarrow \boxed{\Delta x = 45 \text{ km}}$$

9. **(D)** The ball is in a free fall, which means it slows down at a constant acceleration rate of about 10 m/s/s, or it loses 10 m/s of speed each and every second. At the maximum height, its final velocity is zero. To determine the time, divide the initial velocity of 30 m/s by the acceleration rate of 10 m/s/s, which gives 3.0 s.

10. **(D)** The initial velocity is 0 m/s, the height is 15 m, and the time is 1 s. Calculate the acceleration due to gravity:

$$\Delta x = v_0 t + \frac{1}{2} at^2 \rightarrow 15 \text{ m} = 0 + \frac{1}{2}(a)(1 \text{ s})^2 \rightarrow \boxed{a = 30 \text{ m/s}^2}$$

11. **(A)** Knowing the car's initial velocity (0 m/s), the rate of acceleration (3 m/s²), and the distance of the track (150 m), calculate the final velocity as follows:

$$v_f^2 = v_0^2 + 2a\Delta x \rightarrow v_f^2 = (0 \text{ m/s})^2 + 2(3 \text{ m/s}^2)(150 \text{ m}) \rightarrow \boxed{v_f = 30 \text{ m/s}}$$

12. **(C)** For projectiles launched at the same velocity but at different angles (between 0° and 90°), those with complementary angles will have the same range.

13. **(C)** It takes 3.0 s for the stone to drop, and the stone started from rest. So, we can calculate the approximate height of the cliff:

$$\Delta x = v_0 t + \frac{1}{2} at^2 \rightarrow \Delta x = 0 + \frac{1}{2}(10 \text{ m/s}^2)(3.0 \text{ s})^2 \rightarrow \boxed{\Delta x = 45 \text{ m}}$$

14. **(A)** The bicycle's initial velocity was 5.0 m/s, and it slowed at an acceleration of −2.5 m/s² to a stop ($v_f = 0$). The time can be determined from this equation:

$$v_f = v_0 + at \rightarrow (0 \text{ m/s}) = (5.0 \text{ m/s}) + (-2.5 \text{ m/s}^2)t \rightarrow \boxed{t = 2.0 \text{ s}}$$

15. **(D)** If the positive direction is forward, then an object that is moving backward at a constant velocity would have a position vs. time graph that is linear with a negative slope.

16. **(D)**

$$Speed_{Photogate \#1} = \frac{\text{Distance}}{\text{Time}} = \frac{\text{Rod Diameter}}{\text{Eclipse Time}} = \frac{0.012m}{.02s} = 0.6 m/s$$

$$Speed_{Photogate \#2} = \frac{0.012m}{.06s} = 0.2 m/s \quad \boxed{\text{Slows down relative to photogate \#1}}$$

$$\Delta x = v_{ave}\Delta t \rightarrow \Delta t = \frac{\Delta x}{v_{ave}} = \frac{\Delta x}{\left(\frac{v_1 + v_2}{2}\right)} = \frac{0.2m}{\left(\frac{0.6m/s + 0.2m/s}{2}\right)} = \frac{0.20m}{0.4m/s} = 0.5s$$

$$a = \frac{\Delta v}{\Delta t} = \frac{v_2 - v_1}{\Delta t} = \frac{(0.2 - 0.6)m/s}{0.5s} = -0.8\frac{m}{s^2} \rightarrow \boxed{|a| = 0.8\frac{m}{s^2}}$$

17. **(D)** It was determined in the previous problem that the cart was slowing down, which is consistent with the second of the original three diagrams (a cart initially moving to the right, diagonally up an incline plane). Once the cart stops, it will gain speed as it goes back to the left on the incline plane. The slope of a X vs. t graph is defined as velocity, and graph option D starts out with a positive slope, indicating that it has a positive velocity (moving to the right). As the graph flattens, the slope goes to zero indicating the cart is slowing down to a stop. Finally, as the cart reverses directions and speeds back up again, the slope increases negatively.

18. **(C)**

Average velocity is defined as the ration of displacement and elapsed time: $v_{ave} = \dfrac{\Delta x}{\Delta t}$

Solving for displacement: $\Delta x = v_{ave}\Delta t$. For uniform acceleration, the average velocity may be found from the midpoint between the inital and final velocity: $v_{ave} = \left(\dfrac{v_f + v_i}{2}\right)$

$$\Delta x = \left(\frac{v_f + v_i}{2}\right)\Delta t = \left(\frac{0 + 34m/s}{2}\right)(4s) = 68m$$

19. **(A)**

Velocity is defined as the slope of the X vs. t graph. For the first phase of motion, the slope is positive and constant. For the second half of the graph, the slope starts positive and gradually decreases to zero. $\boxed{\text{Graph A}}$ is the only option that begins with a positive constant value of velocity which subsequenty decreases to zero.

20. **(C)**

The masses are all free falling since there is negligible air drag. Free-fall acceleration is independent of mass, so they have the same vertical acceleration.

21. **(D)**

In a vacuum, the trajectory is independent of mass. If fired at the same speed, P1 and P3 would have the same range because their angles are complements, but because P1 has a greater firing speed it will have the greater of the two ranges.P4 will have no range because it's fired straight upward. That leaves the comparison between P1 and P2, which have the same firing speed. It's common knowledge that a $45°$ angle maximizes range, so P2 must have the greatest range.

$$v_{y_i} = 40\sin 45° = 40\left(\frac{\sqrt{2}}{2}\right)m/s = 20\sqrt{2}m/s$$

$$\Delta t_{peak} = \frac{20\sqrt{2}m/s}{10m/s/s} = 2\sqrt{2}s \rightarrow \Delta t_{Up\ and\ Down} = 2\sqrt{2}s + 2\sqrt{2}s = 4\sqrt{2}s$$

$$Range = v_x\Delta t = (40\cos(45°)m/s)4\sqrt{2}s = 40\left(\frac{\sqrt{2}}{2}\right)4\sqrt{2}m = 160m$$

$\boxed{\text{Projectile \#2 has the greatest range of } 160m}$

22. **(D)** Free-fall motion is modeled as uniform acceleration, When the initial velocity is zero, the following equation is obtained:

$$x = x_0 + v_{x0}t + \frac{1}{2}a_xt^2 \rightarrow x - x_0 = (0)t + \frac{1}{2}a_xt^2 \rightarrow \Delta x = \frac{1}{2}a_xt^2 \rightarrow \Delta x \, \alpha \, t^2$$

So if the elapsed time is doubled, the displacement **quadruples**.

23. **(D)** When a position–time graph is horizontal, the velocity of the object is zero. The velocity at any instant in time is the slope of the line tangent to any point on the position–time graph. For this graph, that occurs at 1 s and 3 s.

24. **(A)** At the beginning of region C, the velocity gradually decreases to zero, indicating its speed is decreasing. At point D, the velocity has reached zero (resting instantaneously). At the beginning of region E, the negative velocity indicates that the direction is now negative, and the increasing magnitude of the velocity indicates it is speeding up.

25. **(B)** The displacement is the final position minus the starting position.

The displacement for part A is 125 m − 0 m = +125 m.

The displacement for part B is 100 m − 100 m = 0 m.

The displacement for part C is 125 m − 100 m = +25 m.

The displacement for part D is 0 m − 125 m = −125 m.

26. **(C)** The average speed is the distance traveled divided by the time for each section.

The average speed for part A is (125 m)/10 s = 12.5 m/s.

The average speed for part B is (0 m)/5 s = 0 m/s.

The average speed for part C is (25 m)/5 s = 5 m/s.

The average speed for part D is (125 m)/5 s = 25 m/s.

27. **(C, D)** Velocity is a vector quantity, so constant velocity is achieved when an object moves at a constant speed in a straight line.

28. **(B, D)** Acceleration $\left(\dfrac{\Delta \vec{v}}{\Delta t}\right)$ is a vector quantity, so the direction of the acceleration must remain constant as well as the rate of change of speed. The skydiver's acceleration decreases as she approaches terminal velocity (when $a = 0$), so this choice must be eliminated. The direction of the acceleration of the truck driver is changing throughout the circle (especially with the required centripetal acceleration), so this choice must be eliminated. The hammer is free-falling near the surface of the moon (no atmosphere and a steady gravitational field), which is a constant acceleration model, and the cart is also gaining speed at a steady rate while keeping direction constant.

29. **(A, D)** Option A is correct because speed is the absolute value of velocity, and both carts were moving at 4 m/s. Option D is also correct because, at the 8-second clock reading, Cart 1 was moving at 6 m/s and Cart 2 was moving at 4 m/s. Option C is tempting but incorrect because it had positive velocity for the first half of the trip, indicating that it was moving in the positive direction.

30. (D) The free-fall acceleration near the surface of the Earth is a uniform rate of 10 m/s², meaning each and every second its speed increases by 10 m/s. In two seconds of time, its speed will increase to 25 m/s + 10 m/s + 10 m/s = 45 m/s.

31. (A) At a constant speed, position should change linearly with time, so only options A and B should be considered. At $t = 0$, option A's position is 35 m. Each second after that, its position changes by −25 m each second.

32. (C) The initial position is $x_0 = -12$ m. The initial velocity is $vx_0 = +5$ m/s. The acceleration rate is $a_x = 2$ m/s².

$$x = x_0 + v_{x0}t + \frac{1}{2}a_x t^2 = -12 + 5t + 1t^2$$

This is a projectile motion problem where v = 10.0 m/s, $\Delta y = -45$ m, and $\theta = 45°$.

33. (A) The average velocity of region A is (0 + 30 m/s)/2 = +15 m/s.

Region B is (30 m/s + 30 m/s)/2 = +30 m/s.

Region C is (30 m/s + 0 m/s)/2 = +15 m/s.

Region E is (0 m/s + −30 m/s)/2 = −15 m/s.

34. (D) Information provided is the angle of the kick (30°) and the initial velocity (10.0 m/s). Find the vertical component of the velocity, and solve for t when the ball hits the ground ($y = 0$).

1. Solve for the vertical component of velocity:

$$v_y = v \sin\theta \rightarrow v_y = (10.0 \text{ m/s})(\sin 30°) \rightarrow v_y = 5.0 \text{ m/s}$$

2. Solve for time:

$$\Delta y = v_y t + \frac{1}{2}gt^2 \rightarrow 0 = v_y t + \frac{1}{2}gt^2 \rightarrow 0 = t\left(v_y + \frac{1}{2}gt\right) : t = 0 \text{ is not a}$$

relevant solution

$$v_y + \frac{1}{2}gt = 0 \rightarrow t = \frac{-2v_y}{g} \rightarrow t = \frac{-2(5.0 \text{ m/s})}{(-10. \text{ m/s}^2)} \rightarrow \boxed{t = 1.0 \text{ s}}$$

35. (B) By subtracting the echo time, calculate that the stone takes 8 s to reach the bottom of the well. Now, calculate the vertical distance of the well:

$$\Delta x = v_0 t + \frac{1}{2}at^2 \rightarrow \Delta x = 0 + \frac{1}{2}(10 \text{ m/s}^2)(8 \text{ s})^2 \rightarrow \boxed{\Delta x = 320 \text{ m}}$$

36. (C) The horizontal component of velocity is $v_x = v\cos\theta = (10.0 \text{ m/s})\cos 45° = 7.1$ m/s. The vertical component of velocity is $v_y = v\sin\theta = (10.0 \text{ m/s})\sin 45° = 7.1$ m/s. The time it takes for the arrow to reach the ground is calculated as follows:

$$\Delta y = v_y t + \frac{1}{2}gt^2 \rightarrow -45 \text{ m} = (7.1 \text{ m/s})t + \frac{1}{2}(-10 \text{ m/s}^2)t^2$$

Solving the quadratic equation using the quadratic formula, yields: $t = 3.8$ s
The range of the arrow is calculated as follows:

$$\Delta x = v_x t = (7.1 \text{ m/s})(3.8 \text{ s}) \rightarrow \boxed{\Delta x = 27 \text{ m}}$$

37. (A) To find the displacement, integrate the area under the curve to the t axis. This involves adding the areas of two trapezoids, one in the $0-6$ s time interval and the other in the $6-10$ s time interval.

$$\Delta x = A_{0-6s} + A_{6-10s} \rightarrow \Delta x = \left[\frac{1}{2}(b_1 + b_2)(h)\right] + \left[\frac{1}{2}(b_1 + b_2)(h)\right]$$

$$\Delta x = \left[\frac{1}{2}(3 \text{ s} + 6 \text{ s})(2 \text{ m/s})\right] + \left[\frac{1}{2}(2 \text{ s} + 4 \text{ s})(-2 \text{ m/s})\right]$$

$$\Delta x = [9 \text{ m}] + [-6 \text{ m}] \rightarrow \boxed{\Delta x = 3 \text{ m}}$$

38. (B) The horizontal component of velocity is calculated by $vx = v \cos \theta$, while the vertical component is calculated by $vx = v \sin \theta$. For angles less than $45°$, the cosine is larger than the sine. So, the horizontal component of velocity is larger than the vertical component.

39. (C) Since the slope of the X vs. t graph starts positive and goes to zero in the first 2 seconds, the object is slowing down. Then the slope increases negatively, indicating that the object is gaining speed in the negative direction. The total displacement is $\Delta X = X_f - X_i = 0 - 6m = -6m$. (Note: Option D is incorrect because acceleration is defined as the slope of the velocity vs. clock reading graph. This slope remains negative even after the 2-second clock reading, as the velocity transitions from zero to more negative values.)

40. (B) There are two distinct models of motion for the bicycle's trip. The first 4 seconds is a constant velocity model, and it traveled a distance of $d_1 = vt = v_o t = 4v_o$. The last 6 seconds of the trip may be modelled by a uniform acceleration model:

$$d_2 = \Delta x = v_{ave}\Delta t = \left(\frac{v_i + v_f}{2}\right)\Delta t = \left(\frac{v_0 + 0}{2}\right)6 = 3v_0 \text{ . Thus, the total distance traveled is}$$

$d_{total} = d_1 + d_2 = 4v_o + 3v_o = 7v_o$. Alternate solution: This may be solved graphically by finding the area bounded by the velocity vs. clock reading graph, which is the sum of the area of a rectangle and a triangle.

41. (A) In the absence of air drag, the vertical acceleration of a projectile is a constant, non-zero value of -10 m/s/s near the surface of the Earth. Even when the ball reaches the peak and the vertical velocity instantaneously reaches a value of 0 m/s, the velocity is still changing and thus the lacrosse ball is still accelerating.

42. (D) The direction of velocity is the direction of motion, which is up in the positive direction. Acceleration, on the other hand is the rate of change of velocity. Since the velocity is decreasing (i.e., getting less positive), then the direction of acceleration is down.

43. (A) Assuming negligible air drag, the horizontal velocity of the ball will remain constant while it's in the air. Because of friction on the court, the horizontal velocity must be less after the bounce. Before the bounce, the ball is moving downward and speeding up, so the vertical velocity is getting more negative. After the bounce as the ball rises upward in the air and slows down, so it will have a positive velocity that decreases.

44. List of possible equipment:
- Motion detector or motion encoder: The graph looks like data from a motion detector because of the characteristic fluctuations on the graph. An optical motion encoder may also be used for smoother data. Both devices gather position data, and slopes are calculated to get velocity and acceleration values.
- Dynamics cart or air track shuttle
- Low friction dynamics track or air track

45. The object is at rest for the first two seconds, as evidenced by the zero velocity. A large force is applied for the next quarter of a second that accelerates the object from rest to a velocity of approximately 0.13 m/s. The object coasts for the next two seconds, perhaps on a flat low friction dynamics track or air track. During the last second and a half, the object slows down at a nearly uniform acceleration rate until it stops, perhaps because it's going uphill or there is a constant force pulling or pushing backwards on the object.

46. To estimate the displacement of the object during the first 7 seconds of the trip, find the value of the area under the graph, which may be approximated by a rectangle and a triangle:

$$\Delta x_{0-7s} = \Delta x_{0-2.5s} + \Delta x_{2.5-4.5s} + \Delta x_{4.5-6.5s} + \Delta x_{6.5-7s}$$

$$\Delta x_{0-7s} = 0 + \left(0.13\frac{m}{s}\right)(2.0s) + \left(\frac{0.13\frac{m}{s}+0}{2}\right)(2.0s) + 0 = 0.26m + 0.13m = 0.39m$$

47. The position graph will stay constant starting at an arbitrary position for about 2 seconds. Next, its slope will rapidly change from a zero slope to a slope of 0.13 m/s within about 0.25 seconds, and then remain in that slope for another 2.0 seconds. Finally, for the last 2.0 seconds, the slope will gradually level out to a value 0.39 meters from its starting position (see calculation above). Here is the actual graph from the motion detector:

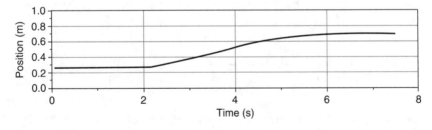

The acceleration vs. time graph is defined as the slope of the velocity vs. time graph. The graph is zero for 2.0 seconds. Next, in an interval of time of about 0.25 seconds, the acceleration will spike up to a value of $a = \dfrac{\Delta v}{\Delta t} = \dfrac{0.13m/s - 0m/s}{0.25\sec} \approx 0.5\dfrac{m}{s^2}$. Then the acceleration remains zero for another 2.0 seconds because the slope is zero. Finally, for the last 2.0 seconds, the slope will go to a value of $a = \dfrac{\Delta v}{\Delta t} = \dfrac{0 - 0.13m/s}{2\sec} \approx -0.07\dfrac{m}{s^2}$. Shown below is the actual graph from the motion detector with all the fluctuations due to variations in the reflected signal and the slope calculations made by the motion detector software:

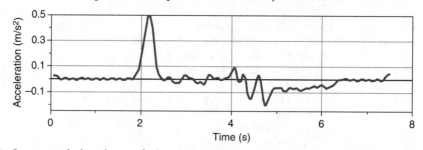

48. Starting with the velocity of +4 m/s, the given graph shows a constant acceleration of 2 m/s each second for the first two seconds; then for the last three seconds the acceleration is −1 m/s each second, as shown in the graph below:

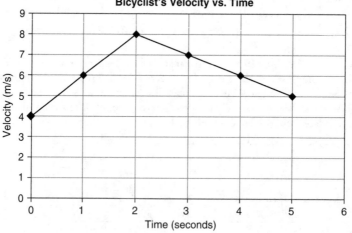

49. The bicyclist starts with a speed of 4 m/s and is moving in the positive direction. She gains 2 m/s each second for two seconds, and for the next three seconds begins to slow down at a rate of 1 m/s each second. For the second half of the trip, as she slows down, her velocities are still positive, indicating that she is still moving in the positive direction.

50. During the first half of the trip, her distance traveled was:

$$x - x_0 = v_{x0}t + \frac{1}{2}a_x t^2 = 4(2) + 0.5(2)(2^2) = 12 \text{ m}$$

At the beginning of the second part of the trip, the velocity was +8 m/s, and the distance is calculated as:

$$x - x_0 = v_{x0}t + \frac{1}{2}a_x t^2 = 8(3) + 0.5(-1)(3^2) = 24 - 4.5 = 19.5 \text{ m}$$

The total distance is 12 m + 19.5 m = $\boxed{31.5 \text{ m, or approximately 32 m.}}$

An alternate method of calculating distance is to determine the magnitude of the area bounded by the velocity–time graph above.

Chapter 2: Dynamics: Newton's Laws

51. (C) According to Newton's second law, the forces acting upon an object are balanced when the acceleration is zero. As shown in the graph, this occurs at 2 s.

52. (C) This problem refers to a single pushing interaction between the mother and the daughter. The mother's push on the daughter forms a Newton's third law pair with the daughter's push on the mother, and thus forms an N3L pair that must be equal in magnitude and opposite in direction.

53. (D) In deep space, there is no gravitational force from a planet and the gravitational attraction between the bodies is negligible. Thus, the only force during the push is the 160-N force of the daughter pushing the mother to the left. Using Newton's second law,

$$\vec{a} = \frac{\vec{F}_{net}}{m} = \frac{160N}{80kg} = \boxed{2\frac{m}{s^2}} \text{ to the left.}$$

54. (D) According to Newton's second law $\left(\vec{a} = \frac{\vec{F}_{net}}{m} \right)$, acceleration is inversely propor-

tional to mass. In order to double the acceleration, the mass must be half as much (for the same net force).

55. (C) The position in the graph is increasing linearly in the positive direction. It is consistent with motion with a constant positive velocity. The constant velocity means that acceleration is zero. According to Newton's second law, when acceleration is zero, there is no net force acting upon it.

56. (D) The gravitational force of the earth on the object in the downward direction is balanced by the supporting force of the spring on the object in the upward direction in order to maintain equilibrium.

57. (D) The box's initial velocity (0 m/s) and mass (10 kg) are known, as well as the girl's applied force (50 N) and the force of friction opposing her (45 N). Use Newton's second law to calculate the rate of the box's acceleration. The box uniformly accelerates to its final velocity of 2 m/s. Calculate the time:

$$a = \frac{F_{net}}{m}$$

$$a = \frac{F_A - F_f}{m}$$

$$a = \frac{(50\ N - 45\ N)}{(10\ kg)}$$

$$a = 0.5\ m/s^2$$

$$v_f = v_0 + at$$

$$2.0\ m/s = 0\ m/s + (0.5\ m/s^2)t$$

$$\boxed{t = 4\ s}$$

58. (D) The acceleration is the slope of a velocity–time graph. In this case, the slope of the graph yields an acceleration of 0.5 m/s². The mass of the crate is 50 kg. From Newton's second law, calculate the force applied:

$$F_{net} = ma$$

$$F_{net} = (50\ kg)(0.5\ m/s^2)$$

$$\boxed{F_{net} = 25\ N}$$

59. (A) From the graph, the acceleration at $t = 1$ s is -2 m/s². The object's mass is 5 kg. So, the net force can be calculated from Newton's second law:

$$F_{net} = ma$$

$$F_{net} = (5\ kg)(-2\ m/s^2)$$

$$\boxed{F_{net} = -10\ N}$$

60. (A) A 10.0-N force pushes the box to the right, while an 8.0-N force pushes it to the left. Since the dominant force is to the right, the acceleration will be to the right. Solve this equation for a:

$$F_{net} = ma$$

$$(10.0\ N - 8.0\ N) = (5\ kg)a$$

$$\boxed{a = 0.4\ m/s^2 \text{ to the right}}$$

61. (D) The force that you exert on the rope is equal to the rope's tension (T). The acceleration of the box is given at 10 m/s² upward. There are only two forces on the box: the upward tension force and the downward gravitational force. Applying Newton's second law to the box system:

$$F_{net} = ma$$

$$T - mg = ma$$

$$T = ma + mg$$

$$T = m(a + g)$$
$$T = (10 \text{ kg})(10 \text{ m/s}^2 + 10 \text{ m/s}^2)$$
$$\boxed{T = 200 \text{ N}}$$

62. (A) Then enter the horizontal component of thrust, the drag force of the wind, and the jet's mass into Newton's second law to find the acceleration:

$$F_{T_x} = F \cos\theta$$
$$F_{T_x} = (20{,}000 \text{ N})(\cos 60°)$$
$$F_{T_x} = 10{,}000 \text{ N}$$
$$F_{net_x} = ma$$
$$a = \frac{F_{net_x}}{m}$$
$$a = \frac{(F_{T_x} - F_{wind})}{m}$$
$$a = \frac{(10{,}000 \text{ N} - 1{,}000 \text{ N})}{(90{,}000 \text{ kg})}$$
$$\boxed{a = 0.1 \text{ m/s}^2}$$

63. (D) The object accelerates only when the forces acting upon it are unbalanced. The net force on the object at $t = 2$ s is $1.2 \text{ N} - 1.0 \text{ N} = 0.2 \text{ N}$. The acceleration is the net force divided by the mass, or $(0.2 \text{ N}/0.1 \text{ kg}) = \boxed{2 \text{ m/s}^2.}$

64. (D) The crate's mass is 10 kg, one force is 10 N, and the rate of acceleration is 0.1 m/s². Solve for the second force using Newton's second law:

$$a = \frac{F_{net}}{m}$$
$$a = \frac{(F_1 - F_2)}{m}$$
$$F_1 - F_2 = ma$$
$$F_2 = F_1 - ma$$
$$F_2 = (10 \text{ N}) - (10 \text{ kg})(0.1 \text{ m/s}^2)$$
$$\boxed{F_2 = 9 \text{ N}}$$

65. (B) Knowing the bullet's initial velocity (0 m/s) and mass (0.010 kg), use Newton's second law to calculate the rate of the bullet's acceleration. The bullet uniformly accelerates over the distance of the musket barrel (1 m) to its final velocity:

$$a = \frac{F_{net}}{m}$$

$$a = \frac{(50 \text{ N})}{(0.010 \text{ kg})}$$

$$a = 5,000 \text{ m/s}^2$$

$$v_f^2 = v_0^2 + 2a\Delta x$$

$$v_f^2 = (0 \text{ m/s}^2) + 2(5,000 \text{ m/s}^2)(1 \text{ m})$$

$$\boxed{v_f = 100 \text{ m/s}}$$

66. **(B)** There are 3 forces acting on the box. The normal force is always perpendicular to the surface, and will be up and to the right in this case. The gravitational force is down toward the center of the earth. The resistive forces of rolling friction and air drag are opposite to the direction of motion, which in this case is up and to the left, parallel to the slope of the hill. Motion is NOT a force and never belongs on a free body diagram.

67. **(C)** Daphne is correct. The acceleration of the dog is zero, and according to Newton's second law ($\vec{a} = \frac{\vec{F}_{net}}{m}$), the net force must also be zero. To obtain a net force of zero, the magnitudes of the normal and gravitational forces must be equal. The two forces do NOT form a Newton's third law pair because forces that constitute a third law pair must act on different systems.

68. **(A)** The force of the rope pulling the 6-kg block to the right and the force of the 6-kg block pulling the rope to the left form a Newton's third law pair. These forces will *always* be equal in magnitude and opposite in direction. The other force pairs *may or may not* be congruent, depending on the state of motion of the system and the presence or absence of friction. The normal force and the gravitational force on the 6-kg box will only be congruent if the vertical acceleration of the elevator system is zero.

69. **(B)** Use Newton's second law (N2L) to calculate the acceleration of the entire 8-kg system:

$$\vec{a} = \frac{\vec{F}_{net}}{m} = \frac{24N}{8kg} = 3\frac{m}{s^2}$$

Next, apply N2L to the 6-kg subsystem:

$$\vec{F}_{net} = m\vec{a} = 6kg\left(3\frac{m}{s^2}\right) = 18N$$

$$24N - T = 18N$$

$$T = 24N - 18N$$

$$\boxed{T = 6N}$$

N2L may also be applied to the 2-kg subsystem, and the same value of tension will be found.

70. (C) Motion is not a force, so options A & B are immediately eliminated. The coefficient of friction of 0.5 demands that the value of friction is half of the normal force. Option C is the only choice left.

71. (B) In order to accelerate, the tire must have traction with the road. When the drive shaft rotates the tire, the tire pushes back against the road without slipping. Newton's third law predicts that the road will push forward on the tire/car system, thus providing the net force it requires to accelerate (as long as that force is greater than any resistive forces like rolling friction and air drag).

72. (B) A system that cruises at a constant velocity has no acceleration. As a consequence, Newton's second law predicts that the system will have no net force. Applying this to the horizontal forces on the airplane/banner system, the forward force on the airplane must equal the combined forces of air drag on the airplane and banner.

73. (D) Block A & B are both free falling, and free-fall acceleration is independent of mass, therefore they will hit the ground at the same time. The mass of block's C & D will not affect their acceleration for the same reason that mass does not affect free-fall acceleration: The mass cancels out of the ratio of net force to mass in Newton's second law. Blocks C & D only have a component of gravitational force accelerating them along the incline, so they have less net force acting on them compared to blocks A & B *and* they must travel along the whole length of the incline, as compare with the direct path of block B. Thus blocks C & D will take more time to reach the ground. Because block C has a greater component of gravitational force than D and a shorter path to travel, its time of travel will be less than D.

74. (A) Acceleration is the ratio between net force and mass:

    I. Net force F applied to a mass M: $a = (F/M)$

    II. Net force 2F applied to a mass M: $a = 2F/M = 2(F/M)$

    III. Net force F applied to a mass $2M$: $a = F/(2M) = (F/M)/2$

    IV. Net force 2F applied to a mass $2M$: $a = (2F)/(2M) = (F/M)$

75. (D) Remember that the force of gravity (mg) must be resolved into x and y components, and that the force of friction (F_f) is related to the normal force (F_N) by $F_f = \mu F_N$. The box does not move above or into the plane, so the forces in the y direction must be balanced. Apply Newton's second law to both the x and y directions to come up with an expression for acceleration:

$$F_{net_y} = 0$$
$$F_N = mg\cos\theta = 0$$
$$F_N = mg\cos\theta$$
$$F_{net_x} = ma$$
$$mg\sin\theta - F_f = ma$$
$$mg\sin\theta - \mu F_N = ma$$
$$mg\sin\theta - \mu(mg\cos\theta) = ma$$
$$g\sin\theta - \mu(g\cos\theta) = a$$
$$\boxed{a = g(\sin\theta - \mu\cos\theta)}$$

76. **(C)** Newton's third law states that an interaction force between two systems is equal in magnitude and opposite in direction. During acceleration, each individual system will have unbalanced forces, but the tension interaction between the two systems is always equal and opposite.

77. **(C)** Sliding friction acts in opposition to the direction of motion, and its magnitude is directly proportional to the normal force.

78. **(D)** The gravitational force on the box, the perpendicular force of the plane on the box (aka the normal force), and the friction force along the surface of the plane beneath the box are the only forces acting on the box. The others mentioned are components of forces, forces the box exerts on its surroundings, or they are misleading.

79. **(A)** Define the positive x-axis along the incline:

$$F_{net_x} = ma$$
$$mg\sin\theta + F = mg$$
$$F = mg - mg\sin\theta$$
$$F = mg(1 - \sin 30°)$$
$$F = mg\left(1 - \frac{1}{2}\right)$$
$$\boxed{F = \frac{mg}{2}}$$

80. **(D)** There is a gravitational field on the surface of the Moon that is about one-sixth the strength of the Earth's field, so they will both accelerate. There is no atmosphere on the Moon, so air drag will not be considered. According to Newton's second law, acceleration is the net force-to-mass ratio. The more massive sphere has a greater gravitational force but in ratio to the greater mass yields the same free-fall acceleration as the less massive sphere.

81. (A) The box exerts a downward force of 1000N. Each cable must exert an upward force (T_y) of 500 N in order to balance that downward force.

$$\sin 30° = \frac{T_y}{T} \rightarrow T = \frac{T_y}{\sin 30°} \rightarrow T = \frac{500N}{0.5} = 1000N$$

82. (B) By applying Newton's second law to the pulley system, derive an equation for acceleration and solve the problem:

$$mg - T = ma$$
$$T - Mg = Ma$$
$$T = Ma + Mg$$
$$mg - (Ma + Mg) = ma$$
$$mg - Ma - Mg = ma$$
$$mg - Mg = ma + Ma$$
$$g(m - M) = a(m + M)$$

$$\boxed{a = g\frac{(m - M)}{(m + M)}}$$

83. (C) A curve on the position versus clock reading graph indicates a changing slope, which is a changing velocity. The straight section between 1.8 and 2.2 s indicates a constant velocity. Newton's first law states that objects will maintain constant velocity as long as there's zero net force acting on it.

84. (C) Both blocks will accelerate at the same rate a, and since they are connected by the same string they will both experience the same magnitude of tension force. By applying Newton's second law to the pulley system, derive an equation for acceleration and solve the problem:

$$F_{net_x} = T = Ma \rightarrow \text{Newton's 2nd law for the table Block } M$$
$$F_{net_y} = mg - T = ma \rightarrow \text{Newton's 2nd law hanging Block } m$$
$$mg - Ma = ma$$
$$ma + Ma = mg$$
$$a(m + M) = mg$$

$$\boxed{a = \frac{mg}{(m + M)}}$$

85. (B) The forces acting upon the skydiver are the downward gravitational force and upward air resistance force (drag). Initially, the net force is high (gravity > air resistance), the skydiver accelerates, and the velocity increases rapidly. Over time, the air resistance increases with speed, so the net force and acceleration decrease. At some point in time the skydiver reaches terminal velocity where there is no net force (gravity = air resistance), acceleration is zero, and the skydiver's velocity is constant.

86. (A) The car travels at constant velocity (its value is irrelevant), so the net force acting on the car is zero according to Newton's first law. Therefore, the resistive forces balance to the forward force on the car.

87. (A, D) A scale reads the normal force acting on the child, not the gravitational force. If the elevator were at rest or moving at a constant velocity, Newton's first and second laws both predict that the scale reading would be 400N in order to balance the child's weight. Since the upward scale reading (300N) is less than the weight (400N), the elevator must be accelerating downward. A downward acceleration may be achieved if the elevator is moving downward and speeding up OR moving upward and slowing down.

88. (A, C) The only object touching the book is the table, and it provides the upward support force (normal force) to balance the downward force of gravity from the interaction of the Earth with the book.

89. (A, C) The upward normal force and the downward gravitational force are the only forces acting on the child. These will be balanced ONLY when the elevator is in a state of constant velocity, meaning it moves at a constant speed in a straight line or if it is at a constant zero velocity (i.e., at rest).

90. (B, C) A free-body diagram would show an upward normal force, a downward gravitational force, a tension force up and to the left at a 30° angle, a frictional force to the right parallel to the surface, and possibly an air drag force to the right that is probably negligible. "Motion" is not a force, and the force of the block on the table is a valid force but does not act on the system of interest (which is the box).

91. (B, C) Mass has an inertial property and a gravitational property. Its inertial property is embedded in Newton's second law in the fact that mass is inversely proportional to acceleration. This means that the more massive something is, the more it resists changes in motion. Its gravitational property describes how the gravitational force attracts two masses (like the force attracting an apple to the Earth and the Earth to the apple).

92. Since the air track is frictionless and the only horizontal force on slider B is shown on the graph, the graph displays the net force. Since the positive force is a pushing force, it will accelerate to the right at the 0.25-second clock reading according to Newton's second law as follows:

$$\vec{a} = \frac{\vec{F}_{net}}{m} = \frac{2N}{0.5kg} = 4\frac{m}{s^2} \text{ to the right}$$

Next, the velocity after accelerating from rest for 0.25 seconds is calculated as follows:

$$v_f = a\Delta t + v_i = (4\frac{m}{s^2})(0.25s) + 0 = 1\frac{m}{s} \text{ to the right}$$

Since the net force is zero between 0.5 and 0.8 seconds, Newton's second law predicts that the acceleration of the system will be zero, and thus the system will continue moving at 1 m/s. For the last 0.2 seconds, similar calculations will be made:

$$\vec{a} = \frac{\vec{F}_{net}}{m} = \frac{-1.5N}{0.5kg} = -3\frac{m}{s^2} \text{ (to the left)}$$

$$v_f = a\Delta t + v_i = (-3\frac{m}{s^2})(0.2s) + 1.0 = 0.4\frac{m}{s} \text{ (still to the right)}$$

Because the motion detector is pointed to the left, the signs on the velocity will be reversed and the following graph will be obtained:

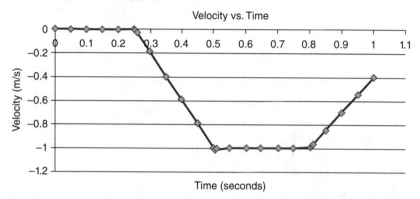

93. Since the force probes are linked together, they measure the same interaction. Thus the forces must be equal in magnitude and opposite in direction according to Newton's third law. Assuming that "right" is the positive direction for both sliders, then a push to the right on slider B is positive while a push to the left on slider A is negative. Thus, when slider B measures a pushing force of +2 N, then slider A simultaneously measures a pushing force of −2 N. Likewise, when slider B measures a pulling force of −1.5 N, then slider A simultaneously measures a pulling force of +1.5 N. The following graph is obtained:

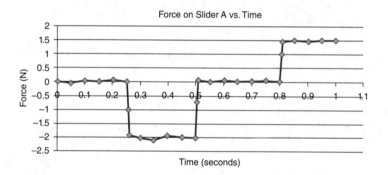

94. To find the displacement of the system, integrate the velocity vs. clock reading graph for each time interval by finding the area bounded:

$$0 - 0.25\,sec \rightarrow \Delta x = 0$$

$$0.25\,sec - 0.5\,sec \rightarrow \Delta x = \text{triangle area} = \frac{1}{2}(0.25s)(-1m\,/\,s) = -0.125m$$

$$0.5\,sec - 0.8\,sec \rightarrow \Delta x = \text{rectangle area} = (0.3s)(-1m\,/\,s) = -0.3m$$

$$0.8\,sec - 1.0\,sec \rightarrow \Delta x = \text{trapezoid area} = \frac{(-1.0m\,/\,s) + (-0.4m\,/\,s)}{2}(0.2s) = -0.14m$$

$$\Delta x_{total} = -0.125m - 0.3m - 0.14m = -0.565m \approx -0.6m$$

95. To return the shuttles to their starting position, a positive displacement of 0.565 meters is needed for the last second of time, which is to the left according to the reference frame of the motion detector. That means slider B will need a net force to the left calculated from the following steps:

$$v_{ave} = \frac{\Delta X}{\Delta t} = \frac{0.565m}{0.5\,sec} = 1.13m/s$$

For a uniform acceleration, the average velocity is the midpoint:

$$v_{ave} = \frac{(v_i + v_f)}{2} \rightarrow 1.13 = \frac{(-0.4 + v_f)}{2} \rightarrow v_f = 2.66m/s$$

$$a = \frac{\Delta v}{\Delta t} = \frac{(2.66 - (-0.4))m/s}{0.5s} = 6.12m/s^2$$

$$F_{net} = ma = (0.5kg)(6.12m/s^2) = 3.06N$$

$$\boxed{F_{net} \approx 3N \text{ to the left}}$$

96. The free-body diagram of this situation looks like this:

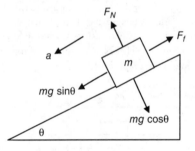

97. Calculate the force of friction by applying Newton's second law:

$$F_{nety} = 0$$

$$F_N - mg\,cos\theta = 0$$

$$F_N = mg\,cos\theta$$

$$F_f = \mu F_N$$

$$F_f = \mu mg\,cos\theta$$

$$F_f = (0.1)(10\,kg)(9.8\,m/s^2)\cos 30°$$

$$F_f = (0.1)(10\,kg)(9.8\,m/s^2)(0.87)$$

$$\boxed{F_f = 8.5\,N}$$

98. The box's acceleration can be calculated by applying Newton's second law:

$$F_{nety} = 0$$
$$F_N - mg \cos \theta = 0$$
$$F_N = mg \cos \theta$$
$$F_{netx} = ma$$
$$mg \sin \theta - F_f = ma$$
$$mg \sin \theta - \mu F_N = ma$$
$$mg \sin \theta \, \mu(mg \cos \theta) = ma$$
$$g \sin \theta - \mu(g \cos \theta) = a$$
$$a = g (\sin \theta - \mu \cos \theta)$$
$$a = (10 \text{ m/s}^2) [\sin 30° - (0.1) \cos 30°]$$
$$a = (10 \text{ m/s}^2) [(0.5) - (0.1) (0.87)]$$
$$\boxed{a = 4.1 \text{ m/s}^2}$$

99. The box started from rest and accelerated down the plane for 2 s. Calculate the final velocity:

$$v_f = v_0 + at$$
$$v_f = (0) + (4.05 \text{ m/s}^2) (2 \text{ s})$$
$$\boxed{v_f = 8.1 \text{ m/s}}$$

100. Calculate the distance that the box moved:

$$v_f^2 = v_0^2 + 2a\Delta x$$
$$(8.1 \text{ m/s})^2 = (0 \text{ m/s})^2 + 2(4.05 \text{ m/s}^2) \Delta x$$
$$\Delta x = 8.1 \text{ m}$$

or

$$\Delta x = v_0 t + \frac{1}{2} at^2$$
$$\Delta x = 0 + \frac{1}{2} (4.05 \text{ m/s}^2) (2 \text{ s})^2$$
$$\boxed{\Delta x = 8.1 \text{ m}}$$

Chapter 3: Circular Motion and the Universal Law of Gravitation

101. (C) For a fixed radius, centripetal acceleration is directly proportional to the square of speed according to $a_c = v^2/r$.

102. (A) Besides the normal force from the horizontal surface pointed out of the page and the gravitational force pointed into the page, the only other force comes from the wall which pushes the ball toward the center of the quarter-circle. This force is the "centripetal force" from the wall, and it points along the line from A toward C.

103. (C) Newton's first law states that objects will keep moving at a constant velocity as long as there is no unbalanced force acting on the object. When the wall no longer provides the centripetal force to keep the ball moving in the arc, there are no forces acting along the horizontal plane of movement, so the object must continue moving with the leftward velocity it had when it reached point B in the diagram.

104. (C) For a fixed radius and fixed speed, centripetal acceleration is independent of mass according to $ac = v^2/r$, so the accelerations will remain the same. (However, the centripetal force would be twice as much.)

105. (A) The tangential velocity is 30 m/s, and the radius of the circle is 10 m. Calculate the centripetal acceleration, which is always toward the center, as follows:

$$a_c = \frac{v^2}{r}$$

$$a_c = \frac{(30 \text{ m/s})^2}{(100 \text{ m})}$$

$$\boxed{a_c = 9 \text{ m/s}^2}$$

106. (D) The force of friction is what holds the car in the circular motion and solely provides the centripetal force. By knowing the mass of the car (1,000 kg), calculate the centripetal force, which acts toward the center:

$$F_c = ma_c$$

$$F_c = (1,000 \text{ kg}) (9 \text{ m/s}^2)$$

$$\boxed{F_c = 9,000 \text{ N}}$$

107. (A) The known quantities include the masses of the satellite (100 kg) and Earth (6×10^{24} kg) and the radius of the satellite's orbit (100 km + radius of the Earth = 100,000 m + 6.4×10^6 m = 6.5×10^6 m). The value of G provided on the constants sheet is 6.7×10^{-11} N·m²/kg². Use Newton's law of gravitation to find the force of gravity:

$$F_g = \frac{Gm_1 m_2}{r^2}$$

$$F_g = \frac{(6.7 \times 10^{-11} \text{ N} \cdot \text{m}^2 / \text{kg}^2)(100 \text{ kg})(6 \times 10^{24} \text{ kg})}{(6.5 \times 10^6 \text{ m})^2}$$

$$\boxed{F_g = 9.5 \times 10^2 \text{ N}}$$

108. (A) The known quantities are the mass of the astronaut (70 kg), the mass of the space-craft (5×10^4 kg), and the distance between them (10 m). Use Newton's law of gravitation to calculate the force of attraction between them:

$$F_g = \frac{Gm_1 m_2}{r^2}$$

$$F_g = \frac{(6.7 \times 10^{-11} \text{ N} \cdot \text{m}^2 / \text{kg}^2)(70 \text{ kg})(5 \times 10^4 \text{ kg})}{(10 \text{ m})^2}$$

$$\boxed{F_g = 2.3 \times 10^{-6} \text{ N}}$$

109. (C) The centripetal acceleration on the car is 1×10^5 m/s^2, and the radius of the turn is 40 m. Use the centripetal acceleration equation to find the car's velocity:

$$a_c = \frac{v^2}{r}$$

$$v^2 = a_c r$$

$$v = \sqrt{a_c r}$$

$$v = \sqrt{(1 \times 10^5 \text{ m/s}^2) \bullet 40m}$$

$$\boxed{v = 2 \times 10^3 \text{ m/s}}$$

110. (A) The minimum speed condition occurs when the cart loses contact with the track (normal force is zero) and the gravitational force solely provides the required centripetal force:

$$F_c = \frac{mv^2}{r} \rightarrow F_g = \frac{mv_{min}^2}{r} \rightarrow mg = \frac{mv_{min}^2}{r}$$

$$v_{min}^2 = gr \rightarrow v_{min} = \sqrt{gr}$$

$$v_{min} = \sqrt{\left(10\frac{m}{s^2}\right)(3.0m)} \rightarrow \boxed{v_{min} = 5.5\frac{m}{s}}$$

111. (B) The warrior spins a slingshot in a horizontal circle above his head at a constant velocity. When it is released, the stone will fly off at that velocity. The known quantities are the stone's mass (50 g = 0.05 kg) and the sling's radius (1.5 m). The tension in the string is equal to the centripetal force (3.3 N), so calculate the velocity:

$$F_c = \frac{mv^2}{r}$$

$$v^2 = \frac{F_c r}{m}$$

$$v = \sqrt{\frac{F_c r}{m}}$$

$$v = \sqrt{\frac{(3.3 \text{ N})(1.5 \text{ m})}{(0.05 \text{ kg})}}$$

$$\boxed{v \approx 10 \text{ m/s}}$$

112. (C) Given: the satellite's altitude (200 km), the mass of the Earth (6.0×10^{24} kg), and the Earth's radius (6.4×10^6 m). Convert the satellite's altitude to m and add the Earth's radius to it to get the satellite's orbital radius. The gravitational force from the planet is the only force acting on the satellite, thus providing the centripetal force:

$$F_{cent} = \frac{mv^2}{r} \rightarrow F_g = \frac{mv^2}{r}$$

Plugging in $\dfrac{GmM}{r^2}$ for F_g :

$$\frac{GmM}{r^2} = \frac{mv^2}{r} \rightarrow \frac{GM}{r} = v^2$$

Solving for v by first cross multiplying :

$$rv^2 = GM \rightarrow v^2 = \frac{GM}{r} \rightarrow v = \sqrt{\frac{GM}{r}}$$

$$v = \sqrt{\frac{(6.7 \times 10^{-11} \text{ N} \cdot \text{m}^2 / \text{kg}^2)(6.0 \times 10^{24} \text{ kg})}{(6.4 \times 10^6 \text{ m} + 2.00 \times 10^5 \text{ m})}}$$

$$\boxed{v = 7.8 \times 10^3 \text{ m/s}}$$

113. (C) Centripetal acceleration and centripetal force are inversely proportional to radius. Thus, tripling the radius (while keeping tangential speed the same) will require one-third the centripetal force.

114. (C) All the coins complete a circle of rotation in the same time period. Coin C traverses the greatest circumference, so it is traveling with the fastest tangential speed.

115. (D) According to Newton's third law, they exert the same magnitude of force on each other, so the difference between the forces is ZERO. This may be shown symbolically as follows:

$$F_{g_{\text{Sun on Mars}}} = \frac{Gm_S m_M}{r^2}$$

$$F_{g_{\text{Mars on Sun}}} = \frac{Gm_M m_S}{r^2}$$

$$F_{g_{\text{Sun on Mars}}} - F_{g_{\text{Mars on Sun}}} = \frac{Gm_S m_M}{r^2} - \frac{Gm_M m_S}{r^2} = \boxed{0}$$

116. (B) Since the car is moving in a vertical circle, it must accelerate toward the center of the circle (centripetal acceleration). Since the center of the circle is downward relative to the car, the acceleration, and consequently the net force, is downward. This implies that the downward gravitational force from the Earth is greater than the upward normal force from the road.

117. (B) During one complete orbit, the distance the carriage travels is the circumference of the circle (πD) and the time of travel is the orbital period. Speed may be calculated by dividing distance by time: $v = \dfrac{\text{Circumference of Orbit}}{\text{Orbital Period}} = \dfrac{\pi D}{T}$

118. (B) Assuming that friction on the carriage is negligible, the tension provides the centripetal force

$$F_{cent} = \frac{mv^2}{R} \rightarrow F_T = \frac{mv^2}{(D/2)} \rightarrow F_T = \frac{2mv^2}{D}$$

Writing this in slope intercept form ($y = \text{slope*}x + b$) with b = 0:

$$F_T = m\left(\frac{2v^2}{D}\right) + 0$$

The slope of the graph of $\boxed{F_T \text{ vs.} \dfrac{2v^2}{D}}$ is the mass of the carriage.

119. (A)

$$|\vec{g}| = \frac{|\vec{F_g}|}{m} \rightarrow |\vec{g}| = \frac{G\dfrac{mM}{R^2}}{m} \rightarrow g = \frac{GM_E}{R_E^2}$$

Cross-multiply and then solve for M_E:

$$GM_E = gR_E^2 \rightarrow \boxed{M_E = \frac{gR_E^2}{G}}$$

120. (B)

At the surface of the Earth, $|\vec{g}| = \dfrac{|\vec{F}_g|}{m} = \dfrac{\frac{GmM}{r^2}}{m} = \dfrac{GM}{r^2}$

At the surface of the "gaseous" Earth, where M is doubled and r is doubled:

$$|\vec{g}| = \dfrac{G(2M)}{(2r)^2} = \dfrac{2GM}{4r^2} = \dfrac{1}{2}\left(\dfrac{GM}{r^2}\right) = \dfrac{1}{2}\left(10\,\dfrac{m}{s^2}\right) = \boxed{5\,\dfrac{m}{s^2}}$$

121. (B) Applying Newton's law of universal gravitation $\left(|\vec{F}_g| = \dfrac{GmM}{r^2}\right)$ to each planet and the equations for each planet using constant terms, G, and the mass of the star (M), the following data about relative gravitation are obtained:

Planet	Relative mass	Relative distance	Gravitational force
A	$2\,m$	r	$|\vec{F}_g| = \dfrac{G(2m)M}{r^2} = 2\dfrac{GmM}{r^2}$
B	m	$0.1\,r$	$|\vec{F}_g| = \dfrac{G(m)M}{(0.1r)^2} = 100\dfrac{GmM}{r^2}$
X	$0.5\,m$	$2\,r$	$|\vec{F}_g| = \dfrac{G(0.5m)M}{(2r)^2} = \dfrac{1}{8}\dfrac{GmM}{r^2}$
Δ	$4\,m$	$3\,r$	$|\vec{F}_g| = \dfrac{G(4m)M}{(3r)^2} = \dfrac{4}{9}\dfrac{GmM}{r^2}$

The planet with the highest gravitational attraction is Planet B.

122. (D) According to Newton's first law, objects maintain constant velocity unless acted upon by an unbalanced force. The string provides the centripetal force that originally keeps the ball moving in a circle. When that force vanishes, the object must maintain a constant, straight-line velocity, which is tangent to the original path. (Note that gravity will also pull the ball toward the Earth, but this curve is not viewable from above.)

123. (C) Since the car is gaining speed, there is a southeast component of acceleration tangent to the curved path. But also, because the car is turning, there is a southwest component of acceleration toward the center of the turn (the centripetal acceleration). These two components sum as vectors to yield a resultant vector that is in the southerly direction. (Note: depending on the magnitudes of the components, the resultant vector may have a slight easterly or westerly component, but the dominant direction will be south.)

124. (B) There must be a net force toward the center of the circular arc, and this net force is called the centripetal force. At the bottom of the swing, the center of the arc is upward, which means the tension force must be greater than the gravitational force.

125. (B) The field will decrease the farther you get away from the center of the Earth, but the decrease is small:

$$\frac{g_{top}}{g_{sea\ level}} = \frac{\left(\dfrac{GM_e}{\left(r_{Earth}+8,848\right)^2}\right)}{\left(\dfrac{GM_e}{r_{Earth}^2}\right)} = \frac{r_{Earth}^2}{\left(r_{Earth}+8,848\right)^2} = \frac{\left(6.4X10^6\right)^2}{\left(6.4X10^6+8,848\right)^2} = 0.997$$

$$\% = (1-0.9976)*100 = 0.28\% \approx \boxed{0.3\%}$$

126. (B, C) All objects moving in a circle must experience a centripetal force and centripetal acceleration (directed toward the center of the orbit). The centripetal force is an unbalanced, or net, force toward the center. Whereas the magnitude of the centripetal acceleration may remain constant, it changes in direction because it is a vector pointed toward the center of the circle. The velocity is not constant because the Moon is constantly changing direction.

127. (C, D) Using $F_g = \dfrac{GM_1M_2}{r^2}$, examine the effect of changing each variable on the gravitational force. Tripling each mass and tripling the distance will result in no change $\left(\dfrac{3\times3}{3^2}=1\right)$. Quadrupling the second mass and doubling the distance will also result in no change $\left(\dfrac{1\times4}{2^2}=1\right)$.

128. (A, D) The only force on Jupiter is the gravitational force from the Sun. This force provides the centripetal force that allows it to stay in orbit. This net force results in a centripetal acceleration toward the center of the orbit.

129. (C, D) Only the rope and the Earth are interacting with the child. A free-body diagram will show an upward tension force and downward gravitational force. The tension will be larger in order to provide the required centripetal force toward the center of the arc.

130. (B, C) $g = \left(\dfrac{GM_{planet}}{r_{planet}^2}\right)$ where G is the universal gravitational constant.

131. (C) Centripetal force is calculated by $\dfrac{mv^2}{r}$, showing that the centripetal force is inversely proportional to the radius. If the mass and speed remain the same, the doubling of the radius will result in one-half the centripetal force.

132. (C) An acceleration of 1 g is approximately 10 m/s². So a "3-g environment" would be approximately 30 m/s². On the graph this corresponds to a radius of approximately 3 m.

133. **(C)** From the graph, notice that a radius of 5 m results in an acceleration of 20 m/s², or approximately 2 G's. Since the astronaut's mass is 70 kg, calculate the magnitude of the centripetal force:

$$F_c = ma_c$$
$$F_c = (70 \text{ kg})(20 \text{ m/s}^2)$$
$$\boxed{F_c = 1400 \text{ N}}$$

134. **(A)** First, the period of revolution for the pebble is calculated by dividing the total time by the total turns: $T = \dfrac{t}{N}$

The speed of the pebble is its circumference divided by the period:

$$v = \frac{2\pi r}{T} \rightarrow v = \frac{2\pi R}{(t/N)} \rightarrow v = \frac{2\pi RN}{t}$$

$$a_c = \frac{v^2}{r} \rightarrow a_c = \frac{\left(\dfrac{2\pi RN}{t}\right)^2}{R} \rightarrow a_c = \frac{4\pi^2 RN^2}{t^2}$$

$$F_c = ma_c \rightarrow F_c = m\frac{4\pi^2 RN^2}{t^2} \rightarrow \boxed{F_c = \frac{4\pi^2 mRN^2}{t^2}}$$

135. **(A)** The maximum speed of the bucket occurs at the bottom of the vertical circle because at this position, the vertical tension must be greater than the gravitational force on the system in order to have the needed centripetal force toward the center of the circle. A free-body diagram at this position shows tension upward and the gravitational force downward, so the centripetal force at the maximum speed is $F_{T_{MAX}} - F_g$. Since the bucket snaps with masses greater than 12 kg, the $F_{T_{MAX}} = 120N$.

$$F_{cent} = \frac{mv^2}{r} \rightarrow \left(F_{T_{MAX}} - F_g\right) = \frac{mv_{max}^2}{r} \rightarrow v_{max}^2 = \frac{r\left(F_{T_{max}} - F_g\right)}{m} \rightarrow v_{max} = \sqrt{\frac{r\left(F_{T_{max}} - F_g\right)}{m}}$$

$$v_{max} = \sqrt{\frac{1.5m(120N - 80N)}{8kg}} \rightarrow \boxed{v_{max} = 2.7\frac{m}{s}}$$

136. **(A)** Centripetal force is directly proportional to centripetal acceleration. Centripetal acceleration is directly proportional to the square of speed. Thus, twice the speed requires four times the centripetal acceleration and friction force.

137. **(D)** Pick any two points on the graph and calculate the centripetal acceleration. Square the velocity, and divide it by the radius. You will find that all of them have approximately the same centripetal acceleration, i.e., 10 m/s².

138. (D) Kepler's third law states that the square of the period of a planet's orbit (T) is proportional to the distance from the Sun (a) cubed. When the period is expressed in Earth years and the orbital radius in AU, then the law is $T^2 \propto a^3$. Knowing that Jupiter's orbital distance is 5 AU, use Kepler's third law to calculate its orbital period:

$$\frac{T^2}{a^3} = \text{constant}$$

$$\frac{(1\,yr)^2}{(1\text{AU})^3} = \frac{(T_J)^2}{(5\text{AU})^3}$$

$$\left(T_J\right)^2 = 5^3\,yr^2$$

$$T = \sqrt{(5)^3}\,yr$$

$$\boxed{T = 11 \text{ years}}$$

139. (B) The frictional force provides the centripetal force. You know the diameter of the ice rink, so calculate its circumference. From the circumference and the period, calculate the tangential velocity. Using the velocity, the radius, and acceleration due to gravity, calculate the coefficient of friction of the ice:

$$F_{cent} = \text{friction force} = \mu F_n$$

$$F_{cent} = mv^2 / r$$

$$\mu F_n = mv^2 / r \rightarrow \mu mg = mv^2 / r \rightarrow \mu = \frac{mv^2 / r}{mg} \rightarrow \mu = \frac{v^2}{rg}$$

$$v = \frac{2\pi r}{T} \rightarrow v^2 = \frac{4\pi^2 r^2}{T^2}$$

Substitute the expression for v^2 into the expression for μ:

$$\mu = \frac{\frac{4\pi^2 r^2}{T^2}}{rg} \rightarrow \mu = \frac{4\pi^2 r}{gT^2}$$

The radius is half of the diameter:

$$\mu = \frac{4\pi^2 (D/2)}{gT^2} \rightarrow \boxed{\mu = \frac{2\pi^2 D}{gT^2}}$$

140. (D) Compare the gravitational force on Satellite A to that on Satellite B using the equations of Newton's law of universal gravitation. Note that the radius of Satellite B is twice that of Satellite A.

$$F_{gA} = \frac{Gm_A m_p}{r_A^2}$$

$$F_{gB} = \frac{Gm_B m_p}{r_B^2}$$

$$r_B = 2r_A \text{ and } m_B = m_A$$

$$F_{gB} = \frac{Gm_A m_p}{(2r_A)^2} \rightarrow F_{gB} = \frac{Gm_A m_p}{4r_A^2}$$

$$\frac{F_{gA}}{F_{gB}} = \frac{\dfrac{Gm_A m_p}{r_A^2}}{\dfrac{Gm_A m_p}{4r_A^2}} = 4 \rightarrow \boxed{F_{gA} = 4F_{gB}}$$

141. (A) The satellite and the Moon are both moving in circles and experiencing the same centripetal acceleration because they have the same speed and the same radius of orbit: $a_c = \dfrac{v^2}{r}$. Since the gravitational force from the Earth is the only force acting on them, the centripetal acceleration is the gravitational acceleration.

142. (D) Centripetal force is the net force on the car toward the center of the circle and is calculated as follows:

$$F_{cent} = \frac{mv^2}{r}$$

$$F_A = \frac{MV^2}{R}$$

$$F_B = \frac{(2M)V^2}{R} = 2\left(\frac{MV^2}{R}\right)$$

$$F_C = \frac{MV^2}{2R} = \frac{1}{2}\left(\frac{MV^2}{R}\right)$$

$$F_D = \frac{M(2V)^2}{2R} = 2\left(\frac{MV^2}{R}\right)$$

Thus, $D = B > A > C$.

143. (B) The coefficient of friction between the rubber tires of a car and dry concrete is $\mu = 0.64$. The radius of the turn is 10.0 m. Calculate the maximum velocity of the car as follows:

$$F_{cent} = \text{friction} = mv^2/r$$

$$\mu F_n = mv^2/r$$

$$\mu mg = mv^2/r$$

$$\mu = \frac{v^2}{gr}$$

$$v^2 = \mu gr$$

$$v = \sqrt{\mu gr}$$

$$v = \sqrt{(0.64)(10 \text{ m/s}^2)(10 \text{ m})}$$

$$\boxed{v = 8 \text{ m/s}}$$

144. The gravitational field strength is independent of satellite mass and decreases inversely with the square of distance from the center of the planet:

$$|g| = \frac{|\vec{F_g}|}{m} = \frac{\frac{GmM}{r^2}}{m} = \frac{GM}{r^2}$$

At the surface of the planet: $|g| == \dfrac{G(10^{24} \text{ kg})}{R^2}$

At the 100-kg satellite's location: $|g| = \dfrac{G(10^{24} \text{ kg})}{(2R)^2} = \dfrac{1}{4}\left(\dfrac{G(10^{24} \text{ kg})}{R^2}\right)$

At the 400-kg satellite's location: $|g| = \dfrac{G(10^{24} \text{ kg})}{(3R)^2} = \dfrac{1}{9}\left(\dfrac{G(10^{24} \text{ kg})}{R^2}\right)$

145. The gravitational force from the planet is the only force acting on the satellites, thus providing the centripetal force:

$$F_{cent} = \frac{mv^2}{r} \rightarrow F_g = \frac{mv^2}{r}$$

Plugging in $\dfrac{GmM}{r^2}$ for F_g :

$$\frac{GmM}{r^2} = \frac{mv^2}{r} \rightarrow \frac{GM}{r} = v^2$$

Solving for v by first cross multiplying :

$$rv^2 = GM \rightarrow v^2 = \frac{GM}{r} \rightarrow v = \sqrt{\frac{GM}{r}}$$

Now, compare the speeds of each satellite:

$$100\text{-kg satellite: } v = \sqrt{\frac{GM}{2R}} \approx 0.71\sqrt{\frac{GM}{R}}$$

$$400\text{-kg satellite: } v = \sqrt{\frac{GM}{3R}} \approx 0.57\sqrt{\frac{GM}{R}}$$

The 100-kg satellite moves about 1.2 times faster than the 400-kg satellite.

146. First calculate the speed of the 400-kg satellite's orbit using the expression derived in the previous problem:

$$v = \sqrt{\frac{GM}{3R}} = \sqrt{\frac{6.67 \times 10^{-11} \frac{m^3}{kg \cdot s^2}(10^{24}\,kg)}{3(2 \times 10^6)m}} = 3334\frac{m}{s}$$

Next, calculate the period as follows:

$$v = \frac{2\pi R}{T} \rightarrow T = \frac{2\pi R}{v} = \frac{2\pi(2 \times 10^6\,m)}{3334 m/s} = 3760\,\text{sec} \approx \boxed{1\text{ hour}}$$

147.

$$|F_g| = \frac{GmM}{r^2}$$

I. $\quad |F_g|_{400 \text{ on } 100} = \dfrac{G(100)(400)}{(3R - 2R)^2} = \dfrac{40000G}{R^2} = 4 \times 10^4\dfrac{G}{R^2}$

II. $\quad |F_g|_{100 \text{ on } 400} = \dfrac{G(400)(100)}{(3R - 2R)^2} = \dfrac{40000G}{R^2} = 4 \times 10^4\dfrac{G}{R^2}$

(I = II due to Newton's third law!)

III. $\quad |F_g|_{\text{Planet on } 100} = \dfrac{G(100)(10^{24})}{(2R)^2} = \dfrac{1 \times 10^{26}G}{4R^2} \approx 3 \times 10^{25}\dfrac{G}{R^2}$

IV. $\quad |F_g|_{\text{Planet on } 400} = \dfrac{G(400)(10^{24})}{(3R)^2} = \dfrac{4 \times 10^{26}G}{9R^2} \approx 4 \times 10^{25}\dfrac{G}{R^2}$

$\boxed{\text{IV} > \text{III} \gg \text{II} = \text{I}}$

Note: The gravitational force between the satellites is negligible compared to the gravitational pull of the planet on the satellites.

148. The free-body diagram of this situation is shown in the following figure, where F_N = Normal Force, F_g = Gravitational Force, and F_f = Static Friction Force.

149. Calculate the car's maximum velocity by applying Newton's second law to the situation. The car's centripetal force is provided by the horizontal component of normal force from the road ($F_c = F_N \sin\theta = mv^2/r$). The car does not accelerate along the y-axis, so the vertical component of the normal force must balance the weight of the car ($mg = F_N \cos\theta$). By dividing these two equations, we get an equation that we can solve for velocity:

$$F_c = F_N \sin\theta = \frac{mv^2}{r}$$

$$mg = F_N \cos\theta$$

$$\frac{F_N \sin\theta = \dfrac{mv^2}{r}}{F_N \cos\theta = mg}$$

$$\tan\theta = \frac{v^2}{rg}$$

$$v^2 = rg \tan\theta$$

$$v = \sqrt{rg \tan\theta}$$

$$v = \sqrt{(300 \text{ m})(10 \text{ m/s}^2) \tan 30°}$$

$$\boxed{v = 42 \text{ m/s}}$$

150. The free-body diagram now looks like this:

The static friction force (F_T) solely provides the centripetal force, and the normal force (F_N) is balanced by the weight, $F_g = mg$:

$$F_c = \frac{mv^2}{r} \rightarrow F_f = \frac{mv^2}{r} \rightarrow \mu(F_N) = \frac{mv^2}{r} \rightarrow \mu(mg) = \frac{mv^2}{r}$$

$$\mu_{min} = \frac{mv^2}{mgr} \rightarrow \boxed{\mu_{min} = \frac{v^2}{gr}}$$

Chapter 4: Simple Harmonic Motion

151. (C) The general equation for this oscillation is $\Delta x = A \cos(2\pi f\, t)$, where A is the amplitude and f is the frequency of vibration. According to the graph, a complete cycle occurs every 2 seconds, which is a frequency of 0.5 cycles per second. The graph also shows an amplitude of vibration of 10 m. This gives the following equation: $\Delta x = 10 \cos(\pi t)$.

152. (D) Without friction, it will swing until its potential energy is equal to the original potential energy, i.e., the horizontal, or 180°.

Questions 153 & 154 refer to the following material:

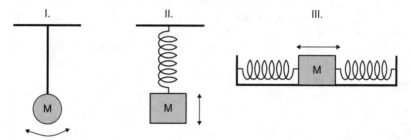

The three systems above are vibrating along the directions shown by the double-headed arrows. The first system is a small mass at the end of a string that's swinging back and forth in a small arc. The second system is a spring-mass system vibrating up and down vertically. The third system is a spring-mass system vibrating back and forth horizontally.

153. (B) The mass of a pendulum has no effect on the frequency of a simple pendulum's oscillation. Larger masses, however, increase the period and decrease the frequency of spring-mass oscillations.

154. (D) Amplitude of vibration has no effect on the frequency of spring-mass oscillators. It has only a slight effect on the frequency of a simple pendulum, but this effect only becomes significant as the amplitude of vibration gets large. Therefore, the amplitude will have no significant effect on any of the system frequencies.

155. (B) The pendulum period equation must be solved for g, the gravitational field strength:

$$T = 2\pi \sqrt{\frac{L}{g}}$$

$$T^2 = 4\pi^2 \frac{L}{g}$$

$$g = (4\pi^2)\frac{L}{T^2} = (4\pi^2)\frac{2.0\,\text{m}}{(4.6\,\text{s})^2} = 3.7\,\frac{\text{m}}{\text{s}^2} = \boxed{3.7\,\text{N/kg}}$$

156. (B) For a periodic vibration to occur, there must be a restoring force. Because the pendulum's mass moves in response to gravity, the restoring force depends on the gravitational force.

157. (D) Use the following equation for the period of a mass-spring system:
$$T = 2\pi \sqrt{\frac{m}{k}} = 2\pi \sqrt{\frac{10kg}{20N\,/\,m}} = 4.44s \approx 4\,\text{sec}\,.$$ This equation applies to both horizontal and vertical spring-mass oscillators.

158. (C) The water tank is 180° out of phase with the ship's hull, so the rolling of the ship is canceled by the rolling of the water in the tank.

159. (A) The equation for oscillation is $\Delta x = A \cos(2\pi f\, t)$, where A is the amplitude and f is the frequency of vibration. Setting $2\pi f = 150$ and solving for f gives 24 Hz.

160. (B) Use the formula for the period of a pendulum, $T_P = 2\pi \sqrt{\dfrac{\ell}{g}} = 2\pi \sqrt{\dfrac{67.17m}{10m/s^2}} = 16\sec.$
(Note that the length of the pendulum is measured from the pivot to the center of bob's mass, so the radius of the bob was added to the length of the string length, but this has a negligible effect on the period because the string is so long.) The frequency is the inverse of the period: $f = \dfrac{1}{T} = \dfrac{1}{16.3\,\dfrac{\sec}{cycle}} = 0.061\,\dfrac{cycles}{\sec}.$

161. (C) The period of a mass-spring system is $T_S = 2\pi \sqrt{\dfrac{m}{k}} = 2\pi \sqrt{\dfrac{8kg}{60N/m}} = 2.3$ s. The frequency is the inverse of the period and equals 0.4 cycle per second (one significant figure).

162. (A) The period of a spring-mass system is given by:

$$T_s = 2\pi \sqrt{\dfrac{m}{k}}$$

If you double the mass and double the spring constant, there will be no change in the period of oscillation. The gravitational field strength does not affect the period of vibration.

163. (D) The maximum force and acceleration occur when the spring is displaced the greatest distance from equilibrium, i.e., when the displacement equals the amplitude. The values are calculated as follows:

$$F_{max} = k\Delta x_{max} = \left(12\,\frac{N}{m}\right)(0.12\ m) = 1.44\ N$$

$$a_{max} = \frac{\vec{F}_{net}}{m} = \frac{1.44\ N}{0.40\ kg} = 3.6\,\frac{m}{s^2}$$

Note that the gravitational force of the hanging mass is not included in the net force calculation because it was already balanced by the spring force when the spring was initially loaded.

An alternate solution could be found using the oscillation acceleration equation:

Acceleration equation: $a(t) = -A(2\pi f)^2 \sin(2\pi ft)$

$|a_{max}| = A(2\pi f)^2 = 4\pi^2 A f^2$

Frequency must be found: $f = \dfrac{1}{T_s} = \dfrac{1}{2\pi\sqrt{\dfrac{m}{k}}} = \dfrac{1}{2\pi\sqrt{\dfrac{0.40kg}{12N/kg}}} = 0.87\,\dfrac{cycles}{s}$

$|a_{max}| = 4\pi^2 A f^2 = 4\pi^2(0.12m)\left(0.87\,\dfrac{cycles}{s}\right)^2 = \boxed{3.6 m/s^2}$

164. (A) Using the formula for the period of a pendulum, $T_p = 2\pi\sqrt{\dfrac{L}{g}}$, solve for L as follows:

$$L = \frac{T^2}{4\pi^2}(g) = \frac{(3.0s)^2}{4\pi^2}(10.m/s^2) = 2.3m$$

165. (B) The frequency of vibration is given, and the period is the inverse of frequency:

$$T = \frac{1}{f} = \frac{1}{6.98 \times 10^{14} \text{ cycles/s}} = 1.43 \times 10^{-15} \text{ s/cycle}$$

166. (C) The equation for the period of the pendulum is $T_p = 2\pi\sqrt{\dfrac{\ell}{g}}$. Mass does not appear in this equation because it does not affect the period of the pendulum. Increased length of the pendulum, however, does increase the period.

167. (D) The equation for the period of the pendulum is $T_p = 2\pi\sqrt{\ell/g}$. Since frequency is the inverse of period, then $f_p = \dfrac{1}{T} = \dfrac{1}{2\pi\sqrt{\ell/g}} = \dfrac{1}{2\pi}\sqrt{\dfrac{g}{\ell}}$. Mass does not appear in this equation because it does not affect the frequency of the pendulum. Increased length of the pendulum, however, does decrease the frequency.

168. (B) The equation for the period of a spring-mass system is $T_s = 2\pi\sqrt{\dfrac{m}{k}}$. Plug in values to compare:

I. $T_s = 2\pi\sqrt{\dfrac{M}{k}}$

II. $T_s = 2\pi\sqrt{\dfrac{2M}{k}}$

III. $T_s = 2\pi\sqrt{\dfrac{M}{2k}}$

IV. $T_s = 2\pi\sqrt{\dfrac{2M}{2k}} = 2\pi\sqrt{\dfrac{M}{k}}$

169. (D) The gravitational field strength has no effect on the period of a spring-mass oscillator. Air density will dampen the oscillation, causing the amplitude to decrease over time, but amplitude has *no effect* on the period of vibration of a spring-mass oscillator.

170. (C) Velocity is the slope of the position vs. time graph, and option D displays this slope. Speed is always positive and is the absolute value of velocity, as displayed in **graph C**. Ignoring the phase shift and the shift in vertical position on the original graph due to the location of the motion detector, these quantities may be represented as follows:

Position equation: $x(t) = A\sin(2\pi f\ t)$

Velocity equation: $v(t) = A(2\pi f)\cos(2\pi f\ t)$

Speed equation: $\text{speed}(t) = A(2\pi f)|\cos(2\pi f\ t)|$

171. (B) Acceleration is the slope of the velocity vs. time graph. It was established in the previous problem that option D displays the velocity vs time. Thus, **graph B** best represents how the slope of graph D changes with time. Ignoring the phase shift and the shift in vertical position on the original graph, these quantities may be represented as follows:

Position equation: $x(t) = A\sin(2\pi f\ t)$

Velocity equation: $v(t) = A(2\pi f)\cos(2\pi f\ t)$

Acceleration equation: $a(t) = -A(2\pi f)^2 \sin(2\pi f\ t)$

172. (D) The spring constant determines the stretch of the spring:

$$F_s = k\Delta x \rightarrow \Delta x = \frac{F_s}{k} \rightarrow \Delta x = \frac{mg}{k} \rightarrow \Delta x = \frac{(12kg)(10m/s^2)}{190N/m} \rightarrow \boxed{\Delta x = 0.63m}$$

The period of a mass-spring system is found by: $T = 2\pi\sqrt{\dfrac{m}{k}} = 2\pi\sqrt{\dfrac{12kg}{190N/m}} = \boxed{1.6s}$

173. (D) The clapper may be modeled as a simple pendulum, and the period of a pendulum depends on its length. So, by making the clapper longer, its period would be longer and out of phase with the bell. Therefore, the bell will ring with a longer clapper. Mass and amplitude of swing have no significant effect on the period of a pendulum.

174. (C) Resonance is a dramatic growth in vibration amplitude that occurs when a system is forced to vibrate at its natural frequency. The natural frequency of a spring-mass system depends on its mass and the spring constant. If the natural frequency of the spring mass system is 6 Hz, then it will resonate with amplitudes considerably greater than 0.2 cm.

175. (C) The ball falls with a uniform acceleration, so use $x - x_0 = v_0\ t + \dfrac{1}{2}at^2$ where v_0 is zero, a is the acceleration of gravity, and t is one-half of the period of the periodic motion. Because the collision of the ball with the plate is elastic, the full energy of the dropped ball is returned to the ball and it will bounce with a period of 2 seconds.

$$x - x_0 = (0)t + \frac{1}{2}(10m/s^2)(1s)^2 = 5m.$$

176. (D) The period of a simple pendulum is directly proportional to the square root of the length. If the length is quadrupled, then the period will increase as the square root of 4, or twice as much.

177. (D) The maximum speed during an oscillation occurs when the mass moves through equilibrium. At equilibrium, the forces are temporarily balanced and the acceleration is instantaneously zero.

178. (D) The equation for oscillation is $\Delta x = A \cos(2\pi f\, t)$, where A is the amplitude and f is the frequency of vibration. The amplitude of vibration is 2.0 cm, which means the cone vibrates forward 2.0 cm from equilibrium and back 2.0 cm from equilibrium. This is half a cycle, and so the total distance traveled for a half cycle is 2.0cm + 2.0 cm = 4.0 cm.

179. (D) The period of a pendulum is defined as the time for one complete back *and forth* swing. When the hooked mass gets to the bottom of the swing, the clock will start when the beam gets blocked. If the clock is turned off the next time the bob blocks the beam, it has only swung through half the swing. Thus, the period may be calculated by doubling the elapsed time between when the beam is blocked and subsequently blocked again.

180. (C) The speed is zero at the position –A because it has to stop as it changes direction.

181. (B) As the mass passes through equilibrium, it has accelerated to its maximum speed.

182. (A) At position –A and +A, the compression/extension of the spring is the greatest distance from equilibrium, giving the largest magnitude of force. This force at position -A is to the right (the positive direction) and yields the largest positive net force. Thus, acceleration, the ratio of net force to mass, is at a maximum at this position.

183. (C) At $t = 0$, the equation $\Delta x = - A \cos\left(\dfrac{2\pi}{T}t\right)$ yields $\Delta x = -A$, which is the initial displacement. One cycle later, when $t = T$, it also yields $\Delta x = -A$. At a quarter of the way into the cycle, when $t = T/4$, it is at a position of zero, which is consistent with the oscillation.

184. (C) The period and frequency of the vibration are independent of amplitude.

185. (B)

$$\frac{T_{P_M}}{T_{P_E}} = \frac{2\pi\sqrt{\dfrac{\ell}{g_m}}}{2\pi\sqrt{\dfrac{\ell}{g_e}}} = \sqrt{\frac{g_e}{g_m}} = \sqrt{\frac{g_e}{\dfrac{g_e}{6}}} = \sqrt{6}$$

186. (B, C) In order to achieve simple harmonic motion, there must be a restoring force that maintains an oscillation about an equilibrium state. Gravity provides the restoring force for the swinging child and the ball in the bowl. The elastic force in the string provides the restoring force for it to continue to vibrate. The bouncing ball and the jumping child rely on gravity and the force from the ground, but these are not considered restoring forces, and the motion is not oscillating about equilibrium.

187. (B, D) Periodic motion repeats itself at regular time intervals. The Moon's orbit has a consistent time period, and the pendulum also has a consistent time period as it swings.

188. (A, D) The most significant variables in the list are the length and the gravitational

field strength $\left(T_p = 2\pi\sqrt{\dfrac{\ell}{g}}\right)$. Mass has absolutely no effect, and amplitude and string char-

acteristics may have only a negligible effect.

189. (A, C) The value of the mass and the spring constant are the variables that have a

significant effect on the period of a spring-mass system $\left(T_s = 2\pi\sqrt{\dfrac{m}{k}}\right)$.

190. (B, C) The value of the mass and the spring constant are the variables that have a significant effect on the period of a spring-mass system:

$$T_s = 2\pi\sqrt{\frac{m}{k}}$$

$$f = \frac{1}{T_S} = \frac{1}{2\pi\sqrt{\dfrac{m}{k}}} = \frac{1}{2\pi}\sqrt{\frac{k}{m}}$$

Increasing the spring constant k will increase the frequency and decreasing the mass, m, will also increase the frequency.

191. The amplitude of vibration remains at 20.0 cm. The period and frequency are calculated as follows:

$$T_s = 2\pi\sqrt{\frac{m}{k}} = 2\pi\sqrt{\frac{2\text{ kg}}{\left(8\dfrac{N}{m}\right)}} = \pi = 3.1\text{ s}$$

$$f_s = \frac{1}{T_s} = \frac{1}{\pi} = 0.32\text{ Hz}$$

192. The standard equation for displacement is $\Delta x = A\cos(2\pi f\ t)$. Plugging in amplitude and frequency yields displacement in $\Delta x = 20\cos(2\ t)$ cm.

193. Graphing the equation from part (b) yields the following graph:

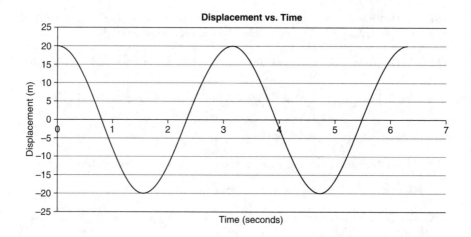

Displacement vs. Time

Time (seconds)

194. $F_{max} = k\Delta x_{max} = \left(8\dfrac{N}{m}\right)(0.20 \text{ m}) = 1.6 \text{ N}$

$a_{max} = \dfrac{F_{net}}{m} = \dfrac{1.6 \text{ N}}{2.0 \text{ kg}} = 0.8 \dfrac{m}{s^2}$

One way to calculate maximum speed is to analyze how much elastic potential energy in the spring transfers to kinetic energy as it passes through equilibrium (the gravitational energy transfer may be ignored in this analysis because a vertical spring oscillation behaves in the same manner as a horizontal oscillation). As it's released, the elastic potential energy is $U_s = \dfrac{1}{2}kx^2 = \dfrac{1}{2}\left(8\dfrac{N}{m}\right)(0.20 \text{ m})^2 = 0.16 \text{ Nm} = 0.16 \text{ J}.$

When this energy is completely transferred to kinetic energy, the speed is maximized:

$K = \dfrac{1}{2}mv^2$

$v_{max} = \sqrt{\dfrac{2K_{max}}{m}} = \sqrt{\dfrac{2*0.16 \text{ J}}{2 \text{ kg}}} = 0.40 \dfrac{m}{s}$

An alternate method is to use the maximum speed relationship for a mass-spring system (not provided on the AP equations sheet):

$$v_{max} = 2\pi Af = 2\pi(0.20 \text{ m})\left(\frac{1}{\pi} \text{ Hz}\right) = 0.40 \frac{m}{s}.$$

195. The maximum speed occurs at the positions where the mass passes through equilibrium ($\Delta x = 0$) because the restoring force had acted for a quarter-period and is switching directions. The maximum magnitude of acceleration occurs at the points when the magnitude spring force (the net force, since gravity is ignored) is maximized, which is at the points of greatest displacement. When the displacement is -20 cm, the spring force is positive, and this represents the point of maximum (positive) acceleration.

196. The period is the time for one full swing of the pendulum, back and forth. It may be measured with a stopwatch, which has an uncertainty close to the human reaction time (approximately $+/- 0.2$ or $+/- 0.3$ s). A photogate placed at the bottom of the swing may also be used to give periods with uncertainties of one-thousandth of a second or better.

197. The independent variable is the length of the pendulum, which is purposely changed. The dependent variable is the variable of interest, which is the period of the pendulum. Controlled variables that are held constant include the mass of the bob, the displacement angle of the swing, and the location (gravitational field).

198. The period is directly proportional to the square root of length and has a shape as follows:

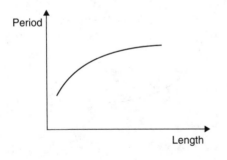

199. The period is independent of mass, so all the periods should be nearly 0.76 s (within the envelope of the measurement uncertainty).

Mass of Bob (g)	Period (s)
10.	0.76
20.	0.76
30.	0.76
40.	0.76
50.	0.76

The length of the pendulum that gives a period of 0.76 may be calculated by solving $T_p = 2\pi\sqrt{\dfrac{\ell}{g}}$ for ℓ:

$$\ell = \frac{g(T_p)^2}{(2\pi)^2} = \frac{\left(10.\frac{m}{s^2}\right)(0.76^2 \text{ s}^2)}{(2\pi)^2} = 0.1463 \text{ m} \approx 15 \text{ cm}$$

200. According to the relationship $T_p = 2\pi\sqrt{\dfrac{\ell}{g}}$, the period is inversely proportional to the square root of the gravitational field, yielding the following graph:

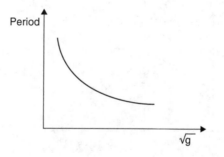

Chapter 5: Impulse, Linear Momentum, Conservation of Linear Momentum, and Collisions

201. (C) Newton defined momentum as the time rate of change of momentum, so the slope of a momentum–time graph is force. Another way of looking at this is using the momentum–impulse theorem: The change in momentum divided by the time interval is the average force exerted on an object:

$$\vec{F} = \frac{\Delta\vec{p}}{\Delta t} = \frac{(10-0)\ \text{kg}\cdot\text{m/s}}{(5-0)\text{s}} = \boxed{2\ \text{N}}$$

202. (C) The impulse theorem states that the momentum change of an object exactly equals the product of the average force acting on the object and the time of application of that force.

203. (A) The mass of the car is 1,000 kg. It's moving at a velocity ($v = +11.0$ m/s). It comes to a complete stop; therefore, the change in velocity ($\Delta v = 0$ m/s $-$ 11 m/s $= -11$ m/s) occurs over a time interval ($\Delta t = 2.0$ s). Use the impulse–momentum theorem to calculate the force acting upon the car:

$$\Delta p = F\Delta t$$
$$\Delta p = m\Delta v$$
$$F\Delta t = m\Delta v$$
$$F = \frac{m\Delta v}{\Delta t}$$
$$F = \frac{(1{,}000\ \text{kg})(-11\ \text{m/s})}{(2.0\ \text{s})} \rightarrow \boxed{F = -5{,}500\ \text{N}}$$

204. (B) The ball has a mass of 2.0 kg. It moves at $+10$ m/s. When it hits the wall, the collision is perfectly elastic, which are collisions where there is no change in kinetic energy in the system. This means the ball's direction of motion is changed and its velocity is now -10 m/s. Calculate the ball's momentum as follows:

$$p = mv$$
$$p = (2.0\ \text{kg})(-10\ \text{m/s}) \rightarrow \boxed{p = -20\ \text{kg}\cdot\text{m/s}}$$

205. (C) The mass of the box is 10 kg, and the box's change in velocity is -10 m/s. The force applied to the box is constant at -10 N. Use the impulse–momentum theorem to calculate the time it takes the box to stop:

$$\Delta p = F\Delta t$$
$$\Delta p = m\Delta v$$
$$F\Delta t = m\Delta v$$
$$\Delta t = \frac{m\Delta v}{F}$$
$$\Delta t = \frac{(10\text{ kg})(-10\text{ m/s})}{(-10\text{ N})} \rightarrow \boxed{\Delta t = 10\text{ s}}$$

206. (B) The balls are of equal mass ($m_A = m_B$). Initially, Ball A moves at a velocity (v_A) of 10 m/s, while Ball B moves at a velocity (v_B) of -5 m/s. After the collision, Ball B moves with a velocity (v'_B) of 8 m/s. Calculate the final velocity of Ball A by conservation of momentum in a perfectly elastic collision:

$$p_A + p_B = p'_A + p'_B$$
$$m_A V_A + m_B v_B = m_A v'_A + m_B v'_B$$
$$m_A = m_B$$
$$v_A + v_B = v'_A + v'_B$$
$$v'_A = v_A + v_B - v'_B$$
$$v'_A = (10\text{ m/s}) + (-5\text{ m/s}) - (8\text{ m/s}) \rightarrow \boxed{v'_A = -3\text{ m/s}}$$

207. (D) The mass of the fullback (m_A) is 140 kg, while the mass of the defender (m_B) is 70 kg. Initially, A is moving at 10 m/s and B at -5 m/s. They collide with a perfect inelastic collision because the defender wraps his arms around the fullback and they travel together. Since there is no net force on the system during the collision, use conservation of momentum for inelastic collisions to find their combined velocity after contact:

$$p_A + p_B = p'_{(A+B)}$$
$$m_A v_A + m_B v_B = (m_A + m_B)v'_{(A+B)}$$
$$v'_{(A+B)} = \frac{m_A v_A + m_B v_B}{(m_A + m_B)}$$
$$v'_{(A+B)} = \frac{(140\text{ kg})(10\text{ m/s}) + (70\text{ kg})(-5\text{ m/s})}{(140\text{ kg} + 70\text{ kg})} \rightarrow \boxed{v'_{(A+B)} = 5\text{ m/s}}$$

208. (C) The explosion of the shell results in forces on all the fragments, but the forces have equal and opposite forces within the system. Thus, there is no net force from the explosion on the system, and the center of mass will continue on its original parabolic trajectory, although the fragments each have unique trajectories.

209. (B) The bat exerts a force of 10.0 N over a time of $\Delta t = 0.005$ s when it strikes a 145-g baseball ($m = 0.145$ kg). Calculate the baseball's change in velocity by the impulse–momentum theorem:

$$\Delta p = F\Delta t$$
$$\Delta p = m\Delta v$$
$$F\Delta t = m\Delta v$$
$$\Delta v = \frac{F\Delta t}{m}$$
$$\Delta v = \frac{(10.0 \text{ N})(0.005 \text{ s})}{(0.145 \text{ kg})} \rightarrow \boxed{\Delta v = 0.345 \text{ m/s}}$$

210. (A) Assume that an object moving to the right is going in the positive direction. The 10-kg cart has a momentum of $+50$ kg · m/s, and the 5-kg cart has -35 kg · m/s. The system has $+15$ kg · m/s of momentum before the collision. After the collision, the combined carts (mass $= 15$ kg) must have the same momentum. Solving for velocity as the ratio of the systems momentum to mass: $\vec{v} = \dfrac{\vec{p}}{m} = \dfrac{+15 \text{ kg}\frac{\text{m}}{\text{s}}}{15 \text{ kg}} = \boxed{+1\frac{\text{m}}{\text{s}}}$

211. (A) The mass of the aircraft is 750 kg. The plane's velocity increases from 100 m/s to 120 m/s ($\Delta v = 20$ m/s). The wind blows for 2 min ($\Delta t = 120$ s). Find the force by the impulse–momentum theorem:

$$\Delta p = F\Delta t$$
$$\Delta p = m\Delta v$$
$$F\Delta t = m\Delta v$$
$$F = \frac{m\Delta v}{\Delta t}$$
$$F = \frac{(750 \text{ kg})(20 \text{ m/s})}{(120 \text{ s})} \rightarrow \boxed{F = 125 \text{ N}}$$

212. (D) To answer this, find the 70.0-kg stunt person's velocity when he hits the airbag. He had been free falling from rest for 2.5 s, so $v \approx (10 \text{ m/s/s})\, t \approx 25$ m/s. He comes to a complete stop ($|\Delta v| = 25$ m/s) after a time interval of 2 s ($\Delta t = 2$ s). Use the impulse–momentum theorem as follows:

$$\Delta p = F\Delta t$$
$$\Delta p = m\Delta v$$
$$F\Delta t = m\Delta v$$
$$F = \frac{m\Delta v}{\Delta t}$$
$$F = \frac{(70 \text{ kg})(25 \text{ m/s})}{(2 \text{ s})} \rightarrow F = 875N \rightarrow \boxed{F \approx 880 \text{ N}}$$

213. (C) The bullet's mass is 4 g (0.004 kg), and its velocity is 950 m/s. The time interval that the rifle exerts on the bullet is ($\Delta t = 0.1$ s). Find the force from the impulse–momentum theorem:

$$\Delta p = F \Delta t$$
$$\Delta p = m \Delta v$$
$$F \Delta t = m \Delta v$$
$$F = \frac{m \Delta v}{\Delta t}$$
$$F = \frac{(0.004 \text{ kg}) (950 \text{ m/s})}{(0.1 \text{ s})} \rightarrow \boxed{F = 38 \text{ N}}$$

214. (C) The masses of the cannon ($m_A = 1{,}000$ kg) and cannonball ($m_B = 15$ kg) are known. The recoil velocity of the cannon (v_A) is -1.5 m/s. Calculate the velocity of the cannonball (v_B) by conservation of momentum:

$$0 = p_A + p_B$$
$$0 = m_A v_A + m_B v_B$$
$$m_B v_B = - m_A v_A$$
$$v_B = \frac{-m_A v_A}{m_B}$$
$$v_B = \frac{-(1{,}000 \text{ kg}) (-1.5 \text{ m/s})}{(15 \text{ kg})} \rightarrow \boxed{v_B = 100 \text{ m/s}}$$

215. (C) In elastic collisions, the total kinetic energy of a system is the same before and after the collision. Thus, the system must have a total of 10 + 8 = 18 joules of kinetic energy.

216. (B) Newton's third law states that the magnitudes of the forces are the same during a collision, regardless of the mass or speeds of the objects involved. With the same forces and different masses, the net force to mass ratio will be different, so the accelerations will be different according to Newton's second law. With the same forces and the same time of contact, the magnitude of the impulse will be the same for both vehicles, and impulse is equal to the momentum change according to the impulse–momentum theorem.

217. (B) The collision takes place during the fourth interval of time on the graph, and since both carts are in contact for the same time, only options A & B are possible. Since momentum is conserved for the 2-cart system, the magnitude of the momentum decrease of the 1-kg cart will equal the magnitude of the momentum increase of the 2-kg cart:

$$\Delta p_1 + \Delta p_2 = 0$$
$$m_1 \Delta v_1 + m_2 \Delta v_2 = 0$$
$$m_2 \Delta v_2 = -m_1 \Delta v_1$$
$$\Delta v_2 = \frac{-m_1 \Delta v_1}{m_2} = \frac{-1 kg(-1-3) \text{ units}}{2 kg} = +2 \text{ units}$$

Graph B is the only graph that increases 2 units in one unit of time.

218. (A) With zero net force on the system consisting of both the object and the cart, momentum must be conserved. Therefore, the magnitude of the momentum loss of each object equals the magnitude of the momentum gain of the cart. The largest momentum change corresponds to the greatest speed change.

$$\text{I.} \quad |\Delta p| = \left| 0.05kg \left(-1\frac{m}{s} \right) - 0.05kg \left(2\frac{m}{s} \right) \right| = 0.15kg \cdot \frac{m}{s}$$

$$\text{II.} \quad |\Delta p| = \left| 0.1kg \left(-0.5\frac{m}{s} \right) - 0.1kg \left(1\frac{m}{s} \right) \right| = 0.15kg \cdot \frac{m}{s}$$

$$\text{III.} \quad |\Delta p| = \left| 0.05kg \left(1\frac{m}{s} \right) - 0.05kg \left(2\frac{m}{s} \right) \right| = 0.05kg \cdot \frac{m}{s}$$

$$\text{IV.} \quad |\Delta p| = \left| 0.1kg \left(1\frac{m}{s} \right) - 0.1kg \left(2\frac{m}{s} \right) \right| = 0.1kg \cdot \frac{m}{s}$$

Therefore, I = II > IV > III.

219. (B) Since there is no net force on the system during the collision, momentum conservation may be used to find the post-collision speed:

$$p_A + p_B = p'_{(A+B)}$$
$$m_A v_A + m_B v_B = (m_A + m_B) v'_{(A+B)}$$
$$v'_{(A+B)} = \frac{m_A v_A + m_B v_B}{(m_A + m_B)}$$
$$v'_{(A+B)} = \frac{(1 \text{ kg})(6 \text{ m/s}) + (2 \text{ kg})(0 \text{ m/s})}{(3kg)} \rightarrow v'_{(A+B)} = 2 \text{ m/s}$$

Next, the vertical free-fall time is found for the projectile:

$$\Delta y = v_{yo} t + \frac{1}{2} a_y t^2$$
$$\Delta y = 0t + \frac{1}{2} a_y t^2$$
$$\Delta y = \frac{1}{2} a_y t^2$$
$$t = \frac{2\Delta y}{a_y} \rightarrow t = \frac{2(5m)}{10m/s^2} \rightarrow t = 1 \text{sec}$$

During the 1-second free-fall time, the projectile moves at a constant horizontal speed with no horizontal acceleration:

$$\Delta x = v_{x0}t + \frac{1}{2}a_x t^2$$

$$\Delta x = v_{x0}t + \frac{1}{2}(0m/s^2)t^2$$

$$\Delta x = v_{x0}t$$

$$\Delta x = (2m/s)(1\sec) \rightarrow \boxed{\Delta x = 2m}$$

220. (D) Because there is no net force on the spacecraft/probe system, momentum is conserved:

$$(mv)_{s+p} = m_s v_s' + m_p v_p'$$

$$m_s v_s' = (mv)_{s+p} - m_p v_p'$$

$$v_s' = \frac{(mv)_{s+p} - m_p v_p'}{m_s}$$

$$v_s' = \frac{(550kg)(20m/s) - 50(-40m/s)}{500kg} \rightarrow \boxed{v_s' = 26\frac{m}{s}}$$

221. (D) Using conservation of momentum:

$$p_A + p_B = p_{(A+B)}'$$

$$m_A v_A + m_B v_B = (m_A + m_B)v_{(A+B)}'$$

$$v_{(A+B)}' = \frac{m_A v_A + m_B v_B}{(m_A + m_B)}$$

$$v_{(A+B)}' = \frac{mv + m\left(\frac{v}{2}\right)}{(m+m)}$$

$$v_{(A+B)}' = \frac{\frac{3}{2}mv}{2m} \rightarrow \boxed{v_{(A+B)}' = \frac{3}{4}v}$$

222. (D) First, compare the total kinetic energy of the system before and after the collision.

Before the collision:

$$K_{a+b} = \frac{1}{2}mv^2 + \frac{1}{2}m\left(\frac{v}{2}\right)^2 = \frac{1}{2}mv^2 + \frac{1}{8}mv^2 = \frac{5}{8}mv^2$$

After the collision:

$$K_{a+b} = \frac{1}{2}(2m)\left(\frac{3v}{4}\right)^2 = \frac{9}{16}mv^2$$

What didn't transfer to kinetic energy must have transferred to internal energy (mainly thermal energy and sound energy):

$$U_{int} = K_i - K_f = \frac{5}{8}mv^2 - \frac{9}{16}mv^2 = \frac{1}{16}mv^2 \rightarrow \boxed{U_{int} = \frac{1}{16}mv^2}$$

223. (C) The slope of a momentum–time graph is force. Another way of looking at this is with the momentum–impulse theorem: The change in momentum divided by the time interval is the average force exerted on an object: $\vec{F} = \frac{\Delta\vec{p}}{\Delta t}$. Notice that the momentum is changing more and more rapidly as time elapses (i.e., the slope gets greater), which means the force is increasing.

224. (A) The total momentum of the two-person system before the push-off was 0. Since there is no net force on the system during the push, conservation of momentum may be used as follows:

$$p_C + p_T = 0$$
$$m_C v_C + m_T v_T = 0$$
$$m_T v_T = -m_C v_C$$
$$v_T = \frac{-m_C v_C}{m_T}$$
$$v_T = \frac{-\frac{m}{3}v_C}{m}$$
$$v_T = \frac{-v_C}{3} \rightarrow \boxed{|v_T| = \frac{v_C}{3}}$$

225. (D) According to the impulse–momentum theorem, the average force may be computed as follows:

$$F_C = \frac{\Delta p}{\Delta t}$$
$$F_C = \frac{mv_{C_f} - mv_{C_i}}{\Delta t}$$
$$F_C = \frac{\frac{m}{3}v_C - 0}{\Delta t} \rightarrow \boxed{|F_C| = \frac{mv_C}{3\Delta t}}$$

According to Newton's third law, the teenager will feel the same force, but in the opposite direction.

226. (D) A cue ball ($m_A = 250$ g $= 0.25$ kg) travels at 1.0 m/s ($Vx = 1.0$ m/s, $Vy = 0$ m/s) and hits a numbered ball ($m_B = 170$ g $= 0.17$ kg) at rest ($Vx = Vy = 0$ m/s). The balls move off at angles. The numbered ball moves off at $45°$, while the cue ball moves off at $-45°$. Apply the law of conservation of momentum to the x components and the y components of momentum and solve two equations simultaneously to get each ball's speed:

$$p_{Ax} + p_{Bx} = p'_{Ax} + p'_{Bx}$$
$$m_A v_{Ax} + 0 = m_A v'_{Ax} + m_B v'_{Bx}$$
$$m_A v_{Ax} = m_A v'_A \cos(-45°) + m_B v'_B \cos(45°)$$
$$(0.25 \text{ kg})(1.0 \text{ m/s}) = (0.25 \text{ kg})v'_A (0.707) + (0.17 \text{ kg})v'_B (0.707)$$
$$(0.25 \text{ kg} \cdot \text{m/s}) = (0.177 \text{ kg})v'_A + (0.12 \text{ kg})v'_B$$
$$p_{Ay} + p_{By} = p'_{Ay} + p'_{By}$$
$$0 + 0 = m_A v'_{Ay} + m_B v'_{By}$$

$$0 = m_A v'_A \sin(-45°) + m_B v'_B \sin(45°)$$
$$0 = (0.25 \text{ kg})v'_A(-0.707) + (0.17 \text{ kg})v'_B (7.707)$$
$$0 = (-0.177 \text{ kg})v'_A + (0.12 \text{ kg})v'_B$$

Add the two equations:

$$(0.25 \text{ kg} \cdot \text{m/s}) = (0.177 \text{ kg})v'_A + (0.12 \text{ kg})v'_B$$
$$0 = (-0.177 \text{ kg})v'_A + (0.12 \text{ kg})v'_B$$
$$(0.25 \text{ kg} \cdot \text{m/s}) = (0.24 \text{ kg})v'_B$$
$$v'_B = \frac{(0.25 \text{ kg} \cdot \text{m/s})}{(0.24 \text{ kg})}$$

$v'_B = 1.04$ m/s, now substitute this value into one of the above equations:
$$0 = (-0.177 \text{ kg})v'_A + (0.12 \text{ kg})(1.04 \text{ m/s})$$
$$(0.177 \text{ kg})v'_A = (0.125 \text{ kg} \cdot \text{m/s})$$

$$v'_A = \frac{(0.125 \text{ kg} \cdot \text{m/s})}{(0.177 \text{ kg})}$$
$$v'_A = 0.71 \text{ m/s}$$

227. (A) The mass of the handgun (m_A) is 1.2 kg, and the mass of the bullet (mB) is 7.5 g (0.0075 kg). The bullet travels away at a velocity (vB) of + 365 m/s. Calculate the recoil velocity of the handgun by conservation of momentum:

$$0 = p_A + p_B$$
$$0 = m_A v_A + m_B v_B$$
$$m_A v_A = - m_B v_B$$
$$v_A = \frac{-m_B v_B}{m_A}$$
$$v_A = \frac{-(0.0075 \text{ kg})(365 \text{ m/s})}{(1.2 \text{ kg})} \rightarrow \boxed{v_A = -2.3 \text{ m/s}}$$

228. (B) The magnitude of the momentum for each object is calculated as follows:

I. $p = (90{,}000{,}000 \text{ kg}) * (0.02 \text{ m/s}) = 2 \times 10^6 \text{ kg} \cdot \text{m/s}$

II. $p = (30{,}000 \text{ kg}) * (0 \text{ m/s}) = 0 \text{ kg} \cdot \text{m/s}$

III. $p = (1{,}000 \text{ kg}) * (25 \text{ m/s}) = 25{,}000 \text{ kg} \cdot \text{m/s}$

IV. $p = (1.67 \times 10^{-27} \text{kg}) * (0.90 * 3.0 \times 10^8 \text{m/s}) = 4.5 \times 10^{-19} \text{ kg} \cdot \text{m/s}$

Ranking these from greatest to least: I > III > IV > II

229. (B) The impulse–momentum theorem is solved for force as follows: $\vec{F} = \dfrac{\Delta \vec{p}}{\Delta t}$. To change the car's momentum to zero, the greater the time of the collision, the less the force will be. The process of crushing the car increases the time of impact and decreases the force.

230. (A) It may be assumed that in collisions there is no net force on the system immediately before and immediately after the collision; therefore *momentum will be conserved*, regardless of whether it's an elastic or inelastic collision. In an elastic collision, the total kinetic energy of the system remains the same before and after the collision. Before the collision, the system has 18 J + 1 J = 19 J of kinetic energy. After the collision, the system has 2 J + 9 J = 11 J of kinetic energy. Apparently, 8 J of energy has transferred into other storage modes (e.g., thermal energy), thus classifying this as an *inelastic* collision.

231. (B) According to the impulse–momentum theorem, $\vec{F} \Delta t = \Delta \vec{p}$. In order to change the momentum of the ball the least (i.e., have the smallest exit velocity), a small explosive force would be applied for the least time. *Decreasing the length of the cannon barrel would decrease the time and result in the least velocity.* Decreasing the mass of the cannon ball would actually increase the exit velocity (for the same force and time).

232. (B) First the initial and final velocities are determined from the slope of the graph:

$$v_i = \frac{\Delta X}{\Delta t} = \frac{(0 - 2.5)m}{(0.5 - 0)s} = -4.0\frac{m}{s}$$

$$v_f = \frac{\Delta X}{\Delta t} = \frac{(2.0 - 0)m}{(1.1 - 0.6)s} = 5.0\frac{m}{s}$$

Next, calculate the momentum change:

$$\Delta p = p_f - p_i$$

$$\Delta p = 0.050 \text{ kg}\left(5\frac{m}{s}\right) - 0.050 \text{ kg}\left(-4\frac{m}{s}\right) \rightarrow \boxed{\Delta \vec{p} = +0.45 \text{ kg}\frac{m}{s}}$$

233. (C) With 30 frames per second, a picture is taken each thirtieth of a second. Three frames will be three-thirtieths of a second, or 0.1 second. To find the average force, solve the momentum–impulse theorem for force as follows: $\vec{F} = \dfrac{\Delta \vec{p}}{\Delta t} = \dfrac{+0.45 \text{ kg} \cdot \text{m/s}}{0.1\,s} = +4.5\,\text{N}.$

This is the force of the floor on the wall, which is in the positive direction (to the right). According to Newton's third law, *the force of the ball on the wall* is equal in magnitude and opposite in direction, or -4.5 N (to the left).

234. (A, D) In an elastic collision, the system's kinetic energy is the same before and after the collision. Since $K = \dfrac{1}{2}mv^2$, the kinetic energy will be the same for the ball before and after the bounce because the speed is the same and the collision is elastic. The moving cart, similarly, transfers all its kinetic energy to the other cart; thus the system of both carts maintains its kinetic energy and is elastic. All the other collisions involve losses in kinetic energy of the system.

235. (A, B) Regardless of the type of collision, momentum is the same before and after the collision because there is no net force on the system during the collision. This is due to the fact that the internal collision forces are equal and opposite due to Newton's third law. With no net force on the system, the velocity of its center of mass will not change. Also, in inelastic collisions the kinetic energy does not remain the same usually because of a transfer of energy to thermal energy, whereas in elastic collisions the kinetic energy of the system remains constant (i.e., no change in thermal energy).

236. (B, C) According to the impulse–momentum theorem, the momentum change of a system equals the product of force and time. An increase in either one (or both) will increase the momentum change of the ball.

237. (B, C) Momentum is the product of mass and velocity, and velocity includes both speed and direction. Acceleration and net force energy may be related to the current momentum, but are NOT particularly helpful in finding the instantaneous momentum.

238. (C, D) The momentum of a system is conserved as long as there is no net force on the system, and this applies to both elastic and inelastic collisions as well as explosions. Also, if the center of mass of a system accelerates, then there must be a net force on the system and its momentum would change.

239. (A) Designate Car B as the 800-kg car ($vB = 25.5$ m/s) and Car A as the 1,000-kg car ($vA = 34.7$ m/s). The two cars collide in a sticky collision (perfectly inelastic). Find the combined velocity ($v'A + B$) by the conservation of momentum:

$$p_A + p_B = p'_{(A+B)}$$
$$m_A v_A + m_B v_B = (m_A + m_B)v'_{(A+B)}$$
$$v'_{(A+B)} = \frac{m_A v_A + m_B v_B}{(m_A + m_B)}$$
$$v'_{(A+B)} = \frac{(1{,}000\ \text{kg})(34.7\ \text{m/s}) + (800\ \text{kg})(25.5\ \text{m/s})}{(1{,}000\ \text{kg} + 800\ \text{kg})} \rightarrow \boxed{v'_{(A+B)} = 30.6\ \text{m/s}}$$

240. (C) To classify a collision, compare the total kinetic energy of the system before and after the collision.

Before the collision:

$$K_a = \frac{1}{2}mv^2 = \frac{1}{2}(1{,}000.\ \text{kg})\left(34.7\ \frac{\text{m}}{\text{s}}\right)^2 = 6.02 \times 10^5\ \text{J}$$

$$K_b = \frac{1}{2}mv^2 = \frac{1}{2}(800.\ \text{kg})\left(25.5\ \frac{\text{m}}{\text{s}}\right)^2 = 2.60 \times 10^5\ \text{J}$$

$$K_{a+b} = 6.02 \times 10^5\ \text{J} + 2.60 \times 10^5\ \text{J} = 8.62 \times 10^5\ \text{J}$$

After the collision:

$$K_{a+b} = \frac{1}{2}mv^2 = \frac{1}{2}(1{,}800.\ \text{kg})\left(30.6\ \frac{\text{m}}{\text{s}}\right)^2 = 8.43 \times 10^5\ \text{J}$$
$$\Delta(K_{a+b}) = 8.43 \times 10^5\ \text{J} - 8.62 \times 10^5\ \text{J} = -1.9 \times 10^4\ \text{J}$$

The collision is inelastic because 1.9×10^4 J transferred from kinetic energy to internal energy in the system (i.e., thermal energy in this scenario). In fact, sticky collisions like this are classified as perfectly inelastic collisions, which always involve a loss in the system's kinetic energy.

241. (C) First, the friction force acting on the post-collision, two-car system needs to be found. The normal force is directly proportional to the friction force. Since the system is not accelerating vertically, the normal force balances the weight of the two-car system. The friction force is calculated as final.

$$F_f = \mu_k F_N \text{ where } F_N = (m_A + m_B)g$$
$$F_f = \mu_k (m_A + m_B)g$$
$$F_f = (0.70)(1{,}000 \text{ kg} + 800 \text{ kg})(10 \text{ m/s}^2)$$
$$F_f = 1.26 \times 10^4 \text{ N}$$

The force of friction is negative because it opposes motion. Calculate the time (Δt) it takes for the interlocked cars to stop ($\Delta v = -30.6$ m/s) by using the impulse–momentum theorem:

$$\Delta p = F\Delta t$$
$$\Delta p = m\Delta v$$
$$F\Delta t = m\Delta v$$
$$F_f \Delta t = (m_A + m_B)\Delta v$$
$$\Delta t = \frac{(m_A + m_B)\Delta v}{F_f}$$
$$\Delta t = \frac{(1{,}000. \text{ kg} + 800. \text{ kg})(-30.6 \text{ m/s})}{(-1.26 \times 10^4 \text{ N})} \rightarrow \Delta t \approx 4.37s \rightarrow \boxed{\Delta t \approx 4.4 \text{ s}}$$

242. From 0–2 seconds, the box will gain speed at a constant rate because the constant net force will accelerate the box. From 2–4 seconds, the box will maintain constant velocity because no net force is on the box. From 4–7 seconds, the constant negative net force will slow the box down at a constant rate.

243. Use $\vec{F}\Delta t = \Delta\vec{p}$ as follows (the last column is included to help with part [c]):

Time Interval	$\vec{F}\Delta t$	$\Delta\vec{p}$	$\Delta\vec{v} = \dfrac{\Delta\vec{p}}{m}$
0–1 second	+20 Ns	+20 kg · m/s	+10 m/s
1–2 seconds	+20 Ns	+20 kg · m/s	+10 m/s
2–3 seconds	0 Ns	0 kg · m/s	0 m/s
3–4 seconds	0 Ns	0 kg · m/s	0 m/s
4–5 seconds	−10 Ns	−10 kg · m/s	−5 m/s
5–6 seconds	−10 Ns	−10 kg · m/s	−5 m/s
6–7 seconds	−10 Ns	−10 kg · m/s	−5 m/s

244. The velocity change in each time interval is calculated in the last column in the table above. Starting with a velocity of +3 m/s, 10 m/s is added each of the first two seconds, no velocity is added for the next two seconds, and 5 m/s of velocity is taken away for each of the last three seconds. This gives a final velocity of +8 m/s.

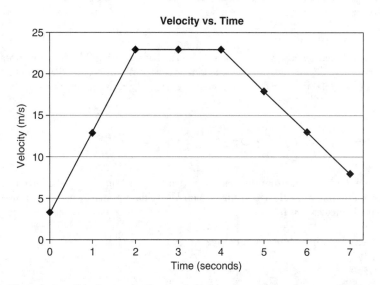

Velocity vs. Time

245. The velocity of the box at the 7-second clock reading is +8 m/s as it strikes the wall for 0.20 second and bounces back at a velocity of –6 m/s. The momentum–impulse theorem is solved for average force as follows:

$$\vec{F} = \frac{\Delta p}{\Delta t}$$

$$\vec{F} = = \frac{2\,\text{kg}\left(-6\,\dfrac{\text{m}}{\text{s}}\right) - 2\,\text{kg}\left(+8\,\dfrac{\text{m}}{\text{s}}\right)}{0.20\,\text{s}} \rightarrow \boxed{\vec{F} = -140\,\text{N}}$$

246. Because there is no net force on the two-body system during the release, momentum must be conserved as follows:

$$p_{2m} + p_m = p'_{2m} + p'_m$$
$$(2m)v + mv = (2m)v_f + m(2v)$$
$$3mv = 2mv_f + 2mv$$
$$2mv_f = mv \rightarrow \boxed{v_f = \frac{v}{2}}$$

247. The ratio of kinetic energies is calculated as follows:

$$\frac{K_{after}}{K_{before}} = \frac{\frac{1}{2}(2m)\left(\frac{v}{2}\right)^2 + \frac{1}{2}m(2v)^2}{\frac{1}{2}(3m)v^2} = \frac{\frac{1}{4}mv^2 + 2mv^2}{\frac{3}{2}mv^2} = \frac{\frac{9}{4}mv^2}{\frac{3}{2}mv^2} = \frac{3}{2}$$

How can the kinetic energy be greater after the release of the spring? Elastic energy from the spring must have transferred into the extra kinetic energy. Assuming any change in thermal energy is negligible, the initial elastic potential energy of the spring may be calculated as follows:

$$U_s = K_{after} - K_{before} = \frac{9}{4}mv^2 - \frac{3}{2}mv^2 = \frac{3}{4}mv^2$$

248. The impulse-momentum theorem states that the area bounded by the force vs. time graph is the momentum change of the system. Using the less-massive cart as the system, F_{max} may be calculated as follows:

Area of graph = Momentum change

$$\frac{1}{2}base * height = mv_f - mv_i$$

$$\frac{1}{2}\Delta t(F_{max}) = m(2v) - mv$$

$$\frac{1}{2}\Delta t(F_{max}) = mv$$

$$F_{max} = \frac{2mv}{\Delta t}$$

$$F_{max} = \frac{2(0.500kg)(1.2m/s)}{(0.2s)} \rightarrow \boxed{F_{max} = 6N}$$

249. First, remember that the spring mass in negligible and it is attached to the more-massive cart. According to Newton's third law (N3L), the force of the spring on the less-massive cart is equal in magnitude and opposite in direction to the force of the less-massive cart on the spring. The following graph is obtained:

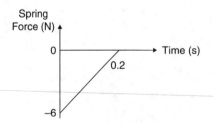

250. There is no net force on the two-cart system during the release because the friction on the track is negligible and the release forces are equal and opposite within the system (N3L). With no net force on the system, the acceleration of the center of mass of the system must be zero. Thus the velocity of the center of mass of the system **equals** the starting velocity, $+v$. This may also be shown with calculation of the post-release velocity of the center of mass as follows:

$$v_{cm} = \frac{m_1 v_1 + m_2 v_2}{m_1 + m_2} = \frac{2m\left(\dfrac{v}{2}\right) + m(2v)}{2m + m} = \frac{3mv}{3m} = +v$$

Chapter 6: Work, Energy, and Conservation of Energy

251. (D) Points A and C are at the same height from the ground and thus have the same gravitational potential energy: $U_g = mg\Delta y$.

252. (A) The car will move the fastest at the point with the most kinetic energy, which is the lowest point, E, where most of the gravitational energy in the car-earth system has transferred to the kinetic energy.

253. (D) The total mechanical energy is the sum of the kinetic energy and gravitational potential energy. It is the same at all points because there is no change in internal energy of the system (air drag and track friction are negligible).

254. (D) The force exerted by the man is 100 N in the direction of motion. The mass of the box is irrelevant to the solution since the box in not lifted vertically. The distance is 60 m, and the time interval is 2 min ($\Delta t = 120$ s). Calculate the power as follows:

$$P = \frac{\Delta E}{\Delta t}$$
$$P = \frac{Fd}{t}$$
$$P = \frac{(100 \text{ N})(60 \text{ m})}{(120 \text{ s})} \rightarrow \boxed{P = 50 \text{ W}}$$

255. (A) Kinetic energy is directly proportional to the square of the speed. Thus, when the speed doubles, the kinetic energy quadruples.

256. (D) The area of the F_{net} vs. displacement graph has units of N * m = Joules and is equivalent to the energy transferred.

257. (C) The force on the box is 10 N at an angle ($\theta = 60°$) over a distance (d) of 50 m. Only the component of force in the horizontal direction contributes to the work done on the box. Find the x component of force, and use it to calculate the work:

$$W = F_x d$$
$$F_x = F \cos\theta$$
$$W = F \cos\theta d$$
$$W = (10 \text{ N})(\cos 60°)(50 \text{ m}) \rightarrow \boxed{W = 250 \text{ J}}$$

258. (C) The mass of the box and the diagonal sliding distance are irrelevant. The height of the hill (h) is 10 m. The box starts from rest and reaches an unknown final velocity (v_f). The box's change in gravitational potential energy is equal to its change in kinetic energy. Calculate the box's final velocity from conservation of energy:

$$K_i + U_{gi} = K_f + U_{gf}$$
$$0 + U_{gi} = K_f + 0$$
$$K_f = U_{gi}$$

$$\frac{1}{2}mv_f^2 = mg\Delta y$$
$$\frac{1}{2}v_f^2 = g\Delta y$$
$$v_f^2 = 2g\Delta y$$
$$v_f = \sqrt{2g\Delta y}$$
$$v_f = \sqrt{2(10 \text{ m/s}^2)(10 \text{ m})} \rightarrow \boxed{v_f = 14 \text{ m/s}}$$

259. (D) The mass of the arrow (m) is 20 g, or 0.02 kg. The archer exerts an average force ($F = 75$ N) to pull the bowstring back ($d = 20$ cm $= 0.20$ m), and so it is assumed that the bow will apply the same force back on the arrow through the same displacement. Calculate the final velocity of the arrow using the work–energy theorem:

$$W = \Delta \text{KE}$$
$$Fd = \frac{1}{2}m(v_f)^2 - \frac{1}{2}m(v_i)^2$$
$$v_i = 0$$
$$2Fd = m(v_f)^2$$
$$2Fd = mv_f^2$$
$$v_f^2 = \frac{2Fd}{m}$$

$$v_f = \sqrt{\frac{2Fd}{m}}$$

$$v_f = \sqrt{\frac{2(75 \text{ N})(0.20 \text{ m})}{(0.02 \text{ kg})}} \rightarrow \boxed{v_f = 39 \text{ m/s}}$$

260. (D) The mass of the car is 1,000 kg. As the car skids to rest, its kinetic energy transfers to thermal energy over a distance (d) of 10 m. Calculate the force by the work–energy theorem:

$$W = \Delta K$$

$$F_{\parallel}d = \frac{1}{2}mv_f^2 - \frac{1}{2}mv_i^2$$

$$F_{\parallel} = \frac{\frac{1}{2}mv_f^2 - \frac{1}{2}mv_i^2}{d}$$

$$F_{\parallel} = \frac{\frac{1}{2}m(v_f^2 - v_i^2)}{d}$$

$$F_{\parallel} = \frac{\frac{1}{2}(1{,}000 \text{ kg})(0^2 - 30^2)}{10}$$

$$F_{\parallel} = -4.5 \times 10^4 \text{ N} \rightarrow \boxed{|F_{\parallel}| = 4.5 \times 10^4 \text{ N}}$$

261. (B) When released, the elastic potential energy stored in the spring transfers to kinetic energy in the moving box. Assuming the horizontal surface is frictionless, the maximum kinetic energy occurs when all the elastic potential energy transfers to the motion of the box:

$$U_s = \frac{1}{2}kx^2$$

$$U_s = \frac{1}{2}\left(2{,}500 \frac{\text{N}}{\text{m}}\right)(0.12 \text{ m})^2 \rightarrow \boxed{U_s = 18 \text{ J}}$$

262. (D) The spring has a constant of 100 N/m and is displaced ($x = -0.2$ m). The mass of the block is 1 kg. Calculate the block's velocity as it passes equilibrium by conservation of energy:

$$K_i + U_{si} = K_f + U_{sf}$$

$$0 + U_{si} = K_f + 0$$

$$K_f = U_{si}$$

$$\frac{1}{2}mv_f^2 = \frac{1}{2}kx^2$$

$$mv_f^2 = kx^2$$

$$v_f^2 = \frac{kx^2}{m}$$

$$v_f = \sqrt{\frac{kx^2}{m}}$$

$$v_f = \sqrt{\frac{(100 \text{ N/m})(-0.2 \text{ m})^2}{(1 \text{ kg})}} \rightarrow \boxed{v_f = 2 \text{ m/s}}$$

263. (C) The mass of the aircraft is 750 kg. The plane's velocity increases from 100 m/s to 120 m/s. The wind blows for 1,200 m. The work done by the tailwind on the aircraft equals the increase of kinetic energy of the aircraft, and from this the force may be found:

$$W = \Delta K$$

$$F_\| d = \frac{1}{2}mv_f^2 - \frac{1}{2}mv_i^2$$

$$F_\| = \frac{\frac{1}{2}mv_f^2 - \frac{1}{2}mv_i^2}{d}$$

$$F_\| = \frac{\frac{1}{2}m(v_f^2 - v_i^2)}{d}$$

$$F_\| = \frac{\frac{1}{2}(750 \text{ kg})(120^2 - 100^2)}{1,200} \rightarrow \boxed{F_\| = 1,400 \text{ N}}$$

264. (A) The worker exerts a component (Fx) of the 20-N force (F) in the horizontal by applying the force at an angle ($\theta = 60°$). The lawn mower moves a horizontal distance (d) of 100 m in a time interval (Δt) of 5 min (300 s). Only the horizontal component of force does work, so resolve the force into components, and use that to calculate the power:

$$P = \frac{\Delta E}{\Delta t}$$

$$\Delta E = Fd \rightarrow F = F \cos \theta$$

$$\Delta E = F \cos \theta d$$

$$P = \frac{F \cos \theta d}{\Delta t}$$

$$P = \frac{(20 \text{ N})(\cos 60°)(100 \text{ m})}{(300 \text{ s})} \rightarrow \boxed{P = 3 \text{ W}}$$

265. (C) The known quantities are the mass of the payload (1,000 kg), the mass of the Earth (6×10^{24} kg), the Earth's radius (6.4×10^6 m), and the height of the orbit (150 km). Calculate the change in gravitational potential energy of the payload when it reaches orbit:

$$\Delta U_G = U_{G_f} - U_{G_i} = \left(\frac{-Gm_1m_2}{R+r}\right) - \left(\frac{-Gm_1m_2}{R}\right)$$

$$\Delta U_G = \left(\frac{-Gm_1m_2}{R+r}\right) - \left(\frac{-Gm_1m_2}{R}\right)$$

$$\Delta U_G = Gm_1m_2\left(\frac{-1}{R+r} + \frac{1}{R}\right)$$

$$\Delta U_G = (6.7\times10^{-11}\ \text{N}\cdot\text{m}^2/\text{kg}^2)\,(1{,}000\ \text{kg})\,(6\times10^{24}\ \text{kg})\left(\frac{-1}{(6.4\times10^6\ \text{m}+1.5\times10^5\ \text{m})} + \frac{1}{6.4\times10^6\ \text{m}}\right)$$

$$\boxed{\Delta U_G = +1.4\times10^9\ \text{J}}$$

266. (B) In an inelastic collision, some of the system's energy transfers to internal energy, primarily thermal energy in this case. As a result, the kinetic energy decreases during the collision, and consequently the mechanical energy (the sum of K and U_g in this scenario) decreases. The gravitational potential energy decreases as the bob swings down and increases as the bob/clay swing up.

267. (C) Work is defined as the area bounded by the net force-displacement graph:

Work = Area of F vs. Δx

Work = $\frac{1}{2}(base)(height)$

Work = $\frac{1}{2}(5\ m)(30\ N) = 75\ J$

Work = ΔK

Work = $K_f - K_i$

$K_f = \text{Work} + K_i$

$K_f = \text{Work} + \frac{1}{2}mv_i^{\,2}$

$K_f = 75\ J + \frac{1}{2}(3.0\ \text{kg})\,(4.0\ \text{m/s})^2$

$K_f = 75\ J + 24\ J \rightarrow \boxed{K_f = 99\ J}$

268. (C) This can be a tricky question, so we'll start with the "easy" answer. A vertical spring-mass system oscillating about equilibrium behaves identically to a horizontal oscillator. Thus, setting the zero spring potential at equilibrium, the only change in mechanical energy is due to spring:

$$\Delta ME = \Delta U_s$$

$$\Delta ME = \frac{1}{2}kx_f^2 - \frac{1}{2}kx_i^2$$

$$\Delta ME = \frac{1}{2}kd^2 - 0 \rightarrow \boxed{\Delta ME = \frac{1}{2}kd^2}$$

How can this be? Why is the change in gravitational energy not show up in this expression? First, we have to consider that the spring was stretched by the weight of the box when it was initially loaded to the equilibrium position. Thus, the system has initially had spring potential energy when it's at rest in equilibrium (where the spring force balanced the weight, *mg*, resulting in a net force of zero) relative to when the spring was not stretched at all (before the weight was added). The change in spring potential energy as its stretched an additional distance *d* from equilibrium is found as follows:

$$\Delta U_s = U_{sf} - U_{si}$$

$$\Delta U_s = \frac{1}{2}k(d + x_e)^2 - \frac{1}{2}kx_e^2$$

$$\Delta U_s = \frac{1}{2}k(d^2 + 2dx_e + x_e^2) - \frac{1}{2}kx_e^2$$

$$\Delta U_s = \frac{1}{2}kd^2 + kdx_e + \frac{1}{2}kx_e^2 - \frac{1}{2}kx_e^2$$

$$\Delta U_s = \frac{1}{2}kd^2 + kx_e d$$

In equilibrium, the spring force must balance the weight *mg* :

$$F_s = kx \rightarrow mg = kx_e \rightarrow \text{Substitute this into the } \Delta U_s \text{ equation:}$$

$$\Delta U_s = \frac{1}{2}kd^2 + mgd$$

Thus we can find the desired change in mechanical energy of the spring-mass-earth system as follows:

$$\Delta ME = \Delta U_s + \Delta U_g$$

$$\Delta ME = \left(\frac{1}{2}kd^2 + mgd\right) + mg\Delta y$$

$$\Delta ME = \frac{1}{2}kd^2 + mgd + mg(-d) \rightarrow \boxed{\Delta ME = \frac{1}{2}kd^2}$$

269. (B) According to the law of conservation of energy, all energy must be accounted for. Since all of the gravitational potential energy did not transfer to kinetic energy, then 25 J − 23 J = 2 J that must be stored as thermal energy due to the friction the box encounters as it slides down the incline.

270. (C) According to conservation of energy, the gravitational potential energy of the person-earth system transfers to kinetic energy during the fall. The airbag must do work to dissipate the stunt person's kinetic energy. Solve this scenario by applying conservation of energy for the fall and the work−energy theorem for the airbag collision as follows:

$$K_i + U_{gi} = K_f + U_{gf}$$
$$0 + U_{gi} = K_f + 0$$
$$K_f = U_{gi}$$

$$\frac{1}{2}mv_f^2 = mg\Delta y$$
$$W = \Delta KE$$
$$Fd = \frac{1}{2}mv_f^2$$

$$Fd = mg\Delta y$$
$$F = \frac{mg\Delta y}{d}$$
$$F = \frac{(70\text{ kg})(10\text{ m/s}^2)(125\text{ m})}{(5.0\text{ m})} \rightarrow \boxed{F = 1.8 \times 10^4 \text{ N}}$$

271. (B) Because all four objects start at the same height relative to the ground, they all begin with the same gravitational energy. With negligible surface friction and air drag, all of that gravitational energy transfers to kinetic energy as they arrive at the ground level. Since objects B, C, and D all start at rest, the analysis looks like this:

$$\Delta U_g = K_f$$
$$mg\Delta y = \frac{1}{2}mv_f^2 \rightarrow \text{mass cancels from both sides}$$
$$v_f^2 = 2g\Delta y$$
$$v_f = \sqrt{2g\Delta y}$$

Therefore, objects B, C, & D all arrive at the ground with the same speed (albeit at different times). In contrast, object A already has kinetic energy when it's released, so its analysis differs as follows:

$$K_i + \Delta U_g = K_f$$
$$\frac{1}{2}mv^2 + mg\Delta y = \frac{1}{2}mv_f^2 \rightarrow \text{mass cancels from both sides}$$
$$v_f^2 = mv^2 + 2g\Delta y$$
$$v_f = \sqrt{mv^2 + 2g\Delta y}$$

Thus, object A arrives at a greater speed. The final ranking is as follows:

$$\boxed{v_A > v_B = v_C = v_D}$$

272. **(A)** According to Newton's third law, the hoops will experience forces that are equal in magnitude and opposite in direction. Hooke's law expressions will be set equal. Using the slope of the graph that is given, the spring constant for the black spring is $k_B = 78$ N/m and the spring constant for the white spring is $k_W = 30$ N/m.

Hooke's law for the black-hoop spring $\rightarrow F_{s_B} = k_B \Delta x_B = 78\dfrac{\text{N}}{\text{m}}\Delta x_B$

Hooke's law for the white-hoop spring $\rightarrow F_{s_W} = k_W \Delta x_W = 30\dfrac{\text{N}}{\text{m}}\Delta x_W$

Newton's third law $\rightarrow F_{s_B} = F_{s_W}$
$$k_B \Delta x_B = k_W \Delta x_W$$

$$\Delta x_B = \frac{k_W \Delta x_W}{k_B} = \frac{\left(30\dfrac{\text{N}}{\text{m}}\right)(5.0 \text{ cm})}{78\dfrac{\text{N}}{\text{m}}} \rightarrow \boxed{\Delta x_B \approx 1.9 \text{ cm}}$$

273. **(B)** The elastic energy stored in the spring transfers to kinetic energy.

$$U_{s_i} = K_f$$
$$\frac{1}{2}kx^2 = \frac{1}{2}mv_f^2$$
$$v_f^2 = \frac{k}{m}x^2$$
$$v_f = x\sqrt{\frac{k}{m}}$$

$$v_f = (0.050m)\sqrt{\frac{78 \text{ N/m}}{1 \text{ kg}}} \rightarrow \boxed{v_f = 0.44\dfrac{\text{m}}{\text{s}}}$$

274. (B)

The final speed of the black-hoop cart was found in the previous solution:

$$v_{f_B}^2 = \frac{k_B}{m_B} x_B^2$$

To have the same speed as the black-hoop cart, the white-hoop cart needs a kinetic energy of:

$$K_W = \frac{1}{2} m_W v_f^2$$

$$K_W = \frac{1}{2} m_W \frac{k_B}{m_B} x_B^2$$

All of the elastic potential of the white spring transfers into kinetic:

$$U_{sW_i} = K_W$$

$$\frac{1}{2} k_W x_W^2 = \frac{1}{2} m_W \frac{k_B}{m_B} x_B^2$$

$$x_W^2 = \frac{k_B m_W}{k_W m_B} x_B^2$$

$$x_W = \sqrt{\frac{k_B m_W}{k_W m_B}} x_B$$

$$x_W = \sqrt{\frac{(78\ \text{N/m})(0.500\ \text{kg})}{(30\ \text{N/m})(1.000\ \text{kg})}} (0.050\ \text{m}) \rightarrow \boxed{x_W = 0.057\ \text{m}}$$

275. (A) When F_1 is applied, a vertical component of the force acts opposite the velocity vector and slows the spacecraft down, but the horizontal component only changes its direction because it's perpendicular to the velocity. As the spacecraft's speed slows, the K *decreases*. When F_2 is applied, it only changes the spacecraft's direction because it remains perpendicular to the velocity vector, thus the K will *not change*. When F_3 is applied, the vertical component of force acts as a net force in the same direction of the velocity vector and speeds the spacecraft up, but the horizontal component only changes its direction because it's perpendicular to the velocity. As the spacecraft speeds up, the K *increases*.

276. (C) Use conservation of energy to find the velocity of the box:

$$K_i + U_{gi} = K_f + U_{gf}$$
$$0 + U_{gi} = K_f + 0$$
$$K_f = U_{gi}$$

$$\frac{1}{2} m v_f^2 = mg\Delta y$$

$$\sin\theta = \frac{\Delta y}{d}$$
$$\Delta y = d\sin\theta$$
$$\frac{1}{2} v_f^2 = gd\sin\theta$$
$$v_f^2 = 2gd\sin\theta$$

$$v_f = \sqrt{2gd \sin \theta}$$

$$v_f = \sqrt{2(10 \text{ m/s}^2)(10 \text{ m})(\sin 45°)} \rightarrow \boxed{v_f = 12 \text{ m/s}}$$

277. (D) The force of friction works against the motion of the box to bring it to a stop. First calculate the force of friction, and then use the work–energy theorem to find the distance the box travels:

$$W = F_f d$$

$$\Delta K = \frac{1}{2}m(v_f)^2 - \frac{1}{2}m(v_i)^2 = -\frac{1}{2}m(v_i)^2$$

$$W = \Delta K$$

$$F_f d = -\frac{1}{2}m(v)^2$$

$$F_f = \mu F_N$$

$$F_N = mg$$

$$F_f = -\mu mg$$

$$2\mu mgd = m(v_i)^2$$

$$2\mu gd = (v_i)^2$$

$$d = \frac{(v_i)^2}{2\mu g}$$

$$d = \frac{(12 \text{ m/s})^2}{2(0.6)(10 \text{ m/s}^2)} \rightarrow \boxed{d = 12 \text{ m}}$$

278. (C) Both cannons fire balls of the same mass (m) and use the same amount of powder to supply identical forces (F). The length of Cannon 2 (d_2) is two times longer than that of Cannon 1 (d_1). Apply the work–energy theorem to both cannons:

$$Fd_1 = \frac{1}{2}mv_1^2$$

$$Fd_2 = \frac{1}{2}mv_2^2$$

$$d_2 = 2d_1$$

$$F(2d_1) = \frac{1}{2}mv_2^2$$

$$Fd_1 = \frac{1}{4}mv_2^2$$

$$\frac{1}{4}mv_2^2 = \frac{1}{2}mv_1^2$$

$$\frac{1}{4}v_2^2 = \frac{1}{2}v_1^2$$

$$v_2^2 = 2v_1^2$$

$$v_2 = \sqrt{2v_1^2}$$

$$v_2 = \sqrt{2}\sqrt{v_1^2}$$

$$v_2 = \sqrt{2}v_1 \rightarrow \boxed{v_2 = 1.4v_1}$$

279. (C) This problem cannot be solved using energy alone because some of the initial kinetic energy of the child will be transferred into internal energy (mainly thermal energy) during the sticky inelastic collision with the tire. Divide the solution into two parts:

Step 1: Use energy transfer during the swinging phase to find the post-collision speed of the child and tire. The kinetic energy child and tire transfer to gravitational potential energy.

$$K_i + U_{gi} = K_f + U_{gf}$$

$$K_i + 0 = 0 + U_{gf}$$

$$K_i = U_{gf}$$

$$\frac{1}{2}(2m + m)v_{C\&T}^2 = (2m + m)g\Delta y$$

$$\frac{1}{2}v_{C\&T}^2 = g\Delta y$$

$$v_{C\&T}^2 = 2g\Delta y$$

$$v_{C\&T} = \sqrt{2gd} = v'_{C\&T}$$

Step 2: Use conservation of momentum for an inelastic collision to find the child's initial velocity:

$$p_C + p_T = p'_{(C\&T)}$$
$$m_C v_C + m_T v_T = (m_C + m_T)v'_{C\&T}$$
$$2mv_C + 0 = (2m + m)v'_{C\&T}$$
$$2mv_C = (3m)v'_{C\&T} \rightarrow m \text{ cancels}$$
$$\boxed{v_C = \frac{3}{2}v'_{C\&T} \rightarrow \boxed{v_C = \frac{3}{2}\sqrt{2gd}}}$$

280. (D) The two carts have equal masses ($mA = mB = 0.5$ kg). Cart A moves at 0.2 m/s, and Cart B is at rest ($vB = 0$ m/s). Both carts move away at 0.1 m/s. Calculate the kinetic energies of the carts before and after the collision. Since knowing that energy must be conserved, the difference between the kinetic energies before and after represents energy lost as heat. (Neither cart has potential energy because they remain at the same height on the track.)

$$KE_A + KE_B = KE'_A + KE'_B + Heat$$
$$KE_A + 0 = KE'_A + KE'_B + Heat$$
$$KE_A = KE'_A + KE'_B + Heat$$
$$Heat = KE_A - KE'_A - KE'_B$$
$$Heat = \frac{1}{2}m_A v_A^2 - \frac{1}{2}m_A v_A'^2 - \frac{1}{2}m_B v_B'^2$$
$$m_A = m_B$$
$$Heat = \frac{1}{2}m_A v_A^2 - \frac{1}{2}m_A v_A'^2 - \frac{1}{2}m_A v_B'^2$$
$$Heat = \frac{1}{2}m_A \left(v_A^2 - v_A'^2 - v_B'^2\right)$$
$$Heat = \frac{1}{2}(0.5 \text{ kg})\left[(0.2 \text{ m/s})^2 - (0.1 \text{ m/s})^2 - (0.1 \text{ m/s})^2\right]$$
$$Heat = 0.005 \text{ J}$$
$$KE_A = \frac{1}{2}m_A v_A^2 = \frac{1}{2}(0.5 \text{ kg})(0.2 \text{ m/s})^2 = 0.01 \text{ J}$$
$$\frac{Heat}{KE_A} = \frac{(0.005 \text{ J})}{(0.01 \text{ J})} = 0.5 = \boxed{50\%}$$

281. **(B)** The ratio is found as follows:

$$\frac{U_{s2}}{U_{s1}} = \frac{18\,\text{J}}{2\,\text{J}} = 9$$

$$\frac{U_{s2}}{U_{s1}} = \frac{\frac{1}{2}kx_2^2}{\frac{1}{2}kx_1^2} = \frac{x_2^2}{x_1^2} = \left(\frac{x_2}{x_1}\right)^2 = 9$$

$$\frac{x_2}{x_1} = \sqrt{9} \rightarrow \boxed{\frac{x_2}{x_1} = 3}$$

282. **(D)** The work done by the wind equals the change in kinetic energy of the boat:

$$W = \Delta K$$

$$F_{\|}d = \frac{1}{2}mv_f^2 - \frac{1}{2}mv_i^2$$

$$F_{\|} = \frac{\frac{1}{2}mv_f^2 - \frac{1}{2}mv_i^2}{d}$$

$$F_{\|} = \frac{\frac{1}{2}m(v_f^2 - v_i^2)}{d}$$

$$F_{\|} = \frac{\frac{1}{2}(14{,}300\,\text{kg})\left(9^2\,\frac{\text{m}^2}{\text{s}^2}\right)}{850\,\text{m}} \rightarrow \boxed{F_{\|} = 681\,\text{N}}$$

The total force of the wind, F, is found as follows:

$$\sin(60) = \frac{F_{\|}}{F}$$

$$F = \frac{F_{\|}}{\sin(60)} = \frac{681\,\text{N}}{\sin(60)} = 786 \rightarrow \boxed{F \approx 790\,\text{N}}$$

283. **(D)** Kinetic energy is directly proportional to mass and directly proportional to the square of speed:

$$\frac{K_{truck}}{K_{car}} = \frac{\frac{1}{2}(2M)\left(\frac{v}{2}\right)^2}{\frac{1}{2}(M)(v)^2}$$

$$\frac{K_{truck}}{K_{car}} = 2\left(\frac{1}{4}\right) \rightarrow \boxed{\frac{K_{truck}}{K_{car}} = \frac{1}{2}}$$

284. (C) The gravitational potential energy is $\Delta U_g = mg\Delta y$. If mass is doubled and the vertical height is also doubled, then its gravitational energy must quadruple: $4 \times 50\,\text{J} = 200$ J. Note that the starting speed of 4 m/s has no effect on the calculation. Since the new box is released from rest, all of the 200 J of gravitational energy will transfer to kinetic energy.

285. (A) The gravitational potential energy is calculated using $\Delta U_g = mg\Delta y$.

I. A 2-kg object held at rest 3 m above the ground:

$$\Delta U_g = (2\,\text{kg})\left(10\,\frac{\text{N}}{\text{kg}}\right)(3\,\text{m}) = 60\,\text{J}$$

II. A 2-kg object falling down at a rate of 5 m/s at the instant it's 3 m off the ground:

$$\Delta U_g = mg\Delta y = (2\,\text{kg})\left(10\,\frac{\text{N}}{\text{kg}}\right)(3\,\text{m}) = 60\text{J}$$

III. A 1-kg object falling down at a rate of 10 m/s at the instant it's 3 m off the ground:

$$\Delta U_g = mg\Delta y = (1\,\text{kg})\left(10\,\frac{\text{N}}{\text{kg}}\right)(3\,\text{m}) = 30\text{J}$$

IV. A 3-kg object at rest 2 m above the ground:

$$\Delta U_g = mg\,\Delta y = (3\,\text{kg})\left(10\,\frac{\text{N}}{\text{kg}}\right)(2\text{m}) = 60\text{J}$$

Therefore, $\text{I} = \text{II} = \text{IV} > \text{III}$

286. (D) The elastic potential energy of a spring is given by $U_s = \frac{1}{2}kx^2$, so the energy is directly proportional to the square of the stretch distance. Thus, if you quadruple stretch from 5 cm to 20 cm, you'll increase the energy storage by 4^2, or 16 times the original amount.

287. (A) The friction force provides the net force stop for each car. The work–energy theorem is used as follows:

$$Fd = \Delta K$$

$$(F_{\text{friction}})d = \frac{1}{2}mv_f^2 - \frac{1}{2}mv_i^2$$

$$(-\mu F_N)d = -\frac{1}{2}mv_i^2$$

$$(\mu\, mg)d = \frac{1}{2}mv_i^2 \rightarrow \text{mass cancels from both sides}$$

$$\mu\, g\, d = \frac{1}{2}v_i^2$$

$$d = \left\{\frac{1}{2\,\mu\, g}\right\}v_i^2$$

Since skid distance (d) is directly proportional to the square of the initial speed (and independent of mass), the car going at twice the speed will have **four times** the skid distance.

288. **(C, D)** Mechanical energy includes spring potential energy and gravitational potential energy (as well as kinetic energy). The spring force and the gravitational force will be responsible for transfers of energy *within* the spring-mass-earth system, but are not responsible for changing the total mechanical energy. Friction and air drag forces are non-conservative forces that are path-dependent, and they are ultimately responsible for transferring energy to internal energy, primarily by dissipating energy to thermal energy.

289. **(B, D)** In both cases, identical objects are pushed the same vertical distance up the incline, so the change in gravitational potential energy ($\Delta U_g = mg\Delta y$) is the same. Work is the product of force and displacement, and displacement is the same as well as the applied force, since the objects are not accelerating and the applied force must balance the friction force in order to maintain constant velocity (note that friction force does not depend on the speed). Since it will take twice the amount of time pushing the box at 3 m/s, the power required is different ($P = \Delta E / \Delta t$).

290. **(A, C)** As the stone rises, its speed decreases, so its *kinetic energy will decrease*. As its height off the ground increases, its gravitational potential energy will increase. Its total mechanical energy ($K + Ug$) stays constant.

291. **(A, D)** Work is the amount of energy transferred from one storage mode to another. Work occurs when a force is applied through a displacement, but only if a component of the force is parallel with that displacement ($W = F_\parallel\, d = F\, d\, \cos\theta$). In circular motion, the force is toward the center and is always perpendicular to the displacement along the circular path; thus the gravitational force on the Moon does no work. The football player pushing on the wall also does no work because there is no displacement. The other two options all involve a force applied in the direction of a displacement, resulting in work done on the object.

292. **(B, C)** A net force is applied by the floor of the elevator to accelerate the child-earth system. Since this force is applied along the direction of the displacement, work is done to the system to change its mechanical energy. Also, the system's kinetic energy increases since the system gains speed, and the gravitational potential energy increases as well because its height from the ground increases.

293. Here are some possible assumptions. Different assumptions may be made, but they may affect answers in the questions that follow:

Assumption 1: The mass of the rope is negligible in comparison to the mass of Gretchen. If the rope had significant mass, her impact with the rope would need to be modeled as an inelastic collision, and the rope's change in gravitational potential energy would also need to be considered as it swings up.

Assumption 2: The child's center of mass is level with the end of the rope. This will insure the length of the rope equals the radius of her circular swing.

Assumption 3: Air drag and pivot friction are negligible. These are very hard to model and should not have much of an effect through a single circular swing.

Assumption 4: The radius of the circle does not change significantly as the rope winds up around the horizontal swing support bar. This will make the circular motion and energy analysis much simpler.

294. The minimum speed condition at the top occurs when the gravitational force alone provides the needed centripetal force, i.e., the tension of the rope vanishes:

$$F_C = ma_C$$

$$F_C = \frac{mv^2}{r}$$

$$mg = \frac{mv^2_{min}}{\ell} \rightarrow \text{mass cancels}$$

$$v^2_{min} = \ell g \rightarrow \boxed{v_{min_{TOP}} = \sqrt{\ell g}}$$

295. Conservation of energy may be used for the girl-earth system, where the initial state is at the bottom of the circle and the final state is at the top.

$$K_i + U_{gi} = K_f + U_{gf}$$

$$K_i + 0 = K_f + U_{gf}$$

$$\frac{1}{2}mv_i^2 = \frac{1}{2}mv^2_{min_{TOP}} + mg\Delta y \rightarrow \text{Cancel mass and multiply both sides by 2}$$

$$v_i^2 = v^2_{min_{TOP}} + 2g\Delta y \rightarrow \text{At the top, } \Delta y = 2\ell$$

$$v_i^2 = v^2_{min_{TOP}} + 4\ell g \rightarrow \text{Substitute } v^2_{min_{TOP}} = \ell g$$

$$v_i^2 = \ell g + 4\ell g \rightarrow \boxed{v_i = \sqrt{5\ell g}}$$

Using an estimated rope length of 3 meters and a gravitational field strength of 10 N/kg, her minimum speed is 12 m/s, which is about as fast as Usain Bolt, one of the fastest human runners in history . . . not a very realistic speed for a child!

296. The tension will be the greatest at the bottom of the circle, because it must be greater than the gravitational force in order to provide the required net upward (centripetal) force.

$$F_c = ma_c$$

$$F_c = m\frac{v^2}{r}$$

$$T - mg = m\frac{v_i^2}{\ell}$$

$$T - mg = m\frac{5\ell g}{\ell}$$

$$T = mg + 5mg \rightarrow \boxed{T = 6mg}$$

Thus, the tension in the rope must be six times the weight of the child.

297. The amount of work is the area bounded by the force–displacement graph. The work for the first 4 m of displacement is the area of the 12 N by 4 m rectangle, which is 48 J. The work for the next 4 m of displacement is the area of the 12 N by 4 m triangle, which is ½ (4) (12) = 24 J. The total amount of work done on the object is 48 J + 24 J = 72 J.

298. The work–energy theorem is used to find the final kinetic energy of the object:

$$W = \Delta K$$

$$W = K_f - \frac{1}{2}mv_i^2$$

$$K_f = W + \frac{1}{2}mv_i^2$$

$$K_f = 72\,\text{J} + \frac{1}{2}(15\,\text{kg})\left(4.0\,\frac{\text{m}}{\text{s}}\right)^2$$

$$K_f = 72\,\text{J} + 120\,\text{J} \rightarrow \boxed{K_f = 192\,\text{J}}$$

299. The final velocity is found as follows:

$$K_f = \frac{1}{2}mv_f^2$$

$$v_f = \sqrt{\frac{2K_f}{m}}$$

$$v_f = \sqrt{\frac{2(192\,\text{J})}{15\,\text{kg}}} \rightarrow \boxed{v_f = 5.1\,\text{m/s}}$$

300. As the spring compresses and the object stops, all of the 192 J of kinetic energy will transfer to elastic potential energy of the spring:

$$(K + U_s)_{\text{initial}} = (K + U_s)_{\text{final}}$$

$$(K + 0)_{\text{initial}} = (0 + U_s)_{\text{final}}$$

$$192\,\text{J} = \frac{1}{2}kx^2$$

$$x = \sqrt{\frac{2(192\,\text{J})}{650\,\frac{\text{N}}{\text{m}}}} \rightarrow \boxed{x = 0.77\,\text{m}}$$

Chapter 7: Torque and Rotational Motion

Questions 301–315 are easier practice questions designed to allow the student to review specific AP learning objectives and essential knowledge of torque and rotational motion.

301. (A) Rotational kinetic energy is directly proportional to the square of the angular speed $\left(K = \frac{1}{2}I\omega^2\right)$, so if the angular speed triples, the rotational kinetic energy is nine times as much.

302. (D) Since there is no net torque applied to the skater system, her angular momentum will remain the same. Extending her arms outward will increase her rotational inertia, and her angular velocity will decrease proportionately to keep $\vec{L} = I\vec{\omega}$ constant.

303. (B) The angular acceleration is given as a uniform value of -2 rad/s². The other quantities are calculated as follows:

$$\omega = \omega_o + \alpha t = +6\frac{rad}{s} + \left(-2\frac{rad}{s^2}\right)4\sec = -2\frac{rad}{\sec}$$

$\alpha = \frac{\tau_{net}}{I} \rightarrow \tau_{net} = I\alpha \therefore$ The net torque is in the same direction (negative) as the angular acceleration.

304. (A) The beam is in equilibrium when it is held by the guide rope, so the sum of all the torques must be zero. The guide rope is 23 m from the fulcrum, and the center of mass is 2 m from the end. The weight of the beam is F = mg = (5.0 kg/m * 50.0 m) * 10 N/kg = 2,500 N.

$$\Sigma\tau = 0$$
$$r_\perp F + r_\perp F = 0$$
$$-(2\text{ m})(2{,}500\text{ N}) + (23\text{ m})F = 0$$
$$F = 217\text{ N} \rightarrow \boxed{F \approx 220\text{ N}}$$

305. (D) Angular momentum must be conserved in the system, so as the skater draws his arms into his body, he is decreasing his rotational inertia. Thus, his angular velocity must increase to conserve his angular momentum.

306. (D) According to Newton's first law, objects maintain constant velocity as long as there is no net force acting on it. The ball flies off in a straight line tangent to the circle because the string is no longer providing a net (centripetal) force on the ball. Since the velocity remains constant and its path is tangent to the original surface, its angular momentum ($\vec{L} = m\vec{v}\vec{r}$) remains the same. Moreover, since there is no net torque on the puck system (even when the string breaks), angular momentum must be conserved.

307. (A) The angular velocity must first be converted to radians per second:

$$\omega = \left(12\,\frac{\text{rev}}{\text{sec}}\right)\left(2\pi\,\frac{\text{rad}}{\text{rev}}\right) = 24\pi\,\frac{\text{rad}}{\text{sec}}$$

Next, the angular momentum is calculated as follows:

$$L = I\omega$$
$$L = (mR^2)(24\pi) \rightarrow \boxed{L = 24\pi(mR^2)}$$

308. (D) The distance traveled in a complete orbit is the circumference of the orbit, and the time is the period. Speed is the ratio of distance to time:

$$v = \frac{d}{t} = \frac{2\pi R}{\text{period}}$$

$$v = \frac{2\pi\,(385{,}000{,}000\text{ m})}{(27.3\ \cancel{\text{days}}) * \left(24\,\frac{\cancel{\text{hours}}}{\cancel{\text{day}}}\right)\left(3{,}600\,\frac{\text{sec}}{\cancel{\text{hour}}}\right)} \rightarrow \boxed{v = 1{,}030\text{ m/s}}$$

309. (C) Every point on the rotating platform makes the same number of revolutions per second, and thus has the same angular speed.

310. (B) Linear speed is the amount of meters covered each second. The girl is making a circle with twice the circumference (circumference = $2\pi R$) in the same amount of time and thus has twice the linear speed.

311. (A) The initial velocity is $\omega_0 = 0$, the angular acceleration is $\alpha = 12$ radians/sec^2, and the angular displacement is $\Delta\theta = 90° = \dfrac{\pi}{2}$ radians.

$$\Delta\theta = \omega_0 t + \frac{1}{2}\alpha t^2 = (0)t + \frac{1}{2}\alpha t^2$$
$$\Delta\theta = \frac{1}{2}\alpha t^2$$

Solving for t:

$$t = \sqrt{\frac{2\Delta\theta}{\alpha}}$$

$$t = \sqrt{\frac{2\left(\dfrac{\pi}{2}\,\text{rad}\right)}{12\,\dfrac{\text{rad}}{s^2}}} \rightarrow \boxed{t = 0.51\text{ s}}$$

312. (C) The angular displacement is calculated as follows:

$$\Delta\theta = w_0 t + \frac{1}{2}\alpha t^2$$

$$\Delta\theta = \left(11\frac{rad}{s}\right)(6.0\ s) + \frac{1}{2}\left(-1.5\frac{rad}{s^2}\right)(6.0\ s)^2 \rightarrow \boxed{\Delta\theta = 39\ \text{radians}}$$

313. (D) The initial angular speed is $w_0 = 150\frac{rad}{s}$, the final angular speed is zero, and the angular acceleration is $\alpha = -25\frac{rad}{s^2}$.

$$w = w_0 + \alpha t$$

$$t = \frac{w - w_0}{\alpha} =$$

$$t = \frac{0 - 150\frac{rad}{s}}{-25\frac{rad}{s^2}} \rightarrow \boxed{t = 6.0\ s}$$

314. (D) The seesaw is in equilibrium, so the sum of all the moments must be zero.

$$\Sigma\tau = 0$$

$$r_\perp F + r_\perp F = 0$$

$$(2.0\ m)\left(42\ kg * 10\frac{N}{kg}\right) - (R)\left(35\ kg * 10\frac{N}{kg}\right) = 0$$

$$(2.0\ m)\left(42\ kg * 10\frac{N}{kg}\right) = (R)\left(35\ kg * 10\frac{N}{kg}\right) \rightarrow \boxed{R = 2.4\ m}$$

315. (D) The initial angular speed is not relevant in this problem. The rotational inertia, I, is determined as follows:

$$\vec{\alpha} = \frac{\vec{\tau}_{net}}{I}$$

$$I = \frac{\vec{\tau}_{net}}{\vec{\alpha}}$$

$$I = \frac{55\ Nm}{5.0\frac{rad}{s^2}} \rightarrow \boxed{I = 11\ kg \cdot m^2}$$

316. (D) Angular acceleration is the ratio of net torque to rotational inertia: $\alpha = \dfrac{\Sigma \tau}{I}$. Assume the forces act at a distance R from the axis of rotation.

I. $|\alpha| = \dfrac{FR}{I}$

II. $|\alpha| = \dfrac{2FR}{I} = 2\left(\dfrac{FR}{I}\right)$

III. $|\alpha| = \dfrac{2FR - FR}{I} = \dfrac{FR}{I}$

IV. $|\alpha| = \dfrac{2FR}{2I} = \dfrac{FR}{I}$

Thus $\boxed{\text{II} > \text{I} = \text{III} = \text{IV}}$

317. (A) When a wheel rolls without slipping and air drag is negligible, there will be no change in internal energy of the wheel-earth system. Thus, the mechanical energy will be conserved. However, one must consider the rotational kinetic energy of the large wheel as it reaches the bottom of the incline. Energy conservation yields:

$$mgh = \frac{1}{2}mv^2 + \frac{1}{2}I\omega^2$$

$$\boxed{\therefore mgh > \frac{1}{2}mv^2}$$

318. (C) Before the collision, the dart has a linear momentum of $\vec{p} = m\vec{v}$. When it hits the 25-cm-tall target 5 cm above the hinge, it moves horizontally at 2.5 m/s at a distance of 20 cm above the hinge (25 cm – 5 cm). Its angular momentum is the product of the linear momentum times the perpendicular distance to the axis:

$$\vec{L} = R_\perp \vec{p} = R_\perp (m\vec{v})$$

$$\vec{L}_{initial} = (0.020 \text{ m})\left(0.012 \text{ kg} * 2.5\frac{\text{m}}{\text{s}}\right) = 0.0060 \frac{\text{kg m}^2}{\text{s}}$$

Because there is no external torque on the dart/target system, the angular momentum is conserved, so the final angular momentum of the dart/target system after the collision

remains the same: $\boxed{\vec{L}_{final} = 0.0060 \dfrac{\text{kg m}^2}{\text{s}}}$.

319. **(A)** After the collision, the dart/target system's angular momentum may be written as $\vec{L} = I\vec{\omega}$, with the rotational inertia of the dart/target system found as the sum of the contributions of each (treat the dart as a point particle and the target as a plank pinned on one end):

$$I = I_{dart} + I_{target} = m_{dart}\,R_\perp^2 + \frac{1}{3}M_{target}\,L^2$$

$$I = (0.012 \text{ kg})\,(0.20 \text{ m})^2 + \frac{1}{3}(0.095 \text{ kg})\,(0.25 \text{ m})^2$$

$$I = (0.00048 + 0.00198)\,\text{kg} \cdot \text{m}^2$$

$$I = (0.00246)\,\text{kg} \cdot \text{m}^2$$

Knowing the angular momentum from part (a), solve $\vec{L} = I\vec{\omega}$ for angular speed:

$$\vec{\omega} = \frac{\vec{L}}{I}$$

$$\vec{\omega} = \frac{0.0060\,\dfrac{\text{kg m}^2}{\text{s}}}{0.00246 \text{ kg m}^2} \rightarrow \boxed{|\vec{\omega}| == 2.4\,\frac{\text{rad}}{\text{s}}}$$

320. **(A)** Because the hanging mass is accelerating downward, the magnitude of the tension force is less than the gravitational force Mg, so the net torque on the pulley is less than MgR. Since $|\alpha| = \dfrac{\vec{\tau}_{net}}{I}$, then $|\alpha| < \dfrac{MgR}{I}$.

One can also analyze the pulley-mass system and come to the same conclusion. To determine the angular acceleration of the system of the pulley and the hanging mass, the rotational inertia of the hanging mass relative to the axis of rotation must be considered:

$$|\alpha| = \frac{\tau_{net}}{I_{system}}$$

$$|\alpha| = \frac{MgR}{I + MR^2}$$

Thus, considering this extra rotational inertia, $\boxed{|\alpha| < \dfrac{MgR}{I}}$.

321. **(B)** In order to apply the conservation of angular momentum there must be zero net torque on the system. The putty collision applies a torque about the hinge of the door, resulting in an angular momentum change for the door system. Likewise, the putty's angular momentum about the door hinge changes during the collision because it experiences a net torque from the door. The torques are equal and opposite, however, due to Newton's third law. Thus, if you consider the door and putty as the system, angular momentum must remain the same before and after the collision.

322. (C) In order for angular velocity to be constant, there must be zero net torque on the rod:

$$\tau_{net} = 0$$

$$-F\left(\frac{L}{2}\right) + F_?\left(\frac{L}{4}\right) = 0$$

$$F_?\left(\frac{L}{4}\right) = F\left(\frac{L}{2}\right)$$

$$F_? = \frac{F\left(\frac{L}{2}\right)}{\left(\frac{L}{4}\right)} \rightarrow \boxed{F_? = 2F}$$

323. (B) The net torque on the system is calculated as follows:

$$\tau_{net} = -F\left(\frac{L}{2}\right) + F\left(\frac{L}{4}\right)$$

$$\tau_{net} = \frac{-F}{4}$$

With a negative (clockwise) net torque, the initial positive angular velocity must decrease to zero and then reverse directions by getting more negative.

324. (C) The final angular velocity is calculated from the rotational kinetic energy:

$$K = \frac{1}{2}I\omega^2$$

$$\omega = \sqrt{\frac{2K}{I}} = \sqrt{\frac{2(800 \text{ J})}{4 \text{ kg m}^2}} = 20\,\frac{\text{rad}}{\text{s}}$$

Next, the elapsed time, Δt, for the acceleration is found as follows:

$$\omega = \omega_0 + \alpha\,\Delta t$$

$$\Delta t = \frac{\omega - \omega_0}{\alpha}$$

$$\Delta t = \frac{(20 - 0)\frac{\text{rad}}{\text{s}}}{5\,\frac{\text{rad}}{\text{s}^2}} \rightarrow \boxed{\Delta t = 4 \text{ s}}$$

325. (D) The rotational kinetic energies may be equated and solved for the rotational velocity of Object 2:

$$K_1 = K_2$$

$$\frac{1}{2} I_1 \omega_1^2 = \frac{1}{2} I_2 \omega_2^2$$

$$\omega_2^2 = \frac{I_1}{I_2} \omega_1^2$$

$$\omega_2^2 = \frac{8 \text{ kg m}^2}{2 \text{ kg m}^2} \left(1 \frac{\text{rad}}{\text{s}}\right)^2 = 4 \left(\frac{\text{rad}}{\text{s}}\right)^2$$

$$\omega_2 = \sqrt{4 \left(\frac{\text{rad}}{\text{s}}\right)^2} \rightarrow \boxed{\omega_2 = 2 \frac{\text{rad}}{\text{s}}}$$

326. (B) Angular momentum is directly proportional to angular speed ($L = I\omega$), so if the angular speed doubles *and* the rotational inertia doubles, the angular momentum will **quadruple**.

327. (A) The following relationship on the equation guide may be solved for elapsed time:

$$\Delta L = \tau\, \Delta t$$

$$\Delta t = \frac{\Delta L}{\tau}$$

$$\Delta t = \frac{L_2 - L_1}{\tau}$$

$$\Delta t = \frac{I\omega_2 - I\omega_1}{\tau} \rightarrow \boxed{\Delta t = \frac{I(\omega_2 - \omega_1)}{\tau}}$$

328. (D) The rotational kinetic energy of the tire transfers to thermal energy. To calculate the rotational kinetic energy, first convert the rotational speed of the tires into radians per second:

$$\omega = \left(25 \frac{\text{rev}}{\text{s}}\right) \left(\frac{2\pi \text{ rad}}{1 \text{ rev}}\right) = 157 \frac{\text{rad}}{\text{s}}$$

According to the work–energy theorem, the energy transferred to heat equals the change in kinetic energy of the tire:

$$E = \frac{1}{2} I\omega_f^2 - \frac{1}{2} I\omega_i^2$$

$$E = \frac{1}{2} (1.5 \text{ kg m}^2) \left(157 \frac{\text{rad}}{\text{s}}\right)^2 - 0 \rightarrow \boxed{E = 19{,}000 \text{ J}}$$

329. (D) During the collision there is no net force on the puck/rod system, so linear momentum is conserved:

$$p_i = p_i$$

$$-mv = m\left(\frac{v}{2}\right) + 4mv_{rod}$$

$$4mv_{rod} = -mv - \frac{mv}{2}$$

$$v_{rod} = \frac{-\dfrac{3mv}{2}}{4m} \rightarrow \boxed{|v_{rod}| = \frac{3v}{8}}$$

Since there is no net torque on the puck/rod system, angular momentum is also conserved:

$$\vec{L}_i = \vec{L}_i$$

$$-mv\left(\frac{\ell}{2}\right) = m\frac{v}{2}\left(\frac{\ell}{2}\right) + I\omega_{rod}$$

$$I\omega_{rod} = -\frac{mv\ell}{2} - \frac{mv\ell}{4}$$

$$I\omega_{rod} = -\frac{3mv\ell}{4} \rightarrow \boxed{|\omega_{rod}| = \frac{3mv\ell}{4I}}$$

330. (D) Angular momentum is the sum of the angular momentum of all the components. The masses have a linear velocity of $v = R\omega$, and since they are located at a distance of half the rod length $\left(\dfrac{L}{2}\right)$ from the center of the barbell, this may be written as $v = \dfrac{L}{2}\omega$. Their linear momentum is calculated as $p = mv = m\left(\dfrac{L}{2}\omega\right)$. The angular momentum of these masses is found by multiplying this linear momentum by the distance from the axis to the line of motion of the object: $L = m\left(\dfrac{L}{2}\omega\right)\left(\dfrac{L}{2}\right) = m\omega\left(\dfrac{L}{2}\right)^2$.

The total angular momentum of the rod and the two masses is calculated as follows:

$$L_{total} = L_{rod} + L_{mass\ 1} + L_{mass\ 2}$$

$$L_{total} = I\omega + m\omega\left(\frac{L}{2}\right)^2 + m\omega\left(\frac{L}{2}\right)^2$$

$$L_{total} = I\omega + \frac{m\omega(L)^2}{2}$$

$$L_{total} = \left(I + \frac{m(L)^2}{2}\right)\omega$$

$$L_{total} = \left(1.5 \text{ kg m}^2 + \frac{3.0 \text{ kg}(2.2 \text{ m})^2}{2}\right)\left(0.50 \frac{\text{rad}}{\text{s}}\right) \rightarrow \boxed{L_{total} = 4.4 \frac{\text{kg} \cdot \text{m}^2}{\text{s}}}$$

331. (C) Torque is calculated by $\tau = r_\perp F = r F_\perp$. Assuming the rod length L, the individual torques are calculated as follows:

I. $|\tau| = r F_\perp = LF$

II. $|\tau| = r F_\perp = LF - (L/2) F = \dfrac{LF}{2}$

III. $|\tau| = r F_\perp = (L/2) F + L(F/2) = LF$

IV. $|\tau| = r F_\perp = L[2F \cos(30°)] = LF$

The rank is as follows: $\boxed{\text{I} = \text{III} = \text{IV} > \text{II}}$

332. (B) The angular acceleration may be written as $\alpha = \dfrac{\Delta\omega}{\Delta t} = \dfrac{\omega - 0}{\Delta t} = \dfrac{\omega}{\Delta t}$.

The angular displacement is $\Delta\theta = \omega_0 t + \dfrac{1}{2}\alpha t^2 = 0 + \dfrac{1}{2}\alpha(\Delta t)^2$.

Substituting the first equation into the second: $\Delta\theta = \dfrac{1}{2}\left(\dfrac{\omega}{\Delta t}\right)(\Delta t)^2 = \dfrac{\omega\Delta t}{2}$ rads

Converting radians to revolutions: $\Delta\theta = \left(\dfrac{\omega\Delta t}{2}\ \text{rad}\right)\left(\dfrac{1\ \text{revolution}}{2\pi\ \text{rad}}\right) \rightarrow \boxed{\Delta\theta == \dfrac{\omega\Delta t}{4\pi}}$

333. (D) The period of rotation, T, is the amount of seconds for each revolution. First, the angular speed is converted into revolutions per second:

$$f = \omega\left(\dfrac{\text{rad}}{s} \cdot \dfrac{rev}{2\pi\ \text{rad}}\right) = \dfrac{\omega}{2\pi}\ \text{revolutions per second}$$

The period is the inverse of frequency:

$$T = \dfrac{1}{f} = \dfrac{1}{\dfrac{\omega}{2\pi}} \rightarrow \boxed{T = \dfrac{2\pi}{\omega}\ \text{seconds for each revolution}}$$

334. (A) The ratio is calculated as follows:

$$\dfrac{K_{\text{translation}}}{K_{\text{rotation}}} = \dfrac{\dfrac{1}{2}mv^2}{\dfrac{1}{2}I\omega^2}$$

$$\dfrac{K_{\text{translation}}}{K_{\text{rotation}}} = \dfrac{\dfrac{1}{2}mv^2}{\dfrac{1}{2}\left(\dfrac{2}{5}mR^2\right)\omega^2} \rightarrow \boxed{\dfrac{K_{\text{translation}}}{K_{\text{rotation}}} = \dfrac{5v^2}{2R^2\omega^2}}$$

335. (D) The gravitational force from the Sun is the *only* force acting on the comet. Since this force is pointed directly at the Sun, it will not have a lever arm to apply a net torque to the comet system about the Sun. With zero net torque on the comet, its angular momentum must **stay constant** in order for angular momentum to be conserved.

336. (D) As the comet moves toward the Sun, the gravitational potential energy, $U_g = -\dfrac{Gm_{comet}m_{Sun}}{r}$, decreases (becomes more negative) as the radial distance, r, from the Sun decreases. Since there is no net force on the comet/sun system, it's mechanical energy must remain constant. Thus, with the gravitational potential energy decreasing, the kinetic energy must increase.

337. (C, D) When the force goes through the axis of rotation, no torque is applied, so this eliminates choices A and B. Choices C and D both have forces that do not go through the axis of rotation and have a component perpendicular to the lever arm, and thus torque is applied.

338. (A, C) The rotational inertia is the rotational equivalent of inertial mass, and thus is the resistance something has to rotational motion. It may be found from the rotational analogue to Newton's second law:

$$\vec{\alpha} = \frac{\vec{\tau}_{net}}{I}$$

Solving for I:

$$I = \frac{\vec{\tau}_{net}}{\vec{\alpha}}$$

Thus, the rotational inertia is the ratio between torque and angular acceleration. Method A may be used to find rotational inertia, since the torque is known and the angular acceleration is found from the slope of the angular velocity versus time graph. Video analysis in option D is not sufficient to determine I because it would only provide the angular acceleration, not the net torque.

Option C uses conservation of energy:

$$U_{g_{top}} = K_{trans_{bottom}} + K_{rot_{bottom}}$$
$$mg\Delta y = \frac{1}{2}mv^2 + \frac{1}{2}I\omega^2, \text{ where } \omega = v/R$$

Option C provides all the quantities needed to solve this expression for the rotational inertia, I. For option B, mass and radius alone are not sufficient to find I since the distribution of mass is not known.

339. (A, B) An object moving in a circle must be accelerating toward the center with an inward ("centripetal") linear acceleration, so choice A must be correct. The merry-go-round may also spin with an angular acceleration if there is net torque acting on it, so choice B is possible.

340. (B, D) When a solid object rotates with a constant angular acceleration, its angular velocity changes at a steady rate. A constant net torque is responsible for a constant angular acceleration according to $\vec{\alpha} = \dfrac{\vec{\tau}_{net}}{I}$.

341. (B, D) A rotational inertia is the resistance a body has to rotation. The more mass the body has and the farther the mass is separated from the axis of rotation, the greater the rotational inertia. The rotational inertia does NOT depend on the state of motion of the body, so choices A and C must be eliminated.

342. The net torque on the rod is the sum of the torque contributions from each force. The 12-N force tends to rotate the rod counterclockwise (positive torque), and the 24-N force clockwise (negative torque).

$$\tau_{net} = \tau_{10} + \tau_{20} = r\,F_\perp + r\,F_\perp = (1.5\text{ m})12\cos(60°) - (1.5\text{ m})(24\text{ N})$$
$$\tau_{net} = -27\text{ Nm (clockwise)}$$

343. The rotational inertia for a thin rod pinned at the center is:

$$I = \frac{1}{12}ML^2$$
$$I = \frac{1}{12}(12\text{ kg})(3.0\text{ m})^2$$
$$I = 9.0\text{ kg}\cdot\text{m}^2$$

344. Angular acceleration is calculated using the rotational expression of Newton's second law:

$$\vec{\alpha} = \frac{\vec{\tau}_{net}}{I}$$
$$\vec{\alpha} = \frac{-27\text{ Nm}}{9.0\text{ kg m}^2} = -3.0\text{ rad/s}^2$$

345. The angular displacement must first be in radians: $\Delta\theta = -90° = -\dfrac{\pi}{2}$ radians (clockwise).

To solve this, it is inferred that the torque (and thus the angular acceleration) remains constant throughout the rotation because the forces remain at the same angles relative to the rod throughout the rotation. Thus, the following displacement equation for uniform angular acceleration may be used:

$$\Delta\theta = \omega_0 t + \frac{1}{2}\alpha t^2$$

Since it starts from rest, the initial angular velocity, ω_0, is zero, and you can solve for time as follows:

$$\Delta\theta = \frac{1}{2}\alpha t^2$$

$$t = \sqrt{\frac{2\Delta\theta}{\alpha}}$$

$$t = \sqrt{\frac{2\left(-\frac{\pi}{2}\right)\text{rad}}{-3.0\,\frac{\text{rad}}{\text{s}^2}}} = 1.023\text{ s} \rightarrow \boxed{t \approx 1.0\,\text{sec}}$$

346.

$$\Delta\theta = \frac{1}{2}\alpha t^2 = \frac{1}{2}\left(-3.0\,\frac{\text{rad}}{\text{s}^2}\right)(5.0\text{ s})^2 = -37.5\text{ rad}$$

$$\Delta\theta = (-37.5\text{ rad})\left(\frac{1\text{ rev}}{2\pi\text{ rad}}\right) = -6\text{ rev} \rightarrow \boxed{6\text{ revolutions}}$$

347. The key physics principle here is conservation of angular momentum of the child/merry-go-round system. Since there is no net torque on a system, its initial angular momentum must be equal to its final angular momentum. This applies to the landing and walking phases of the problem. Some key assumptions are as follows:

Assumption 1: There is negligible axle friction on the merry-go-round. Otherwise, friction would apply a net torque on the system, changing its angular momentum.

Assumption 2: There is negligible air drag. Otherwise, air drag would also apply a net torque to the system.

Assumption 3: The child drops straight down off the branch, thus having no horizontal component of landing velocity. A horizontal velocity would add angular momentum to the system relative to the axis of rotation. (Note: The vertical landing velocity is parallel to the axis of rotation and has no contribution to the angular momentum, so the height, h, has no relevance in the solution.)

348. The angular momentum of the child-merry-go-round system is conserved:

$$\vec{L}_i = \vec{L}_f$$

$$I_{disk}w_o = (I_{disk} + I_{child})w_{drop}$$

$$w_{drop} = \frac{I_{disk}w_o}{(I_{disk} + I_{child})}$$

$$w_{drop} = \frac{\left[\frac{1}{2}(10m)R^2\right]w_o}{\left[\frac{1}{2}(10m)R^2 + m\left(\frac{R}{2}\right)^2\right]} = \frac{5mR^2 w_o}{\left(5mR^2 + \frac{mR^2}{4}\right)}$$

$$w_{drop} = \frac{5mR^2 w_o}{\left(\frac{21mR^2}{4}\right)} = \frac{20w_o}{21}$$

$$\% = \left(\frac{\frac{20w_o}{21} - w_o}{w_o}\right) * 100$$

$$\% = -\frac{1}{21} * 100 = 4.76 \rightarrow \boxed{5\% \text{ decrease in angular velocity}}$$

349. While the child walks outward, there is still no net torque on the system, so angular momentum is conserved:

$$L_i = L_f$$

$$I_{R/2}w_{drop} = I_R w_R$$

$$w_R = \frac{I_{R/2}w_{drop}}{I_R}$$

$$w_R = \frac{\left[\frac{1}{2}(10m)R^2 + m\left(\frac{R}{2}\right)^2\right]w_{drop}}{\left[\frac{1}{2}(10m)R^2 + m(R)^2\right]}$$

$$w_R = \frac{\left(\frac{21}{4}mR^2\right)w_{drop}}{(6mR^2)} \rightarrow \boxed{w_R = \frac{21}{24}w_{drop}}$$

350. The friction between the shoes and the pavement provide a net torque that slows the rotation of the system:

The net torque is due to the friction force $F_f = \mu F_N = \mu F_y$ acting $\perp$ to the lever arm R:

$\vec{\tau}_{net} = r_\perp F = -R(\mu F_y) = -\mu R F_y$ (note that the $\vec{\tau}_{net}$ is considered negative because it decreaes ω)

$\vec{\alpha} = \dfrac{\vec{\tau}_{net}}{I_R}$ where $I_R = 6mR^2$ as derived in the previous problem

$\vec{\alpha} = \dfrac{-\mu R F_y}{6mR^2} = \dfrac{-\mu F_y}{6mR}$

$\omega_f = \omega_i + \alpha \Delta t$

$\Delta t = \dfrac{\omega_f - \omega_i}{\alpha}$

$\Delta t = \dfrac{0 - \omega_R}{\left(\dfrac{-\mu F_y}{6mR}\right)} \rightarrow \boxed{\Delta t = \dfrac{6mR\omega_R}{\mu F_y}}$

Chapter 8: Electric Charge and Electric Force

351. (D) The negatively charged rod induces a charge separation in the sphere. The rod repels some of the sphere's valance electrons to the right hand side (like charges repel). The remaining positive charges in the left hand side of the sphere are attracted to the negative rod. Barring a nuclear event, positive charges will not break free from the nucleus. Also, since no contact is made, the sphere will not gain or lose charge.

352. (A) The conductor is charged positively by contact. This occurs because many of the (negative) freely moving valence electrons in the conductor are attracted to the positively charged glass rod and transfer to the rod. The previously neutral conductor is now missing electrons and is positively charged. Protons are fixed in the nucleus and do not flow from atom to atom in a solid object.

353. (C) The electric charge of a single proton is $+1.6 \times 10^{-19}$ C. The object has a charge of $+8.0 \times 10^{-19}$ C. So, divide the object's charge by the single proton charge to find that it has five more protons than electrons.

354. (C) The charge on a proton is 1.6×10^{-19} C. The distance between the protons is 1×10^{-6} m. The protons have the same charge, so the force will be repulsive. Use Coulomb's law to find the magnitude of the force:

$F = \dfrac{kq_1 q_2}{r^2}$

$F = \dfrac{(9 \times 10^9 \ \text{N} \cdot \text{m}^2/\text{C}^2)(1.6 \times 10^{-19}\text{C})(1.6 \times 10^{-19}\text{C})}{(1.0 \times 10^{-16}\text{m})^2} \rightarrow \boxed{F = 2.3 \times 10^{-16}\text{N}}$

355. (B) The fact that the paper bits accelerated upward is evidence that the upward electrostatic force is greater than the downward gravitational force.

356. (C) The fundamental charge is 1.6×10^{-19} C, which is the magnitude of the charge of an electron or proton, and all charges are integer multiples of this value. Millikan discovered this quantity in 1909 with his famous oil drop experiment. No charge less than this value has ever been detected.

357. (A) According to Coulomb's law, electric force is inversely proportional to the square of the distance between the objects. If the distance is doubled, then the force decreases to one-fourth of what it was.

358. (D) According to Coulomb's law, electric force is directly proportional to the product of the two charges. If one charge is doubled, the electric force doubles. If the other charge is tripled, that triples the already doubled force. Thus, the force is six times the original force.

359. (D) Coulomb's law may be used to find the value of the electric repulsive force:

$$\left|\vec{F}_E\right| = k \frac{|q_1 q_2|}{r^2}$$

$$\left|\vec{F}_E\right| = 9.0 \times 10^9 \, \frac{\text{Nm}^2}{\text{C}^2} \frac{\left|\left(6.4 \times 10^{-8}\text{C}\right)\left(6.4 \times 10^{-8}\text{C}\right)\right|}{\left(0.0056 \, \text{m}\right)^2}$$

$$\left|\vec{F}_E\right| 1.2 \, N$$

360. (A) The charge of a single electron is -1.6×10^{-19} C, so the total number of electrons may be found as follows:

$$\text{\# of elecrons} = (-8 X 10^{-6} C) \left(\frac{1 \, \text{electron}}{-1.6 X 10^{-19} C} \right) = \boxed{5 \times 10^{13} \text{ electrons}}$$

361. (D) The only change is that one of the charges is doubled. Since the electrostatic force is directly proportional to charge, the force must double from 100 N to 200 N.

362. (B) In good conductors, the valence electrons may move freely from atom to atom. Protons stay fixed in the nucleus.

363. (A) In the field of electrostatics, objects become charged when electrons transfer between objects (protons are fixed in the nucleus of the atom and will not transfer from atom to atom). When an object becomes positively charged, it must lose electrons. Thus the silk gains electrons and the glass loses electrons.

364. (A) The electron has a charge of -1.6×10^{-19} C, and two protons have a charge of $2(+1.6 \times 10^{-19}$ C$) = +3.2 \times 10^{-19}$ C. Coulomb's law needs to be solved for the radial distance, r:

$$\left|\vec{F}_E\right| = k \frac{|q_1 q_2|}{r^2}$$

$$r = \sqrt{k \frac{|q_1 q_2|}{\left|\vec{F}_E\right|}}$$

$$r = \sqrt{9.0 \times 10^9 \frac{\text{Nm}^2}{\text{C}^2} \frac{\left(-1.6 \times 10^{-19}\text{C}\right)\left(+3.2 \times 10^{-19}\text{C}\right)}{4.8 \times 10^{-7}\,\text{N}}}$$

$$r = 3.1 \times 10^{-11}\,\text{m} \rightarrow \boxed{r = 31\ \text{pm}}$$

365. (A) Electrical attraction occurs between oppositely charged objects but also occurs between neutral objects and charged objects. One can say for certain that at least one of the pieces of tape is charged.

366. (A) Newton's third law states that forces between two interacting systems are equal in magnitude, therefore $F_{e_{\alpha}\text{ on p}} = F_{e_{\text{p on }\alpha}}$ and $F_{g_{\alpha}\text{ on p}} = F_{g_{\text{p on }\alpha}}$. Electric forces are significantly stronger than gravitational forces on the atomic scale. Therefore,

$$\boxed{F_{e_{\alpha}\text{ on p}} = F_{e_{\text{p on }\alpha}} \gg F_{g_{\alpha}\text{ on p}} = F_{g_{\text{p on }\alpha}}}$$

367. (D) Millikan's oil drop experiment determined the fundamental charge of a single electron to be approximately 1.6×10^{-19} C. All drops are charged ("quantized") to integer multiples of this value because they have one, two, three, or more electrons on them. Some expected values for charge are as follows:

$2 * 1.6 \times 10^{-19}$ C $= 3.2 \times 10^{-19}$ C

$3 * 1.6 \times 10^{-19}$ C $= 4.8 \times 10^{-19}$ C

$4 * 1.6 \times 10^{-19}$ C $= 6.4 \times 10^{-19}$ C

$5 * 1.6 \times 10^{-19}$ C $= 8.0 \times 10^{-19}$ C

$6 * 1.6 \times 10^{-19}$ C $= 9.6 \times 10^{-19}$ C

$7 * 1.6 \times 10^{-19}$ C $= 11.2 \times 10^{-19}$ C

Trial 3 is clearly flawed, because it has about half the charge of an electron. All other trials are close to being integer multiples of the fundamental charge. Trial 4 has the biggest variation from the expected value: $\% = \dfrac{(3.41 - 3.20)}{3.20} * 100 = 6.6 \approx 7\%$.

368. (B) According to the law of conservation of charge, charge cannot be created or destroyed. Thus, the net charge of an isolated system must remain constant. In order for the system to remain neutral, the magnitude of the charge on the negative rubber rod must equal the magnitude of the positive charge on the wool fabric.

369. (B) Since the paper is an insulator, the electrons tend to stay within their individual atoms. The positive tape can attract the (negative) electrons within the atoms to the side closest to the tape, and an attraction occurs. This phenomenon is known as electric polarization. Note: The protons are fixed within the nucleus and do not flow through objects; electrons are the "fluid" responsible for electrostatic phenomena.

370. (B) Protons are fixed within the nucleus and do not flow from atom to atom through objects.

371. (D) The leaves are repelling each other, so they both have the same charge, either positive or negative. The electroscope must have been touched by a charged object at some point in time.

372. (C) Electrons are the only subatomic particle which can flow easily through conductors. The (negative) electrons in the electroscope flow up toward the positive rod because opposites attract. Thus the gold leaves are now positive because they are missing electrons. The like-charged leaves now repel.

373. (B) In a positive electroscope, the leaves stand apart because they have like charges. If they come together, that means that they must be approaching the neutral state, and this is achieved by sending electrons to the leaves. A negative rod held near the metal ball will do just that by inducing (negative) electrons to move into the leaves. Note: A positive electroscope still has valance electrons that can flow freely through the electroscope, so transfer of electrons from the rod into the electroscope is not necessary.

374. (A) The charges and masses of the particles are available in the AP "Constants and Conversion Factors" table. Coulomb's law may first be used to find the force of attraction between the particles:

$$\left|\vec{F}_E\right| = k\frac{|q_1 q_2|}{r^2}$$

$$\left|\vec{F}_E\right| = k\frac{|q_{electron} q_{proton}|}{r^2}$$

Next, the acceleration may be found by using Newton's second law. Since the electron has less mass, it will accelerate at a great rate.

$$a = \frac{\vec{F}_{net}}{m} = \frac{\vec{F}_E}{m_{electron}} = \frac{k\frac{|q_{electron} q_{proton}|}{r^2}}{m_{electron}}$$

$$a = \frac{9.0 \times 10^9 \frac{Nm^2}{C^2}\left|\left(-1.60 \times 10^{-19} C\right)\left(1.60 \times 10^{-19} C\right)\right|}{\left(1.5 \times 10^{-10}\ m\right)^2}{9.11 \times 10^{-31}\ kg} \rightarrow \boxed{a = 1.12 \times 10^{22}\ \frac{m}{s^2}}$$

375. **(D)** Electrons and protons have the same magnitude of charges, so the force from the proton at (0, 1) is the same magnitude as the force from the electron at (1, 0). The proton applies an upward attractive force on the electron at the origin. The electron at (0, 1) applies a leftward repulsive force on the electron at the origin. The net force on the electron is up and to the left on the coordinate plane, at an angle of 135 degrees.

376. **(D)** The electric force is found from Coulomb's law, and the gravitational force is found from the universal law of gravitation:

$$\frac{\left|\vec{F}_E\right|}{\left|\vec{F}_g\right|} = \frac{k\dfrac{\left|q_{electron}q_{proton}\right|}{r^2}}{G\dfrac{\left|m_{electron}m_{proton}\right|}{r^2}}$$

$$\frac{\left|\vec{F}_E\right|}{\left|\vec{F}_g\right|} = \frac{k\left|q_{electron}q_{proton}\right|}{G\left|m_{electron}m_{proton}\right|}$$

$$\frac{\left|\vec{F}_E\right|}{Fg} = \frac{9.0\times10^9\,\dfrac{Nm^2}{C^2}\left|\left(-1.60\times10^{-19}C\right)\left(1.60\times10^{-19}C\right)\right|}{6.67\times10^{-11}\,\dfrac{Nm^2}{kg^2}\left|\left(9.11\times10^{-31}kg\right)\left(1.67\times10^{-27}kg\right)\right|}$$

$$\frac{\left|\vec{F}_E\right|}{\left|\vec{Fg}\right|} = 2.27\times10^{39}$$

377. **(D)** This sphere is positive, so it must have more protons than electrons. Divide the net charge by the fundamental charge as follows:

$$\text{Excess \# of protons} = \frac{+4.0\times10^{-15}C}{+1.6\times10^{-19}\,\dfrac{C}{proton}} \rightarrow \boxed{25,000 \text{ extra protons}}$$

378. **(D)** Objects B and C must be charged in the same way (and not neutral) since they repel. Since the positive Object A is attracted to Object B and opposites attract, B must be negative (note that attraction may also be observed between charged objects and neutral objects, but it has been established that Object B is charged). Since the negative Object B is repelled from Object C and like charges repel, C must be negative. Since the negative Object C is attracted to Object D, then D must be positive or neutral.

379. **(D)** The net charge on both spheres is 12 μC − 8 μC = +4 μC. Since they are both identical conductors, the electrons will quickly seek equilibrium where they share the same charge. When separated, they will each have +2 μC.

380. (D) The positive glass rod will attract many valance electrons to the left sphere. When the spheres are separated, those electrons are now trapped on the left sphere, making it negatively charged. The sphere on the right is missing electrons, and is thus equally positively charged.

381. (D) Neutral objects attract both positive and negative objects. Thus the foil *may be neutral.* Positive and negative objects also attract. Thus the foil *may also be positive* to attract to the negative balloon.

382. (B) The balloon is an insulator, so the charge will not flow throughout the balloon but will rather stay in the location where the friction with the wool cloth caused the charge separation. Since the balloon is negative, excess electrons are on the balloon in the location where it was rubbed on the wool.

383. (C) This process is called "charging by induction and grounding." The negative rod repels many of the valance electrons in the conducting sphere to the person. When the person disconnects his finger, the sphere is now positive because it's missing electrons.

384. (C) Since the nuclei are positive and electrons are negative, the force will be attractive. The force of the nucleus on the electron is equal to the force of the electron on the nucleus because all interaction forces are equal and opposite according to Newton's third law. This can be also be shown with Coulomb's law, $\left|\vec{F}_E\right| = k\dfrac{|q_1 q_2|}{r^2}$, because the same electrostatic force is calculated regardless of which charge is q_1 and which is q_2.

385. (A) Sphere A must have gained electrons in the charging process (the protons stay fixed in the nucleus and are not transferred in solids in an electrostatic experiment). The number of excess electrons on Sphere A are calculated as follows:

$$\text{Excess \# of electrons} = \frac{-1.28 \times 10^{-13} \text{C}}{-1.60 \times 10^{-19} \dfrac{\text{C}}{\text{electron}}} = 800,000 \text{ electrons}$$

The mass of these extra electrons is calculated as follows:

$$800,000 \text{ electrons} \left(9.11 \times 10^{-31} \frac{\text{kg}}{\text{electron}} \right) = \boxed{7.29 \times 10^{-25} \text{ kg}}$$

386. (B) Coulomb's law may be solved for the distance between the charges:

$$\left|\vec{F_E}\right| = k\frac{|q_1 q_2|}{r^2}$$

$$r = \sqrt{k\frac{|q_1 q_2|}{\left|\vec{F_E}\right|}}$$

$$r = \sqrt{k\frac{|(e)(4e)|}{F}}$$

$$r = \sqrt{k\frac{4e^2}{F}}$$

$$r = \sqrt{k\frac{(2e)^2}{F}} \rightarrow \boxed{r = 2e\sqrt{\frac{k}{F}}}$$

387. (A) When Sphere A and Sphere B touch, the net charge is $+ 10 \ \mu C - 6 \ \mu C = +4$ μC, and so each sphere gets $+2 \ \mu C$ when they are separated. Now, when Sphere B and Sphere C touch, the net charge is $+ 2 \ \mu C - 4 \ \mu C = -2 \ \mu C$, and so each sphere gets -1 μC when the spheres are separated.

388. (A) The nuclei have the same charge, so the hydrogen nucleus will be repelled from the helium nucleus. Coulomb's law $\left(\left|\vec{F_E}\right| = k\frac{|q_1 q_2|}{r^2}\right)$ predicts that the force between them will decrease significantly as the distance between them increases. Since Newton's second law $\left(a = \frac{\vec{F}_{net}}{m}\right)$ states that acceleration is directly proportional to the net force, and it's known that force decreases with distance, then the hydrogen nucleus will move away from the helium nucleus with a *decreasing acceleration rate*.

389. (B, D) The fundamental charge is 1.6×10^{-19} C, which is the magnitude of the charge of an electron or proton, and all charges are integer multiples of this value (e.g., there cannot be a half of an electron or proton charge). Options B and D yield integer values of the fundamental charge.

390. (A, D) Coulomb's law $\left(\left|\vec{F_E}\right| = k\frac{|q_1 q_2|}{r^2}\right)$ demonstrates that the magnitude of the electric force depends on the charges of each object and the distance, r, that they are separated.

391. (A, C) Since the two-sphere system is isolated from its surroundings, the total charge of the system must be conserved. The total charge before the spheres touch is: $q_1 + q_2 = +5\mu C - 17 \mu C = -12\mu C$, and so the sum of the charges after they touch must also be the same:

Option A's charges add up properly: $q_1 + q_2 = -4\mu C - 8\mu C = -12\mu C$.

Option C's charges also add up properly: $q_1 + q_2 = -6\mu C - 6\mu C = -12\mu C$.

392. (A, B) Oppositely charged objects attract. Also, neutral objects attract both positive and negative objects. Objects that are charged in the same way cannot attract each other.

393. (A, B) Coulomb's law $\left(\left|\vec{F_E}\right| = k\dfrac{|q_1 q_2|}{r^2}\right)$ may be used to reason through this answer. If both electrons are replaced with protons, they will still repel, and since they have the same magnitude of charge, the magnitude of the force will be the same. (If only one electron is replaced with a proton, the magnitude of the force will remain the same, but the force will change to an attractive force.) Since the electrostatic force is directly proportional to the product of the charges, then if both charges are doubled, the force will quadruple. However, the fact that the distance is doubled cancels this quadrupling effect, because the electrostatic force is inversely proportional to the square of the distance.

394. The $-1.6\ \mu C$ charge repels the $-3.2\ \mu C$ charge to the left, and the $+4.8\ \mu C$ charge attracts the $-3.2\ \mu C$ charge to the left:

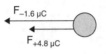

395. The net force is to the left and is the sum of the two forces in the diagram above. Using Coulomb's law:

$$\left|\vec{F_E}\right| = k\frac{q_1 q_2}{r^2}$$

$$\left|\vec{F_E}\right| = \left(9.0\times10^9\ \frac{\text{Nm}^2}{\text{C}^2}\ \frac{\left|\left(+4.8\times10^{-6}\ \text{C}\right)\left(-3.2\times10^{-6}\ \text{C}\right)\right|}{\left(0.0040\ \text{m}\right)^2}\right)$$

$$+ \left(9.0\times10^9\ \frac{\text{Nm}^2}{\text{C}^2}\ \frac{\left|\left(-1.6\times10^{-6}\ \text{C}\right)\left(-3.2\times10^{-6}\ \text{C}\right)\right|}{\left(0.0020\ \text{m}\right)^2}\right)$$

$$\left|\vec{F_E}\right| = \left(8{,}640\ \text{N}\right) + \left(11{,}520\ \text{N}\right) =$$
$$\left|\vec{F_E}\right| = 2.016\times10^4\ \text{N} \rightarrow \boxed{\left|\vec{F_E}\right| \approx 2.0\times10^4\ \text{N}}\ \text{to the left}$$

396. The acceleration is calculated from Newton's second law:

$$a = \frac{F_{\text{net}}}{m}$$

$$a = \frac{2.016\times10^4\ \text{N}}{0.075\ \text{kg}} \rightarrow \boxed{a = 2.7\times10^5\ \frac{\text{m}}{\text{s}^2}}\ \text{(to the left)}$$

397. When the $-6.4\ \mu C$ pith ball touches the neutral pith ball and then separates, they each will share the charge of $-3.2\ \mu C$.

398. The force diagram looks like this:

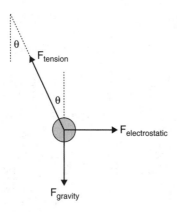

399. The gravitational force is $F_g = \left(10 \dfrac{N}{kg}\right)(0.024 \text{ kg}) = 0.24$ N. The electrostatic force is calculated from Coulomb's law:

$$\left|\vec{F}_E\right| = k \frac{|q_1 q_2|}{r^2}$$

$$\left|\vec{F}_E\right| = 9.0 \times 10^9 \frac{\text{Nm}^2}{\text{C}^2} \frac{\left|(-3.2 \times 10^{-6} \text{ C})(-3.2 \times 10^{-6} \text{ C})\right|}{(0.52 \text{ m})^2} \rightarrow \boxed{\left|\vec{F}_E\right| = 0.34 \text{ N}}$$

400. The angle theta in the force diagram is half the angle between the threads. To keep the pith ball in equilibrium, the angle is calculated by:

$$\theta = \tan^{-1}\left(\frac{F_{\text{electrostatic}}}{F_{\text{gravity}}}\right)$$

$$\theta = \tan^{-1}\left|\frac{0.34 \text{ N}}{0.24 \text{ N}}\right| = 55°$$

Therefore, the total angle between the threads is 110°.

Chapter 9: DC Circuits

401. (B) First, find the equivalent resistance of the resistors by adding the resistances. Then, use Ohm's law to find the current:

$$R_{eq} = R_1 + R_2 + R_3$$
$$R_{eq} = 3\,\Omega + 1\,\Omega + 2\,\Omega$$
$$R_{eq} = 6\,\Omega$$
$$I = \frac{V}{R_{eq}}$$
$$I = \frac{(12 \text{ V})}{(6\,\Omega)}$$
$$I = 2 \text{ A}$$

402. (D) In a series circuit, the current is equal in all parts of the circuit according to conservation of charge. However, the voltage drops across each resistor following Ohm's law $(\Delta V = IR)$. Since R_1 has the greatest resistance and it has the same current as the other resistors, it has the greatest voltage drop across it.

403. (D) First, find the equivalent resistance of the resistors by adding the resistances. Then, use Ohm's law to find the current:

$$R_{eq} = R_1 + R_2 + R_3$$
$$R_{eq} = 3\,\Omega + 1\,\Omega + 2\,\Omega$$
$$R_{eq} = 6\,\Omega$$
$$I = \frac{V}{R_{eq}}$$
$$I = \frac{(12\text{ V})}{(6\,\Omega)} = 2\text{ A}$$

The total power dissipated by the resistors is the same as the power output of the battery. Power is the product of the total voltage drop (12 V) and the current (2 A):

$$P = IV$$
$$P = (2\text{ A})(12\text{ V}) \rightarrow \boxed{P = 24\text{ W}}$$

404. (B) As the temperature increases, the resistivity of the wire increases. Since resistance is directly proportional to resistivity, the resistance increases. For a fixed potential difference, the current is inversely proportional to resistance, so the current decreases with increasing resistance.

405. (A) In a parallel circuit, each device has the same potential difference across it, which is 12.0V in this case.

406. (D) In a parallel circuit, the current gets divided among the branches and the voltage is the same across each device. According to Ohm's law $\left(I = \dfrac{\Delta V}{R}\right)$, current is inversely proportional to the resistance when voltage is fixed. Therefore, since $R_3 > R_1 > R_2$, then $I_2 > I_1 > I_3$.

407. (C) First, calculate the current from the charge and time. Then, find the voltage from Ohm's law:

$$I = \frac{\Delta q}{\Delta t}$$
$$I = \frac{(40\text{ C})}{(80\text{ s})} = 0.5\text{ A}$$
$$V = IR$$
$$V = (0.5\text{ A})(10\,\Omega) \rightarrow \boxed{V = 5.0\text{ V}}$$

408. **(C)** Combine Ohm's law and the power equation, and then solve for the resistance:

$$P = IV$$
$$V = IR$$
$$P = I(IR)$$
$$P = I^2 R$$

$$R = \frac{P}{I^2}$$
$$R = \frac{(1 \times 10^5 \text{ W})}{(5 \text{ A})^2}$$
$$R = 4 \times 10^3 \text{ } \Omega \rightarrow \boxed{R = 4 \text{ k}\Omega}$$

409. **(D)** First, calculate the equivalent resistance of the resistors in series; then use Ohm's law to find the value of the battery voltage:

$$R_{eq} = R_1 + R_2 + R_3$$
$$R_{eq} = 20 \text{ } \Omega + 10 \text{ } \Omega + 30 \text{ } \Omega$$
$$R_{eq} = 60 \text{ } \Omega$$
$$V = IR_{eq}$$
$$V = (2 \text{ A}) (60 \text{ } \Omega) \rightarrow \boxed{V = 120 \text{ V}}$$

410. **(D)** Use Ohm's law to calculate the voltage drop across the 30-Ω resistor when the current is 5 A:

$$\Delta V_3 = IR_3$$
$$\Delta V_3 = (5 \text{ A}) (30 \text{ } \Omega) \rightarrow \boxed{\Delta V_3 = 150 \text{ V}}$$

411. **(A)** According to Kirchhoff's laws, the sum of all the voltages around a closed loop is zero.

412. **(C)** The potential difference V across a device is the amount of energy transferred for each coulomb of electric charge that flows through the device. By definition of units, $V = \dfrac{J}{C}$. Thus, a 12-volt car battery transfers 12 joules of energy for each and every coulomb of electric charge that passes through it.

413. (B) First, calculate the equivalent resistance of the parallel branch of the circuit ($Req_{\parallel}$). Use that to calculate the equivalent resistance of the series circuits:

$$\frac{1}{R_{eq\parallel}} = \frac{1}{R_2} + \frac{1}{R_3}$$

$$\frac{1}{R_{eq\parallel}} = \frac{1}{(10\,\Omega)} + \frac{1}{(20\,\Omega)}$$

$$\frac{1}{R_{eq\parallel}} = 0.15\,\Omega^{-1}$$

$$R_{eq\parallel} = 6.7\,\Omega$$

$$R_{eq} = R_1 + R_{eq\parallel} + R_4$$

$$R_{eq} = 10\,\Omega + 6.7\,\Omega + 45\,\Omega = 61.7\,\Omega$$

Now, use Ohm's law to calculate the current moving through the circuit. That current must be equal between the first resistor, the parallel branch of resistors, and the final resistor. So, the current leaving the parallel branch must be the same as that which entered it (Kirchhoff's law):

$$I = \frac{\Delta V}{R_{eq}}$$

$$I = \frac{(120\text{ V})}{(61.7\,\Omega)} \rightarrow \boxed{I = 1.9\text{ A}}$$

414. (A) When the resistor is used in normal operating conditions, its resistance stays constant. Ohm's law ($I = \dfrac{\Delta V}{R}$) shows that current and potential difference are directly proportional. Thus, when the voltage is doubled, its current doubles proportionately.

415. (B) The relationship between these variables is given as $R = \dfrac{\rho\ell}{A}$. The cross-sectional area must first be converted to meters: $A = (4.0\text{ mm}^2)\left(\dfrac{(10^{-3})^2\text{ m}^2}{\text{mm}^2}\right) = 4.0\times10^{-6}\text{ m}^2$

$$R = \frac{(1.7\times10^{-8}\,\Omega\text{m})(1.5\text{ m})}{(4.0\times10^{-6}\text{ m}^2)}$$

$$R = 6.4\times10^{-3}\,\Omega$$

416. (B) The law of conservation of charge may be applied at the junction at the top of the circuit where the three wires come together using Kirchhoff's junction rule. The current flowing into the junction equals the current flowing out, thus $I_1 = I_2 + I_3$. Since resistor #1 and resistor #4 are in series within the same branch of the circuit, they must have the same current according to the law of conservation of charge. Therefore, $\boxed{I_1 = I_4 = I_2 + I_3}$.

417. (D) First, apply Kirchhoff's loop rule (conservation of energy) to the small, left-hand loop of the circuit:

$$\Delta V - I_1 R_1 - I_2 R_2 + I_4 R_4 = 0$$

Since resistors #1 and #4 are in series, they have the same current according to the law of conservation of charge. Thus,

$$\Delta V - I_1 R_1 - I_2 R_2 + I_1 R_4 = 0 \rightarrow \boxed{\Delta V - I_1 (R_1 + R_4) - I_2 R_2 = 0}$$

418. (D) When the switch is open, there is no pathway for current to flow through bulb #2 so it will not light. Identical bulbs #1 and #3 are now in series and will get the same current according to the law of conservation of change. With the same current and the same resistance (identical bulbs), they must have the same potential difference across them. Power is the rate at which energy transfers in a device and is used to compare brightness. Since power is the product of current and voltage, bulb #1 and #3 have the same brightness.

419. (D)

The power of a bulb is $P = I\Delta V$. Combining this with Ohm's law $\Delta V = IR$:

$$P = I(IR)$$
$$P = I^2 R$$

Let I be the current flowing through bulb #1 and R be resistance of each bulb, then $P_1 = I^2 R$

As the current flows from bulb #1 into the junction into bulbs #2 and #3, Kirchhoff's junction rule predicts $I = I_2 + I_3$. Since bulbs #2 and #3 are identical, then $I_2 = I_3 = \dfrac{I}{2}$. Now applying the derived power equation above:

$$P_2 = P_3 = \left(\frac{I}{2}\right)^2 R$$

$$P_2 = P_3 = \frac{1}{4} I^2 R$$

Thus, bulb #2 has one-fourth the power of bulb #1.

420. (A) When the switch is closed, the resistance of the entire circuit decreases because there is another pathway for current to flow. With less circuit resistance, the current will increase through the battery and bulb #1. With more current running through it (and the same resistance), Ohm's law predicts that the potential difference across bulb #1 will also increase.

421. (C) The relationship between resistance and cross-sectional area is embedded in the following relationship: $R = \dfrac{\rho L}{A}$. In their experiment, length and resistivity should have been controlled, so resistance is inversely proportional to cross-sectional area.

422. (A) The relationship between resistance and cross-sectional area is embedded in the following relationship:

$$R = \frac{\rho L}{A}$$

$$R = \left(\frac{\rho}{A}\right)L$$

The second form of the equation above shows that when they graph resistance vs. length, the slope should be $\dfrac{\rho}{A}$. Solving for resistivity yields $\boxed{\rho = slope * A}$

423. (B) Resistivity (and thus resistance) depends on the temperature of the wire, and this will have a significant effect on the experimental results if it's not controlled. Differing voltages will result in proportionate changes in current without affecting the resistance (assuming that temperature is not affected). The incremental changes in the independent variable (in this case, wire length) will *not* affect the resistance of the wire or the slope of the graph. In order to measure current in the wire, the ammeter must be placed in series, so this was also not a problem in their experiment.

424. (B) Voltage across the resistors is as follows:
  I. The same potential difference, V, will be measured for the battery and the resistor.
  II. According to Kirchhoff's loop rule (conservation of energy), the voltages must add up to the voltage provided by the battery, so each resistor will measure the voltage V/2.
  III. Voltage is constant in parallel, so each resistor will get the full voltage of the battery, V.
  IV. According to Kirchhoff's loop rule (conservation of energy), the voltages must add up to the voltage provided by the battery, so since the battery has a voltage 2V, each resistor will measure the voltage V.

425. (C) In all parts of a series circuit with different resistors, the resistances are different, the voltage drops are different, and the current is the same.

426. (C) The resistance of a wire is given by $R = \dfrac{\rho \ell}{A}$. This shows that resistance is directly proportional to length and inversely proportional to cross-sectional area. Doubling the length will double the resistance. Doubling the area will reduce the resistance to one-half of its value. Changing both variables will result in no change to the resistance and thus no change to the current flowing through it.

427. **(A)** The resistivity (ρ) of a wire increases with temperature because greater molecular vibrations in the atoms of the wire make it more difficult for the electrons to flow. Resistance is directly proportional to resistivity $\left(R = \dfrac{\rho \ell}{A} \right)$.

428. **(C)** Power is the rate at which energy transfers from a device; thus the energy transfer may be found by multiplying the power by the time:

$$P = I \Delta V = \left(\frac{\Delta V}{R} \right) \Delta V = \left(\frac{\Delta V^2}{R} \right)$$

$$P = \left[\frac{(120 \text{ V})^2}{12 \ \Omega} \right] = 1,200 \text{ W} = 1,200 \ \frac{\text{J}}{\text{s}}$$

$$E_{\text{transferred}} = P \Delta t = \left(\frac{\Delta V^2}{R} \right) \Delta t$$

$$E_{\text{transferred}} = \left(1,200 \ \frac{\text{J}}{\text{s}} \right)(7,200 \text{ s}) \rightarrow \boxed{E_{\text{transferred}} = 8.6 \times 10^6 \text{ J}}$$

429. **(D)** According to Kirchhoff's junction rule (i.e., conservation of charge flow), the currents of the two resistors in parallel must add together and feed into the series part of the circuit. Thus, 1.5 A + 1.5 A = 3.0 A. Since current is constant in series, both the 20-Ω resistor and the power supply will get 3.0 A.

430. **(B)** In a series circuit, the equivalent resistance is $R + R = 2R$. Therefore, using Ohm's law, the circuit's current is $I = \dfrac{\Delta V}{R_{\text{series}}} = \dfrac{\Delta V}{2R}$. Plugging this into the power equation:

$$P = I \left(\Delta V \right)$$

$$P = \frac{\Delta V}{2R} \left(\Delta V \right) = \frac{\Delta V^2}{2R} \rightarrow \boxed{P = \frac{\Delta V^2}{2R}}$$

431. **(A)** Power is the rate at which energy transfers in a device, so this is what needs to be found. In a series circuit, the equivalent resistance is $R + R = 2R$. Therefore, using Ohm's law, the circuit's current is $I = \dfrac{\Delta V}{R_{\text{series}}} = \dfrac{\Delta V}{2R}$. Since current is constant in series, each individual resistor gets this current. The power equation needs to be arranged in terms of current and individual resistance using Ohm's law as follows:

$$P = I \left(\Delta V \right) = I \left(IR \right) = I^2 R$$

Plugging the earlier expression for current in this new expression:

$$P = \left(\frac{\Delta V}{2R} \right)^2 R \rightarrow \boxed{P = \frac{\Delta V^2}{4R}}$$

432. (C) Power is the rate at which energy transfers in a device, so this is what needs to be found. Since voltage is constant across each device in parallel, each individual resistor gets the full voltage. The power equation needs to be arranged in terms of this voltage and individual resistance using Ohm's law as follows:

$$P = I(\Delta V)$$

$$P = \frac{\Delta V}{R}(\Delta V) \rightarrow \boxed{P = \frac{\Delta V^2}{R}}$$

433. (D) According to $R = \frac{\rho \ell}{A}$, resistance is inversely proportional to cross-sectional area A and directly proportional to length ℓ. Therefore, halving the length will reduce the resistance to one-half as much. Doubling the area alone will also reduce the resistance to one-half as much. Changing both variables will result in one-fourth as much resistance.

434. (B) The junction rule states that the current flowing into any junction in a circuit equals the current flowing out of that same junction. Since current is the rate of flow of electric charge, Kirchhoff's junction rule is an expression of the law of conservation of charge. Kirchhoff's loop rule, on the other hand, states that the sum of the potential differences around any complete loop of a circuit must be zero. Electric potential difference (sometimes called voltage) is the energy transferred per unit of charge in a device. As you proceed around a circuit, some devices add energy to the circuit (e.g., a battery) and have a positive potential difference. Other devices transfer energy out of a circuit (e.g., a resistor) and have a negative potential difference. Energy cannot be created or destroyed, so in the end the positive and negative differences in potential must sum to zero. This is an expression of the law of conservation of energy.

435. (B) The parallel circuit II behaves like two basic circuits because each bulb gets the full voltage of the battery, thus circuit II will pull twice the current compared to circuit I. With two series resistors, circuit II has twice the resistance of circuit I, and so circuit II will only pull half the current of circuit I. Therefore, $I_{\mathrm{II}} > I_{\mathrm{I}} > I_{\mathrm{III}}$.

436. (D) Since all the bulbs are identical, they all have the same resistance. Bulbs 1, 2, and 3 all have the same potential difference across them from the battery and will draw the same current according to Ohm's Law $\left(I = \frac{\Delta V}{R}\right)$. They will also output energy at the same rate according to the power equation $P = I\Delta V$, and power measures brightness. The bulbs in circuit III each have half of the potential difference provided by the battery according to Kirchhoff's loop rule and will also draw half the current according to Ohm's law. Thus they each transfer power at a quarter of the rate $\left(P = \frac{I}{2} \cdot \frac{\Delta V}{2} = \frac{I\Delta V}{4}\right)$. The final ranking is $\boxed{B_1 = B_2 = B_3 > B_4 = B_5}$.

437. **(A)** First, combine the power equation $\left(P=I\Delta V\right)$ and Ohm's law $I=\dfrac{\Delta V}{R}$ to write an expression for power in terms of R and ΔV only:

$$P=\left(\frac{\Delta V}{R}\right)\Delta V=\frac{\Delta V^2}{R}$$

Circuit I: $P=\dfrac{\Delta V^2}{R}$

Circuit II: $P=\Delta V^2\left(\dfrac{1}{R_P}\right)=\Delta V^2\left(\dfrac{1}{R}+\dfrac{1}{R}\right)=2\dfrac{\Delta V^2}{R}$

Circuit III: $P=\dfrac{\Delta V^2}{R_S}=\dfrac{\Delta V^2}{R+R}=\dfrac{1}{2}\dfrac{\Delta V^2}{R}$

Total Power = $P=\dfrac{\Delta V^2}{R}+2\dfrac{\Delta V^2}{R}+\dfrac{1}{2}\dfrac{\Delta V^2}{R}\rightarrow\boxed{P=\dfrac{7}{2}\dfrac{\Delta V^2}{R}}$

438. **(A, D)** Every element in a series circuit has the same current, and the equivalent resistance is the sum of all the resistances.

439. **(B, D)** The resistance of a wire is given by $R=\dfrac{\rho\ell}{A}$. The ratio of voltage to current is a constant for a wire, so their individual values do NOT affect the resistance.

440. **(B, D)** The battery is neutral and has energy to move electrons that already exist throughout the entire circuit, including the battery itself. According to the law of conservation of charge, electrons cannot be created or destroyed, so the electron flow (the current) will be the same throughout the circuit, and the electrons will remain in it.

441. **(B, C)** Power is defined as the rate of energy transfer in a circuit and is calculated as follows: $P=I\Delta V$.

442. **(A, D)** Energy cannot be created or destroyed. In a simple circuit, the chemical energy stored in the battery is transferred to thermal energy at the resistor. When the battery "dies," the chemical reactions are complete and the resistor and the environment have now been heated.

443. The battery provides the current to both resistor 3's branch and the branch containing the other two resistors (conservation of charge), thus the battery current is the greatest. Since both parallel branches in the circuit have the same potential difference applied from the battery, the branch with less resistance will receive more current according to Ohm's law $\left(I=\dfrac{\Delta V}{R}\right)$. Given $R_1+R_2<R_3$, this means that resistor #3 will get more current than the higher resistance branch containing resistors #1 and #2. Finally, since resistors #1 and #2 are in series, they have will have the same current (conservation of charge). Thus, $I_{BAT}>I_3>I_1=I_2$.

444. The potential difference between points "a" and "b" is the same as the voltage across resistor #2, thus $\Delta V_2 = 4V$. Since resistor #1 and resistor #2 are in series, they have the same current flowing through them (due to the law of conservation of charge), and since those two resistors have the same value of resistance, the potential difference across both of them must be the same according to Ohm's law. Thus $\Delta V_1 = \Delta V_{ab} = 4V$. Looking at the large outer loop in the circuit and applying Kirchhoff's loop rule, the sum of the potential differences across the two identical resistors must equal the potential difference across the battery: $\Delta V_{BAT} = 4V + 4V = 8V$. Finally, since the battery's voltage is impressed across resistor 3, $\Delta V_3 = \Delta V_{BAT} = 8V$.

445. To find the power delivered to the circuit by the battery, the current must be found. First, find the equivalent resistance of the circuit. The two series branch resistance is $R_s = R + R = 2R$. This branch is in parallel with the third resistor, and so the equivalent resistance is:

$$\frac{1}{R_{eq}} = \frac{1}{2R} + \frac{1}{R}$$

$$\frac{1}{R_{eq}} = \frac{1}{2R} + \frac{2}{2R}$$

$$\frac{1}{R_{eq}} = \frac{3}{2R}$$

$$R_{eq} = \frac{2R}{3}$$

Next, the battery current is found from Ohm's law:

$$I = \frac{\Delta V_{BAT}}{R_{eq}}$$

$$I = \frac{\Delta V_{BAT}}{\left(\dfrac{2R}{3}\right)}$$

$$I = \frac{3\Delta V_{BAT}}{2R}$$

Finally, power is calculated as follows:

$$P = I\Delta V_{BAT}$$

$$P = \left(\frac{3\Delta V_{BAT}}{2R}\right)\Delta V_{BAT} \rightarrow \boxed{P = \frac{3\Delta V_{BAT}^2}{2R}}$$

446. The current through the battery will increase. When resistor #2 is shorted, no current will flow through that resistor and the resistance in that upper branch will only be from resistor #1. With less resistance in the upper branch, more current must flow through it. Resistor 3's branch will still have the same current, because it still has the same potential difference across it from the battery. Since the current from the battery equals the sum of the current in both branches (according to the law of conservation of charge), the new circuit will demand more current.

447. The equivalent resistance increases linearly as you increase the number of resistors in series. In contrast, the equivalent resistance decreases as you increase the number of resistors in parallel because more pathways are open.

448. The current in the power supply decreases as you increase the number of resistors in series because current is inversely related to resistance for a fixed voltage (rearrange Ohm's law to get $I = \Delta V / R$) and the equivalent resistance is increasing. In contrast, the current increases linearly as you increase the number of resistors in parallel because the equivalent resistance decreases.

449. In the series circuit, the equivalent resistance increases with an increasing number of resistors, and the power decreases inversely for a fixed potential difference as follows:

$$P = I\Delta V = \left(\frac{\Delta V}{R_{eq}}\right)\Delta V = \left(\frac{\Delta V^2}{R_{eq}}\right)$$

In contrast, in the parallel circuit, the equivalent resistance decreases with an increasing number of resistors, and so the total power increases linearly with the number of resistors.

450. Power is the rate of flow of energy and corresponds to the brightness of the bulbs. Since the current is constant in a series circuit, the power in each individual bulb may be calculated as follows: $P = I\Delta V = I(IR) = I^2 R$. Since the current of the circuit decreases as the number of lightbulbs in the string increases, the brightness of the bulbs also decreases. For a parallel string of lights, the power of each bulb is calculated as follows:

$$P = I\Delta V = \left(\frac{\Delta V}{R}\right)\Delta V = \left(\frac{\Delta V^2}{R}\right)$$

Since each bulb gets the same voltage in parallel, the lights will get the same power and stay equally bright (although this happens within limits).

Chapter 10: Mechanical Waves and Sound

451. (D) According to the AP Physics 1 Course and Exam Description, "A wave is a disturbance that carries energy and momentum from one place to another without the transfer of matter."

452. (B) Amplitude is the vertical distance between the equilibrium position (the zero line) and the crest of the wave, which is 20 cm in this diagram. Wavelength is the horizontal distance of one complete wave, which is approximately 5 cm in this diagram.

453. (B) A wave is classified by the way the medium vibrates as the wave energy travels through it. In a transverse wave, that vibration is perpendicular to the motion of the wave, as opposed to the parallel vibration in the case of a longitudinal wave.

454. (B) The distance between adjacent rarefactions is the wavelength. Use the wave equations to find the wavelength as follows:

$$\lambda = \frac{v}{f}$$

$$\lambda = \frac{340 m/s}{20.0 \times 10^3 \frac{vibrations}{sec}} \rightarrow \boxed{\lambda = 0.017m}$$

455. (C) The two pulses will experience partial destructive interference. The resulting pulse has an amplitude = +A − A/3 = + 2A/3.

456. (C) After the pulses overlap, the pulses continue to travel in their original directions. One pulse (+A) continues traveling to the right while the other pulse (−A/3) continues traveling to the left.

457. (B) We are looking for the length, L, of the air column when the first ($n = 1$) resonance sound is heard. The frequency of the tuning fork is 440 Hz. At the temperature specified, the speed of sound is 343 m/s. First, find the wavelength of the sound wave using the wave equation.

$$\lambda = \frac{v}{f}$$

$$\lambda = \frac{343 \frac{m}{s}}{440 \frac{waves}{s}} = 0.78 \text{ m}$$

The length of a standing wave with one antinode and one node is a quarter of a wavelength, therefore the length of the air column is:

$$L = \frac{\lambda}{4} = \frac{0.78 \text{ m}}{4} \rightarrow \boxed{L = 0.19 \text{ m}}$$

458. (A) The speed of a radio wave is the speed of light (3×10^8 m/s), and the frequency is 100 MHz (1×10^8 Hz). Calculate the wavelength of the radio wave:

$$\lambda = \frac{v}{f}$$

$$\lambda = \frac{(3 \times 10^8 \text{ m/s})}{(1 \times 10^8 \text{ Hz})} \rightarrow \boxed{\lambda = 3 \text{ m}}$$

459. (A) When six waves pass a buoy in 3.0 seconds, two waves must pass by each and every second, so the frequency is 2.0 Hz. The 1.5-m distance between the waves is the wavelength. The speed of the waves is calculated from the wave equation:

$$\lambda = \frac{v}{f}$$

$$v = f\lambda$$

$$v = \left(2 \frac{\text{waves}}{\text{s}}\right)\left(1.5 \frac{\text{m}}{\text{wave}}\right) \rightarrow \boxed{v = 3.0 \frac{\text{m}}{\text{s}}}$$

460. (C) Solve the wave equation for frequency:

$$\lambda = \frac{v}{f} \rightarrow f = \frac{v}{\lambda}$$

$$f = \frac{\left(16 \frac{\text{m}}{\text{s}}\right)}{\left(4 \frac{\text{m}}{\text{wave}}\right)}$$

$$f = 4 \frac{\text{waves}}{\text{s}} \rightarrow \boxed{f = 4 \text{ Hz}}$$

461. (A) Sound beats are a result of the interference between two sounds of almost the same frequency. The observer hears a pitch (the average of the two original frequencies) that pulsates in loudness and a particular frequency (the difference between the two original frequencies).

462. (D) Sound waves travel at a constant speed through a uniform medium. Using the constant rate equation:

$$d = vt$$

$$d = \left(344 \frac{\text{m}}{\text{s}}\right)(2 \text{ s}) \rightarrow \boxed{d = 688 \text{ m}}$$

463. (B) The distance between compressions is the wavelength of the sound wave.

$$\lambda = \frac{v}{f}$$

$$\lambda = \frac{345 \,\frac{m}{s}}{256 \,\frac{waves}{s}} \rightarrow \boxed{\lambda = 1.35 \text{ m}}$$

464. (B) The two-way time is given, so to find the one-way distance, the time is divided in half:

$$d = vt$$

$$d = \left(1{,}400 \,\frac{m}{s}\right)\left(\frac{0.15 \text{ s}}{2}\right) \rightarrow \boxed{d = 105 \text{ m}}$$

465. (C) A Node-Antinode-Node pattern is half of a complete wave. Since half of a wave fits into the 0.50-m tube, its wavelength is 1.00 m. The wave equation is applied as follows:

$$\lambda = \frac{v}{f}$$

$$f = \frac{v}{\lambda}$$

$$f = \frac{343 \,\frac{m}{s}}{1.00 \text{ m}} \rightarrow \boxed{f = 343 \text{ Hz}}$$

466. (A) The diagram shows a characteristic sound beat pattern that occurs when two notes of almost the same frequency are played simultaneously. The sounds interfere to create a pattern with an amplitude (loudness) that increases and decreases at the "beat frequency." Since the graph shows that there are 6 beats in 3 seconds, the beat frequency is 2 beats per second, or 2 Hz. This 2 Hz vibration does not sound like a note because it's infrasonic; rather, it sounds like a note of varying loudness.

467. (B) In the previous question, it was determined that the beat frequency is 2 Hz. The difference between the two frequencies is the beat frequency. Since the first trumpet plays a 256 Hz note, the other trumpet may be playing a 254 Hz note or a 248 Hz note.

468. (D) To find the speed of a wave, the frequency and wavelength are needed. The period of vibration for a spring-mass system is $T_s = 2\pi\sqrt{\dfrac{m}{k}}$, and the frequency of vibration is found from the inverse of period: $f_s = \dfrac{1}{T_s} = \dfrac{1}{2\pi}\sqrt{\dfrac{k}{m}}$. The diagram shows that there are two complete wavelengths the length of the spring, so $\lambda = \dfrac{\ell}{2}$. Finally, speed is found from the wave equation:

$$\lambda = \frac{v}{f}$$
$$v = f\lambda$$
$$v = \left(\frac{1}{2\pi}\sqrt{\frac{k}{m}}\right)\left(\frac{\ell}{2}\right) \rightarrow \boxed{v = \frac{\ell}{4\pi}\sqrt{\frac{k}{m}}}$$

469. (D) The frequency of the disturbance remains the same since the mass and spring constant were not changed. Since the medium is the same (no change in tension or the rope characteristics), the speed will remain the same. Also, recall that the amplitude (vertical vibration distance) of the disturbance has no effect on wavelength, frequency, period, or wave speed.

470. (A, D) If the two transverse wave pulses are both crests, then they will constructively interfere with amplitude 10cm + 15cm = 25cm. If one pulse is a crest and the other is a trough, then they will destructively interfere with amplitude 15cm − 10cm = 5cm.

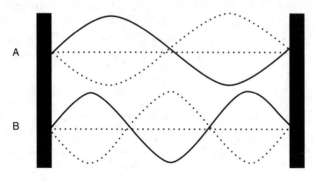

471. (A) The speed of a mechanical wave depends only on the medium, and since the strings are identical and have the same tension, the speeds are the same: $\boxed{v_A = v_B}$. String A's wavelength is one complete length of the string. String B's wavelength is shorter and is only 2/3 of the string length:

Let ℓ = string length

$$\lambda_A = \ell$$

$$\lambda_B = \frac{2}{3}\ell$$

$$\frac{\lambda_A}{\lambda_B} = \frac{\ell}{\frac{2}{3}\ell} = \frac{3}{2}$$

$$\frac{\lambda_A}{\lambda_B} = \frac{3}{2} \rightarrow \boxed{\lambda_A = \frac{3}{2}\lambda_B}$$

472. (C) This is a question about the Doppler effect. As a source of sound approaches an observer, a higher frequency than normal is heard, and as it leaves the observer, a lower frequency is heard. Thus, the observer hears the frequency (pitch) shift from high to low. The wave speed stays the same because the medium does not change.

473. (A) In a transverse wave on a rope, visualize each part of the rope vibrating up and down, perpendicular to the direction that the wave travels. Thus, all pieces of tape are traveling up, traveling down, or are instantaneously at rest. As the leading edge of the crest hits Point A, the tape was moving up but must stop before moving back down again, thus $\boxed{\vec{v}_A = 0}$. As the trailing edge of the trough was moving through point B, the tape was moving up and continues to move up through the equilibrium position as the leading edge of the crest hits it, thus $\boxed{\vec{v}_B = \text{up}}$. Since the trailing edge of the trough is also moving through point B, the tape must move up as it moves toward the equilibrium position, thus $\boxed{\vec{v}_C = \text{up}}$.

474. (C) To find the acceleration, one must look at the slope of the velocity versus time graph. Point A had a positive velocity (up) that's now stopping and transitioning to a negative velocity (down). This will have a negative slope, thus $\boxed{\vec{a}_A \text{ is down}}$. Point B had just sped up to its maximum positive velocity, is leveling off, and will start transitioning to a slower positive velocity. This gives an instantaneous zero slope on the velocity graph, thus, $\boxed{\vec{a}_B = 0}$. Point C has a positive velocity that's getting greater which gives a positive slope on the velocity graph, thus $\boxed{\vec{a}_C = \text{up}}$.

475. (B) Observer 1 is not moving relative to the source, so the passenger will hear the pitch with the same frequency and period as the observer at rest: $T_{\text{rest}} = T_1$. Observer 2 experiences the Doppler effect as the source moves toward her. Because the wave compressions are close together with a shorter wavelength, a higher frequency and shorter time period are measured. Observer 3 also experiences the Doppler effect as the source moves away from him. Because the wave compressions are farther apart with a longer wavelength, a lower frequency and greater time period are measured. Thus, the time periods compare as follows: $\boxed{T_3 > T_{\text{rest}} = T_1 > T_2}$.

476. (D) Amplitude is the size of the vertical vibration and sound #2 clearly has a larger amplitude. More vertical vibration indicates that the air molecules hitting the diaphragm of the microphone had a bigger displacement. For a human observer, this would mean a greater physical vibration of the eardrum which would sound louder. Frequency is how many complete vibrations occur each second. Sound #2 has a lower frequency which a human perceives as a lower pitch.

477. (C) Speed of sound depends solely on the medium and its characteristics. Since the air conditions are the same, the speeds are the same. Higher frequency sounds have shorter wavelengths but still have the same speed. Likewise, high and low amplitude waves also have the same speed.

478. (A) The oscilloscope display indicates the superposition of a high-frequency sound and a low-frequency sound. This is most likely the result of the interference pattern of a high pitch and a low pitch note simultaneously. If a single note is played with varying loudness, the trace would show a signal without the little fluctuations that grows in amplitude. If a single note is played with varying pitch, the trace would show a sine-wave with a period that gets shorter or longer. If two notes of almost the same frequency, were detected, the trace would show a beat pattern similar to the pattern in problem #466.

479. (A) According to the AP Physics 1 content outline, "For standing sound waves, pressure nodes correspond to displacement antinodes, and vice versa. For example, the open end of a tube is a pressure node because the pressure equalizes with the surrounding air pressure and therefore does not oscillate. The closed end of a tube is a displacement node because the air adjacent to the closed end is blocked from oscillating." Thus, the left end is a pressure node and the right end is a pressure antinode. Since the lowest resonant frequency is given, then there are no additional nodes or antinodes in the tube. The adjacent node and anti-node form a sound wave in the tube that is one-quarter of a wavelength. First, the wavelength is calculated from the wave equation, and then the tube length is determined as follows:

$$\lambda = \frac{v}{f} = \frac{340m/s}{170\dfrac{vibrations}{s}} = 2\frac{m}{vibe}$$

$$\text{Tube length} = \frac{\lambda}{4}$$

$$\text{Tube length} = \frac{2m}{4} \rightarrow \boxed{\text{Tube length} = 0.5m}$$

480. (C) At resonance, the open end of the tube has a pressure node and the closed end of the tube has a pressure antinode. Because of this, the second harmonic is skipped and the third harmonic (Node/Antinode/Node/Antinode) forms at 3 times the fundamental frequency of 170Hz. At this resonance, the 0.5-meter-long tube holds three-quarters of the wavelength:

$$\text{Tube length} = \frac{3\lambda}{4}$$

$$\lambda = \frac{4}{3}\left(\text{Tube length}\right)$$

$$\lambda = \frac{4}{3}(0.5m)$$

$$f = \frac{v}{\lambda}$$

$$f = \frac{340m/s}{\frac{4}{3}(0.5m)} \rightarrow \boxed{f = 510Hz}$$

481. (C) The two waves add together due to constructive interference, and the resulting wave will have the amplitude 3A/2.

482. (A) Once a mechanical wave is generated, its frequency is fixed, even when it changes speed from one medium into the next. Thus, according to $v = f\lambda$, wavelength will change proportionately with speed.

483. (A) The distance between compressions is the wavelength of the sound wave:

$$\lambda = \frac{v}{f} = \frac{343\,\frac{m}{s}}{25,000\,\frac{\text{waves}}{s}} \rightarrow \boxed{\lambda = 0.014\,\frac{m}{\text{wave}}}$$

484. (B) To travel to the cave wall and back again, the sound travels a distance of 3.5 m + 3.5 m = 7.0 m. Using $d = vt$ and solving for time:

$$t = \frac{d}{v}$$

$$t = \frac{7.0\text{ m}}{343\,\frac{m}{s}} \rightarrow \boxed{t = 0.020\text{ s}}$$

485. (C) The volume of sound corresponds to amplitude, so a loud sound correlates to a large amplitude. The pitch of the sound corresponds to frequency, so a low pitch is a low frequency. The speed of mechanical waves does not depend on the frequency.

486. (C) As a wave is generated, an increase in frequency results in a smaller wavelength $\left(\lambda = \dfrac{v}{f} \right)$. For a fixed wave speed, frequency and wavelength are inversely proportional. A graph of wavelength versus period (i.e., inverse frequency), however, has a slope equal to the speed of the wave.

487. (D) A sound beat is a changing amplitude (loudness) that occurs at a particular frequency. That frequency is the difference between the two close frequencies making the sound.

488. (D) Wavelength and frequency are inversely proportional, so an increase in frequency will decrease the wavelength. Speed depends solely on the medium and will stay the same in this case.

489. (B) Sound is a longitudinal wave, so the medium (air particles) must vibrate along lines parallel with the motion of the wave energy.

490. (A, D) The speed of sound increases slightly with temperature, going up about 6 m/s for every 10° Celsius above zero. Sound travels about 18 times faster in steel than air.

491. (A, B) Standing waves form when the medium is disturbed at its natural frequency. This resonance occurs because the wave reflects off a boundary and interferes with oncoming waves to form nodes (destructive interference) and antinodes (constructive interference).

492. (C, D) The speed of a mechanical wave depends only on the medium and its characteristics.

493. (A, C) When a wave hits a boundary, three things occur: reflection, transmission (refraction), and absorption. The frequency of a mechanical wave depends only on the frequency of the source, so the frequency will not change when it hits a boundary. A wave cannot gain energy according to the law of conservation of energy.

494. (C, D) Resonance occurs when something is forced to vibrate at its natural frequency and a dramatic growth in amplitude occurs. The tuning fork and the wineglass are perfect examples of this.

495. First, determine the wavelength and amplitude of the wave. Wavelength is the length of one complete vibration (crest and trough). Since there are two-and-a-half waves in the picture, the wavelength is $\lambda = (2.5 \text{ m}) / (5/2) = 1.0$ m. Another way to see this is by dividing the wave into five 0.5-m segments and recognizing that the wavelength is two of those segments.

Speed is calculated with the wave equation: $v = f\lambda = \left(5.0\, \dfrac{\text{vibes}}{\text{s}} \right)\left(1.0\, \dfrac{\text{m}}{\text{vibe}} \right) = 5.0\, \dfrac{\text{m}}{\text{s}}$.

496. The wave must travel 2.5 m to the wall and 2.5 m back, for a total of 5.0 m. Since the speed is 5.0 m for each and every second, the time is one second.

497. Frequency does not affect the speed of a mechanical wave. Frequency and wavelength, however, are inversely proportional. Thus, if frequency is doubled, wavelength is cut in half to 0.5 m.

498. The shape of a wave does not affect the speed, so both waves travel at 0.5 *m/s*. At t = 4 seconds, they will have each moved 2 meters. Thus the pulses completely overlap between the 4*m* and 5*m* position. The pulses will add constructively, so the amplitudes will add as follows:

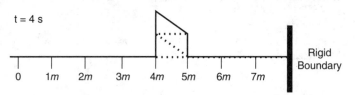

499. The wave pulses travel through each other, so the triangular pulse is still traveling to the left and will have traveled $d = vt = \left(0.5\frac{m}{s}\right)11s = 5.5m$. Since the leading edge of the wave started at 6m, its leading edge is at 0.5m at the 11-second clock reading. The square wave will have traveled 5.5 m to the right which means the front half of the wave will have already hit the rigid boundary and reflected as a trough. The tail-end crest and the front-end trough destructively interfere and the resulting amplitude is zero.

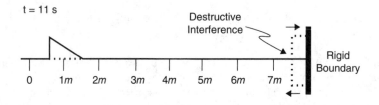

500. Lets begin by assuming that the rope doesn't stretch, in which case elastic potential energy will not be considered. A wave can store kinetic energy of the movement of particles in the medium. At t = 11s particles in the rope are moving either up or down between the 0.5m and 1.5m and thus have kinetic energy. Between the 7.5m position and the rigid boundary the particles also have kinetic energy. Even though the amplitude is temporarily zero due to the destructive interference, the particles are moving downward at that instant as the square wave inverts.